Complete PET

Student's Book *with answers*

Emma Heyderman and Peter May

CAMBRIDGE
UNIVERSITY PRESS

CAMBRIDGE UNIVERSITY PRESS
Cambridge, New York, Melbourne, Madrid, Cape Town, Singapore,
São Paulo, Delhi, Dubai, Tokyo

Cambridge University Press
The Edinburgh Building, Cambridge CB2 8RU, UK

www.cambridge.org
Information on this title: www.cambridge.org/9780521741361

© Cambridge University Press 2010

First published 2010
Reprinted 2010

Printed in the United Kingdom by Latimer Trend

A catalogue record for this publication is available from the British Library

ISBN 978-0-521-74648-9 Student's Book with CD-ROM
ISBN 978-0-521-74136-1 Student's Book with answers with CD-ROM
ISBN 978-0-521-74137-8 Teacher's Book
ISBN 978-0-521-74138-5 Class Audio CDs (2)
ISBN 978-0-521-74141-5 Student's Book Pack
ISBN 978-0-521-74139-2 Workbook with Audio CD
ISBN 978-0-521-74140-8 Workbook with answers and Audio CD

Contents

Map of the units

Speaking	Vocabulary	Grammar
• Discussing a young person's room • Speaking Part 1: Questions and answers	• House and home • Countable and uncountable nouns	• Prepositions of time • Frequency adverbs • Present simple and present continuous • State verbs • *A few, a little, many, much, a lot of, lots of* • Prepositions of place • Question forms
• Talking about typical school days • Talking about changes in your life • Speaking Part 4: Turn-taking and active listening • Talking about work	• *Take, sit, pass, fail, lose, miss, learn, teach, study* • *Earn, have, make, spend, take*	• Past simple and past continuous • *Used to*
• Talking about yourself • Speaking Part 2: Making suggestions and replying politely to suggestions • Pronunciation: Word stress for new information	• Free time • Negative prefixes • Phrasal verbs • People's hobbies	Verbs followed by *to* or *-ing*
Speaking Part 3: Describing photos of places	• Holiday activities • *Travel, journey, trip* • Buildings and places • Adjectives used to describe places	• Comparative and superlative adjectives • Spelling of comparative and superlative adjectives • *A bit, a little, much, far, a lot* • *Not as … as …* • *Big* and *enormous* (gradable and non-gradable adjectives)
• Speaking Part 3: Describing photos • Speaking Part 4: Describing personal experiences	• Personal feelings, opinions, experiences • Relations with others • Adjectives with *-ed* and *-ing* • Adjectives and prepositions • Adjectives of emotion and their opposites	• *Can, could, might, may* (ability and possibility) • *Should, shouldn't, ought to, must, mustn't, have to, don't have to* (obligation and prohibition)
• Talking about entertainment • Speaking Part 4: Talking about activities at home and going out; Talking about the clothes you like to wear	• Television programmes • Going out • *Been/gone, meet, get to know, know, find out* • Describing lost items	• Present perfect • *Yet, already, just* • *Since* and *for* • Present perfect or past simple
• Talking about extreme weather • Speaking Part 2: Giving and asking for reasons and preferences • Pronunciation: Weak forms	• Weather • Transport • Adverbs of degree • *Too/enough* • Prepositions of movement, *on foot/by car*, etc. • Compound words	The future: *will, going to*, present continuous, present simple
• Saying the letters of the alphabet and spelling words • Speaking Part 1: Asking general questions	• Phrasal verbs • Describing people • Prefixes and suffixes	• Zero, first and second conditionals • *When, if, unless* + present, future • *So do I* and *Nor/Neither do I*
• Speaking Part 2: Which sport to take up • Pronunciation: Stressed words	• Health and exercise • Illnesses and accidents • Sports collocations	• *Which, that, who, whose, when* and *where* clauses (defining and non-defining) • Past perfect simple
• Talking about food • Speaking Part 3: Describing objects you don't know the name of	• Types of food and drink • *Course, dish, food, meal, plate* • Shops and services	• Commands • *Have something done*
• Discussing animal facts • Saving water • Speaking Part 4: Saving energy • Giving examples • Pronunciation: Word stress with suffixes • Pronunciation: Weak forms in passives	• The natural world • The environment • Noun suffixes	• The passive: present and past simple • Comparative and superlative adverbs
• Communicating with others • Describing where things are • Speaking Part 3: Describing a photo	• Slang words • *Speak, talk, say, tell, ask for* • Prepositions of place	• Reported speech • Reported commands • Reported speech: other changes • Reported questions • Indirect questions

Introduction

Who this book is for

Complete PET is a stimulating and thorough preparation course for students who wish to take the **Preliminary English Test** from **Cambridge ESOL**. It teaches you the reading, writing, listening and speaking skills which are necessary for the exam as well as essential grammar and vocabulary. For those who are not planning to take the exam in the near future, the book provides skills and language highly relevant to an intermediate level of English (Common European Framework (CEF) level B1).

What the book contains

In the **Student's Book** there are:

- **12 units for classroom study**. Each unit contains:
  - one part of each of the three papers in the PET exam. The units provide language input and skills practice to help you deal successfully with the tasks in each part.
  - essential information on what each part of the exam involves, and the best way to approach each task.
  - a wide range of enjoyable and stimulating speaking activities designed to increase your fluency and your ability to express yourself.
  - a step-by-step approach to doing PET Writing tasks.
  - grammar activities and exercises for the grammar you need to know for the exam. When you are doing grammar exercises you will sometimes see this symbol: ⊙. These exercises are based on research from the **Cambridge Learner Corpus** and they deal with the areas which often cause problems for students in the exam.
  - vocabulary necessary for PET. When you see this symbol ⊙ by a vocabulary exercise, the exercise focuses on words which PET candidates often confuse or use wrongly in the exam.
- **Six unit reviews**. These contain exercises which revise the grammar and vocabulary that you have studied in each unit.
- **Speaking and Writing reference sections**. These explain the possible tasks you may have to do in the Speaking and Reading and Writing papers, and they give you examples together with additional exercises and advice on how best to approach these PET papers.
- A **Grammar reference section** which clearly explains all the main areas of grammar which you will need to know for the PET exam.

- An authentic **past PET exam paper supplied by Cambridge ESOL** for you to practise with.
- A **CD-ROM** which provides you with many interactive exercises, including further listening practice exclusive to the CD-ROM (please use the class audio CDs for the Student's Book listening exercises). All these extra exercises are linked to the topics in the Student's Book.

Also available are:

- **Two audio CDs** containing listening material for the 12 units of the Student's Book plus the Listening Paper for the test supplied by Cambridge ESOL. The listening material is indicated by different coloured icons in the Student's Book as follows: ⌒ CD1, ⌒ CD2.
- A **Teacher's Book** containing:
  - **Step-by-step guidance** for handling the activities in the Student's Book.
  - A number of suggestions for **alternative treatments** of activities in the Student's Book and suggestions for **extension activities**.
  - **Extra photocopiable materials** for each unit of the Student's Book to practise and extend language abilities outside the requirements of the PET exam.
  - **Photocopiable recording scripts** from the Student's Book listening material.
  - **Complete answer keys** including recording scripts for all the listening material.
  - **Four photocopiable progress tests** for every three Student's Book units.
  - **12 photocopiable word lists** (one for each unit) containing vocabulary found in the units. Each vocabulary item in the word list is accompanied by a definition supplied by the corpus-informed *Cambridge Learner's Dictionary*.
- A Student's **Workbook** containing:
  - **12 units for homework and self-study**. Each unit contains further exam-style exercises to practise the reading, writing and listening skills needed in the PET exam. In addition, they provide further practice of grammar and vocabulary, which also use information about common PET candidate errors from the Cambridge Learner Corpus ⊙.
  - A **'Vocabulary Extra'** section, which contains twelve pages of further revision and practice of the essential PET exam vocabulary contained in the Student's Book units.
  - An **audio CD** containing all the listening material for the Workbook.
- The **website** www.cambridge.org/completepet contains a full model PET for Schools practice test.

PET content and overview

Part/timing	Content	Test focus
1 Reading and Writing 1 hour 30 minutes	**Reading** **Part 1** Five very short texts: signs and messages, postcards, notes, emails, labels, etc. followed by five three-option multiple choice questions. **Part 2** Five items in the form of descriptions of people to match to eight short texts. Five questions in which candidates match the descriptions of people to the short texts. **Part 3** Longer text with ten true/false type questions. **Part 4** Longer text with five four-option multiple choice questions. **Part 5** Short text as a four-option multiple choice cloze. Ten questions; candidates select the correct word from each question to complete the text. **Writing** **Part 1** Sentence transformations. Five items that are theme related. Candidates are given sentences and then complete similar sentences using a different structural pattern so the sentence still has the same meaning. **Part 2** Short communicative message. Candidates write a short message of about 35–40 words in the form of a postcard, note, email, etc. **Part 3** A longer piece of continuous writing. There is a choice of two questions, an informal letter or a story.	Parts 1–4: Candidates are expected to read for the main message, global meaning, specific information, detailed comprehension, understanding of attitude, opinion and writer purpose and inference. Part 5: Candidates are expected to show understanding of vocabulary and grammar in a short text, and the lexico-structural patterns in the text. Candidates are mainly assessed on their ability to use and control a range of PET-level language. Coherent organisation, spelling and punctuation are also assessed.
2 Listening Approximately 30 minutes	**Part 1** Short monologues or dialogues with seven three-option multiple choice questions with pictures. **Part 2** Longer monologue or interview (with one main speaker). Six three-option multiple choice questions. **Part 3** Longer monologue. Six gaps to fill in. Candidates write one or more words in each space. **Part 4** Longer dialogue. Six true/false questions. Candidates decide whether the statements are true or false.	Candidates are expected to identify the attitudes and opinions of speakers, and listen to identify key information, specific information and detailed meaning, and to identify, understand and interpret meaning.
3 Speaking 10–12 minutes	**Part 1** A short conversation with the interlocutor. The interlocutor asks the candidates questions in turn, using standardised questions. **Part 2** A two-way conversation between candidates (visual stimulus with spoken instructions). The interlocutor sets up the activity. **Part 3** An individual long turn for each candidate. A colour photograph is given to each candidate in turn and they talk about it for about a minute. Both photographs relate to the same topic. **Part 4** A discussion on topics related to Part 3.	Candidates are expected to be able to ask and understand questions and make appropriate responses, and to talk freely on matters of personal interest.

Unit 1 Homes and habits

Julia

Starting off

1 With a partner, look at the two pictures and the photo of Julia. Which do you think is her room? Why?

2 (2) Listen to Julia, and check your answer.

3 Look at the <u>underlined</u> words from the recording. Match 1–6 to the expressions a–f with similar meanings.

1	I'm <u>out quite a lot</u> then	a	the things I like most
2	it's <u>not a particularly big</u> room	b	somebody visits me
3	I've got <u>all my favourite things</u> there	c	not in very much
4	but <u>there just isn't any space there</u>	d	beginning to improve
5	I'm <u>starting to get better</u>	e	rather a small
6	when <u>I have someone round</u>	f	it's completely full up

Listening Part 4

1 Read these instructions.

- You will hear a conversation between a girl, Zoe, and a boy, Lucas, about daily habits in different countries.
- Decide if each sentence 1–5 is correct or incorrect.
- If it is correct, put a tick (✓) in the box under A for YES. If it is not correct, put a tick (✓) in the box under B for NO.

❷ Before you listen, look at the <u>underlined</u> part of each sentence 1–5 and think of other expressions that mean the same, or the opposite.

	A YES	B NO
1 Lucas says that <u>everywhere closes early</u> in his town.	☐	☐
2 Lucas and Zoe agree that taxis <u>are too expensive</u>.	☐	☐
3 Zoe believes that Lucas's town <u>can be dangerous</u> at night.	☐	☐
4 Zoe says people in the north of Europe <u>get up earlier</u> than those in the south.	☐	☐
5 Lucas thinks it is <u>a good idea</u> to sleep for a short time after lunch.	☐	☐

❸ 🎧³ Now listen to the conversation and tick (✓) the boxes.

Prepositions of time

▶ page 117 *Grammar reference: Prepositions of time*

❹ ⊙ Zoe says <u>at</u> six o'clock and <u>in</u> the evening. PET candidates often make mistakes with prepositions of time. Circle the correct option in *italics* in sentences 1–5.

1 The weather is cold *in / (at)* night.
2 School starts at 8 o'clock *on / in* the morning.
3 We got there *at / on* Friday evening.
4 I'll see you *on / at* 4 o'clock.
5 His birthday is *on / in* July.

❺ With a partner, put these expressions in the correct columns. Then think of more expressions to add to each column.

… ~~the weekend~~   … the morning   … summer
… April 24   … 2010   … the holidays
… half past two   … bedtime   … Saturdays

at	in	on
the weekend		

❻ Discuss these questions about the recording with your partner. Use expressions from Exercise 4.

1 Why do you think different parts of the world often have different daily routines?
2 Which of the daily routines you heard about is more like yours? In what ways?
3 Which do you think is better? Why?

Grammar

Frequency adverbs; question forms

▶ page 117 *Grammar reference: Frequency adverbs*

❶ Look at these words and sentences from the recording and answer the questions below.

… they often go out after that …

… they don't usually have their main meal …

… there are always lots of people around …

… older people go to bed early most nights …

… the school day is normally about the same …

1 Do frequency adverbs like *often* go before or after the main verb?
2 What happens with the verb *be*?
3 Where do frequency expressions like *most nights* go?

❷ Put the words in brackets in the correct position in these sentences.

1 I listen to music on the radio. (occasionally)
   I occasionally listen to music on the radio.
2 I check my email. (every two hours)
3 I'm late for school. (never)
4 I write letters to friends. (sometimes)
5 I don't have lunch at home. (always)
6 I'm sleepy in the morning. (almost every day)
7 I go out on Monday nights. (hardly ever)
8 I stay in bed late. (most weekends)

❸ How true are sentences 1–8 for you? Rewrite those that are not true, using different frequency adverbs and expressions.

I rarely listen to music on the radio.

I listen to music on the radio nearly all the time.

4 Work in groups. Ask about these activities and answer using frequency adverbs plus the correct preposition of time.

arrive at school or work	get home
get up in the morning	go to bed
have breakfast have dinner	have lunch

'When do you get up?'
  'I always get up at 7.30 in the morning.'

5 Ask a partner questions about the following, beginning *Do you ever* or *How often do you … .* Use expressions like *every day, once a week* and *twice a month* in your answers.

chat online	cook a meal	go dancing
read a magazine	send text messages	tidy your room

'Do you ever chat online?'
  'Yes, I chat online every evening.'

'How often do you send text messages?'
  'I send one every half hour!'

6 Now do the same with activities 1–3.

Reading Part 5

1 Work in small groups and answer these questions.

- In what ways are the homes in the pictures different from ordinary homes?
- What are the advantages and disadvantages of living in each?
- Which would you like to live in? Why?

2 Quickly read the text at the top of page 11, without filling in the gaps, and answer these questions.

- What kind of text (e.g. *story*, *article*) is it?
- What is the text about?
- Which of the pictures on the right shows this building?
- Which parts of it are the *sails* and the *balcony*?
- Which **five** of the points below are in the text?

1 The family built a windmill and they now live in it.
2 The Wraysbury windmill is four centuries old.
3 The windmill has the same kind of rooms as a house.
4 Living in a windmill is different from living in a house.
5 There are sometimes fires in the windmill.
6 The windmill has a fire exit.
7 The windmill will make its own power.
8 They used material from abroad to build the windmill.

Glynn & Debbie Larcombe

Teenager Charlie Larcombe lives in an amazing home: a wooden windmill. His parents built the windmill in the pretty English village of Wraysbury, basing their design (1) .....*on*..... a 400-year-old mill in the same area.

Inside, there are five levels. The (2) .... floor is the largest, containing the living room, dining room and kitchen. Upstairs, the first and second floors have bedrooms, a tiny office and the bathroom. The Larcombes use the (3) .... floor for storing things, and the fourth, at the top of the mill, is the part that looks

(4) .... a boat and holds the sails.

Living in a windmill brings a (5) .... changes to normal life. The family found the shape of their new home a little strange at first. All the rooms are round, so there are no (6) .... , and the ceilings seem quite small compared to the floors.

It has central heating and it's very cosy, but fire is a danger (7) .... it is made of wood. There is a water system in each ceiling, so if there is a fire, the people inside can flood every level (8) .... seconds. Also, the balcony around the outside of the mill provides an escape route from the upper floors.

The Larcombes used local materials to build the windmill, including pieces from old cottages and farm buildings in the nearby area. The one last (9) .... is to complete the 8-metre long sails. They hope to use wind energy to create all the (10) .... the mill needs – and perhaps also enough for ten other houses in the village.

❸ **Read the text more carefully, and fill in the gaps with these words.**

as	corners	electricity	few
ground	job	like	in	~~on~~	third

❹ **Read the text below, paying no attention to the gaps for the moment. Decide what kind of text it is, what it is about, and its three main points.**

Exam advice

• Begin by reading the text to get a general idea of the type of text, its topic and the main points.

We often believe that living in a cave is (0) .....C..... from the distant past, the days of cavemen and cavewomen, but nowadays a (1) .... of people are

buying cave homes. The climate is changing and temperatures around the world are (2) ...., but inside a cave it remains cool, even (3) .... summer.

I am sitting in a cave home in Cappadocia, one of the hottest parts of Turkey, (4) .... three o'clock on a July afternoon. Outside it reaches 35 degrees almost (5) .... day, but in

here it is only 18. It never falls much below that, even during the coldest months.

Modern cave homes like this often have a phone, satellite TV and an Internet (6) ...., and they are very comfortable. (7) .... the bedrooms are very quiet, dark and cool, people love sleeping in them. And, they say, it's easy to make more (8) .... for yourself. You just dig a bigger room!

❺ Read the text on page 11 about living in caves again and choose the correct word for each space, A, B, C or D. Use the questions in *italics* to help you.

0   A anything   B everything
     C (something)   D nothing

1   A little   B many
     C few   D lot

Which word goes before 'of' and a noun?

2   A rising   B lifting
     C adding   D raising

Which verb does not need an object?

3   A about   B in
     C on   D round

Which preposition goes with the seasons?

4   A at   B during
     C for   D by

Which preposition usually goes with exact times?

5   A some   B both
     C every   D another

Which word completes the frequency expression?

6   A bridge   B connection
     C relation   D tie

Which word usually goes with 'Internet'?

7   A So   B Since
     C Until   D Even

Which linking word means 'because' at the beginning of a sentence?

8   A area   B floor
     C land   D space

Which word means 'empty', on and above the ground?

❻ Discuss these questions in pairs.

- Would you like to live in a cave home? Why (not)?
- Which other unusual places to live do you know of?

Grammar

Present simple and present continuous; state verbs

▶ page 117 *Grammar reference: Present simple and present continuous*

❶ Match extracts 1–4 from the text with uses a–d of the present simple and present continuous.

1   *I am sitting in a cave*   a   it's always true
2   *the climate is changing*   b   it's happening now
3   *it remains cool, even in summer*   c   it happens regularly
4   *it reaches 35 degrees almost every day*   d   it's in progress

❷ Complete the email with the correct form of the verbs in brackets. Use the present simple or the present continuous.

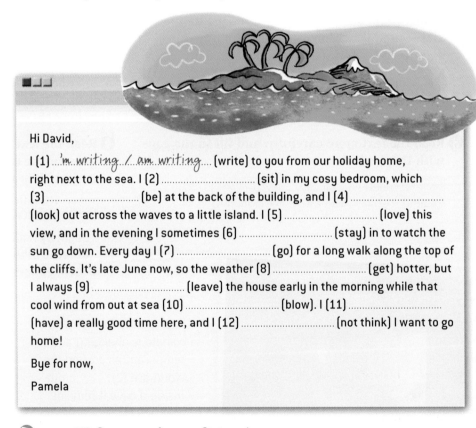

Hi David,

I (1) .....'m writing / am writing.... (write) to you from our holiday home, right next to the sea. I (2) .... (sit) in my cosy bedroom, which (3) .... (be) at the back of the building, and I (4) .... (look) out across the waves to a little island. I (5) .... (love) this view, and in the evening I sometimes (6) .... (stay) in to watch the sun go down. Every day I (7) .... (go) for a long walk along the top of the cliffs. It's late June now, so the weather (8) .... (get) hotter, but I always (9) .... (leave) the house early in the morning while that cool wind from out at sea (10) .... (blow). I (11) .... (have) a really good time here, and I (12) .... (not think) I want to go home!

Bye for now,

Pamela

▶ page 118 *Grammar reference: State verbs*

Verbs that describe states are not normally used in continuous forms:

We often believe that living in a cave … **not** ~~we are often believing~~

inside a cave it remains cool … **not** ~~it is remaining~~

❸ Which of these are state verbs?

belong	change	consist	contain	dream	exist	fill	forget
guess	improve	include	matter	mean	need	own	paint
prefer	relax	remember	seem	suppose	understand		

4 Ask your partner questions using state verbs and note down their answers.

Do you belong to a youth club? Do you ever forget important things?

Now work with a different partner. Ask questions about their first partner.

Does she prefer weekdays or weekends? (Answer: She prefers weekends.)

5 Make questions using the present simple or the present continuous, adding and changing words where necessary. Then answer the questions in full sentences.

1 what / 'state verb' / mean?
What does 'state verb' mean?

State verbs aren't usually used in continuous forms.

2 you / prefer / to get up / early or late?
3 anybody at your house / watch / TV / at the moment?
4 what colour clothes / you / wear / today?
5 which things / in your house / belong / to you?
6 what / you / sometimes / forget / to do / in the morning?

6 Think of a close friend. Tell your partner these things about them:

- facts, e.g. *She lives in …, she belongs to …*
- things they often do, e.g. *He often plays …*
- something they're doing over a period of time, e.g. *She's learning Spanish.*
- what you think they're doing right now, e.g. *He's walking home.*

Vocabulary

House and home; countable and uncountable nouns

▷ page 118 *Grammar reference: Countable and uncountable nouns*

1 Which of these does your home have?

balcony	bathroom	bedroom	corridor
dining room	garage	garden	hall	kitchen
lavatory	living room	stairs

2 With a partner, decide in which room the items in the box would normally be.

armchair	bath	bell	blankets	chest of drawers
cooker	cupboards	cushions	dishwasher
fridge	microwave	mirror	pillow	sink	sofa
taps	toilet	towels	washbasin	washing machine

3 ⊙ The words in the box are all countable nouns, but some words in the home are uncountable, e.g. *heating, air-conditioning*. PET candidates often make mistakes with these. Choose the correct option in *italics* in this sentence, then check your answer with the extract from the *Cambridge Learner's Dictionary*.

I am looking for new *furniture / furnitures* for my bedroom.

> **furniture** *noun* [U]
>
> objects such as chairs, tables, and beds that you put into a room or building *antique furniture*
>
> **Common Learner Error**
>
> **furniture**
>
> Remember you cannot make **furniture** plural. Do not say 'furnitures'.
>
> *I want to buy some new furniture for my bedroom.*

4 Look at the extract again and answer the questions.

- Which symbol tells you the noun is uncountable?
- What do you think the symbol is for a countable noun?

Grammar

A few, a little, many, much, a lot of and *lots of*; prepositions of place

▷ page 118 *Grammar reference:* A few, a little, many, much, a lot of, lots of

1 Study the text with the picture. Then complete the rules and examples on page 14 with *a little, a few, much, many, a lot, a lot of* and *lots of*.

In the garden we have a lot of flowers of many different colours. At this time of the year it rains a lot and there isn't much sunshine, but summer is different. From June to August we only have a little rain, and for a few months we have lots of sunshine almost every day!

1 For small numbers we use .... with countable nouns, e.g. *There are .... plates on the table. Three, I think.*

2 For small amounts we use .... with uncountable nouns, e.g. *Only .... sugar in my coffee, please. I don't like it very sweet.*

3 We use .... only with countable nouns, e.g. *'Are there .... blankets on your bed?' 'No, I don't like to have .... blankets in summer.'*

4 We use .... only with uncountable nouns in questions and negative sentences, e.g. *'Do you have .... free time at weekends?' 'No, I don't have .... free time at all!'*

5 We can use .... with countable and uncountable nouns in any kind of sentence, e.g. *We've got .... food and drinks in the fridge – it's full. If there is no noun, we just use ....,* e.g. *He sleeps ....* .

❷ Fill in the gaps with *a little, a few, much, many, a lot* or *a lot of/lots of*. (Sometimes more than one answer is possible.)

1 I usually like to put ......*a little*...... make-up on, but not ......*a lot*............ . Too much looks terrible, I think.
2 It doesn't take .... time to wash those clothes, but it takes .... hours, usually two or three, to dry them.
3 I've got .... DVDs but I can't buy any more because they cost .... money.
4 Those new light bulbs are very popular. They don't use .... electricity, so .... people are buying them.
5 I don't use .... shampoo, just .... drops. My hair always goes dry if I use ....
6 There isn't .... space in my bedroom so I don't keep .... things there.

▶ page 118 *Grammar reference: Prepositions of place*

❸ ⊙ PET candidates often make mistakes with prepositions of place like *in*, *at* and *on*. Circle the correct option in *italics* in each of these sentences.

1 You can stay *in / at* my house.
2 We're staying *at / in* different rooms.
3 My bedroom is the best room *of / in* my house.
4 It's a large room *at / on* the second floor.
5 I have some photos *in / on* the wall.
6 Also I have a big window *in / on* the left of my bed.

❹ Work in pairs. Talk about your apartment or house, describing each room and what is in it. As your partner listens, he or she draws a picture or plan of your home. When you finish, check your partner's diagram. Then change roles.

Speaking Part 1

❶ Put the words in 1–5 in the correct order. Then match the questions with answers a–e.

1 surname / your / what / is?
  What is your surname?
2 spell / you / it / how / do?
3 live / where / you / do?
4 do / what / do / you?
5 English / do / studying / enjoy / you?

a In Torre del Mar. It's a town on the coast near Málaga, in Spain.
b López.
c Yes, a lot. I studied it at school and now I have lessons at work with the other people there.
d It's L-Ó-P-E-Z.
e I'm a secretary. I work in an insurance company.

❷ Complete the tables with prepositions from a–e above.

...	school	...	a town	...	the coast
	work		a country		a hill
	home		a company		an island

❸ Ask another student the questions in Exercise 1. Your partner should answer about himself or herself, being careful to use the correct prepositions.

❹ Read the dialogue based on Speaking Part 1 questions. Fill in the correct form of the verbs in brackets and prepositions of place and time.

John: Maria, where (1) *do you come* (you / come) from?

Maria: I'm from Vari. It's a small town (2) .... Greece, near Athens.

John: And (3) .... (you / work) or (4) .... (you / be) a student?

Maria: I'm a student, (5) .... a secondary school (6) .... the town.

John: What subjects (7) .... (you / study)?

Maria: All the usual ones like maths and history, but this month we (8) .... (study) modern music, too. It's really interesting.

John: What (9) .... (you / enjoy) doing in your free time?

Maria: Well, I (10) .... (like) listening to music (11) .... home, (12) .... my room. And I sometimes (13) .... (go out) with friends (14) .... the evenings, or (15) .... weekends.

5 🎧⁴ **Listen to the recording and check your answers.**

6 **Work with a different partner. Ask the questions in Exercise 4. Your partner gives true answers.**

Writing Part 1

1 Circle the correct option in italics.

1 We always have a party at my house *in /(on)/at* December 31st.
2 In winter, there's only *a few / a little / a lot* sunlight in this room.
3 It's ten o'clock at night and I *wait / waiting / 'm waiting* for my friend to phone me.
4 I occasionally do some of my homework *at / on / in* school.
5 I don't *rarely / often / sometimes* watch television.

2 What do the sentences in Exercise 1 test? Match sentences 1–5 with grammar points a–e below.

a frequency adverbs [5]
b present tenses [ ]
c prepositions of time [ ]
d quantifiers like *a few, a little*, etc. [ ]
e prepositions of place [ ]

3 Study the second sentence in questions 1–6 opposite. Which grammar point a–e does each of 1–6 test? (One grammar point is not tested.)

1 d

4 Now do the Writing Part 1 exam task in the yellow box.

• Here are some sentences about family life.

• For each question, complete the second sentence so that it means the same as the first, **using no more than three words**.

1 There aren't many days when all my family do the same thing.
There are only ......*a few*...... days when all my family do the same thing.

2 Right now, my mum and dad are out having a meal somewhere.
My parents .... home right now because they're having a meal somewhere.

3 My elder sister Emily is at the swimming pool at the moment.
At the moment, my elder sister Emily .... a swim.

4 She nearly always goes out somewhere during the evening.
She hardly .... stays in during the evening.

5 My brother James doesn't spend much time here in summer.
In summer, my brother James only spends .... time here.

6 He usually prefers to be by the sea with his friends.
He usually prefers to be .... seaside with his friends.

5 Write an email to an English-speaking friend about your own family life.

Unit 2 Student days

Starting off

1 Work in pairs. Choose a phrase from the box for photos A–E.

> have lunch in the school canteen   alarm clock rings
> teacher takes register   catch the school bus   set off for school

2 🔊 You will listen to five different sounds. After each sound, talk to your partner and match it with photos A–E.

1 I think an alarm clock is ringing, so it goes with Photo A.

3 Use the phrases in Exercise 1 to ask and answer questions about your typical school day.

Have you got an alarm clock? Yes. It rings at 7.00 am.

Reading Part 3

> ### Exam advice
> - You read a long factual text and decide if ten sentences are correct or incorrect.
> - The ten sentences follow the order of the text.

1 Work in pairs. Before you read the text on page 17, look at the title, pictures and clocks. What do you think the text is about?

2 Wayne goes to secondary school in Beijing, China. What do you think Wayne does on a typical school day? Use the phrases in Starting off.

I think Wayne's alarm clock rings very early.

3 Read the text quickly to get a general idea of what it is about and find out if you were right about Wayne.

4 Read sentences 1–8 about Wayne's day. Underline the most important words in each.

		A	B
1	Wayne <u>makes breakfast</u> for his <u>sister</u>.	☐	✓
2	Wayne gets a lift to school by car.	☐	☐
3	Wayne is punished if he gets to school later than 07.20.	☐	☐
4	Wayne's school has some sports facilities.	☐	☐
5	At midday, none of the students go home for lunch.	☐	☐
6	Wayne leaves school at 17.20.	☐	☐
7	Wayne does his homework until it's time for dinner.	☐	☐
8	Wayne never sleeps more than six hours a night.	☐	☐

5 Read the text again to decide if each sentence is correct or incorrect. If it is correct, tick (✓) box A. If it is not correct, tick (✓) box B. <u>Underline</u> where you find the information in the text.

6 In your groups, compare your typical school day with Wayne's. In which ways is your day similar and in which ways is it different? Would you like to study at Wayne's school? Why (not)?

Wayne

★ ⋆˙THE DAILY LIFE OF ⋆⋆A BEIJING TEENAGER

5:30 The alarm clock rings. I have to get up. I go to the kitchen to fry myself an egg for breakfast. <u>My sister buys something from the market stalls on the way to school so she can sleep longer.</u>

6:00 I read something. Sometimes I need to learn famous poems or texts in other languages.

6:45 I set off for school. I sometimes go to school by bus. However, I normally go to school by bicycle. In China, drivers have to be older than 18 years old. As I'm 16, I can't drive to school like teenagers in other countries.

7:20 We have to be in school at least 20 minutes before lessons begin. It's a school rule. If you don't arrive on time, you can expect punishment. If you are often late, the teacher will talk to your parents seriously.

7:40 Classes begin. Today we have history, chemistry, geography, maths, English and sport of course. We have sport every day. Our school didn't use to have a football pitch, basketball courts or a running track but now it does.

12:10 All of us eat in the school canteen. We have 30 minutes to eat our lunch and then we have a break for 20 minutes. Sometimes I go to the library to study and sometimes I go outside to play table tennis.

13:00 Afternoon classes begin.

17:20 We finish school but we can't go home; we have an exam after class. School is so hard!

18:00 I'm home again. That means I can have supper early. It takes me 30 minutes to eat and then I have to do my homework. We have lots of homework every day.

00:00 I'm never asleep before midnight. I always wake up less than six hours later.

Vocabulary

Take, *sit*, *pass*, *fail*, *lose*, *miss*, *learn*, *teach* and *study*

❶ **Read this extract from the *Cambridge Learner's Dictionary*.**

Common Learner Error

Take/sit/pass/fail an exam

To **take** an exam means to do an official test. '**Sit**' is slightly more formal than '**take**' in this phrase and is only used in the UK.

We have to take an exam at the end of the course.

~~We have to write an exam at the end of the course.~~

If you **pass** an exam, you are successful because you get a good mark. If you **fail** an exam, you are not successful because you get a bad mark.

Lose or miss?

Usually you **miss** something which happens, such as an event, a train leaving, or an opportunity.

I do not want to miss my class.

~~I do not want to lose my class.~~

Usually you **lose** a thing.

I've lost my umbrella.

Learn, teach or study?

To **learn** is to get new knowledge or skills.

I want to learn how to drive.

When you **teach** someone, you give them new knowledge or skills.

My dad taught me how to drive.

~~My dad learnt me how to drive.~~

When you **study**, you go to classes, read books, etc to try to understand new ideas and facts.

He is studying biology at university.

❷ ⊙ **Work in pairs. PET candidates often make mistakes with verb + noun combinations. Circle the correct option in *italics* in sentences 1–7.**

1 I *made /* ⟨*took*⟩ an exam two weeks ago.
2 I have to go to the university because I'm *sitting / passing* my exam today.
3 I'm in my classroom, *writing / taking* this exam.
4 I began to run because I was afraid of *losing / missing* the school bus.
5 I *learn / study* every weekend for my exams.
6 Near the hotel there is a golf course, so we've decided to go there to *learn / study* golf.
7 I think our new teacher will *learn / teach* us a lot.

❸ **Write five questions using some verb + noun combinations from Exercises 1 and 2.**

How often do you take exams at your school?

❹ **Work in small groups. Ask and answer each other's questions.**

Grammar

Past simple

▶ page 119 *Grammar reference: Past simple*

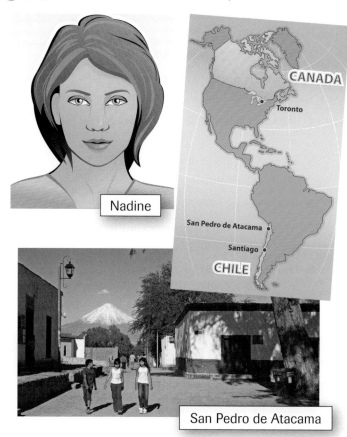

Nadine

San Pedro de Atacama

❶ **Work in small groups. Nadine is from Toronto, Canada. Last year she went to San Pedro de Atacama – a town in Chile – to be an exchange student. What differences do you think she found between her life in Canada and her life in Chile?**

❷ ⒍ **Listen to Nadine talking about these differences and complete the table.**

	in Toronto	in San Pedro de Atacama
clothes	no school uniform	(1) .... *uniform* ....
entertainment	disco (2) .... (3)	none of these thing
Nadine dreams in	English	(4) ....
fun	expensive activities	(5) ....

❸ Work in pairs. Nadine talks about an experience that happened last year. Write the interviewer's questions 1–6 in the correct form of the past simple, using the words given.

1 Where / go / last year? *Where did you go last year?*
a Last year I ....*lived*.......... in Chile.

2 Where / stay?
b I .... in San Pedro de Atacama.

3 How / feel / when / first / arrive?
c I .... scared.

4 Speak / Spanish / before / go?
d Yes, I did. I .... Spanish at school.

5 What subjects / study?
e I .... maths, chemistry, biology, …

6 Be / a good experience?
f Yes, it .... I'm really glad I .... there.

❹ 🎧 Listen to the interview again. Check your questions 1–6 and complete Nadine's answers a–f.

❺ Work in pairs. Look again at Nadine's answers a–f. <u>Underline</u> the *regular* past simple forms and circle the *irregular* past simple forms.

❻ ⊙ PET candidates often make spelling mistakes with regular past tense forms. Correct one spelling mistake in sentences 1–7 and say why it is wrong.

⟫ page 120 *Grammar reference: Spelling of regular past simple*

enjoyed
1 We ~~enjoied~~ ourselves a lot. *'O' is a vowel before 'y', so the 'y' doesn't change.*
2 We plaid football all day.
3 I planed two things for the holiday.
4 He traveled around the world two years ago.
5 It was very hot so I openned the window.
6 I really must tell you what happend to me.
7 My dad studyed French at school.

❼ ⊙ PET candidates also make mistakes with *irregular* past simple forms. Correct one mistake in sentences 1–6.

⟫ page 132 *Grammar reference: Irregular verbs*

ate
1 We ~~eated~~ spaghetti at lunchtime.
2 She buyed us a lot of presents.
3 I choosed a part-time course because I didn't have a lot of free time.
4 I was riding my bike when I felt off it.
5 He had short hair and he weared glasses.
6 In your email you writed you had a lot of exams.

Past simple and past continuous

⟫ page 119 *Grammar reference: Past simple and past continuous*

❶ Look at the pictures. What happened to Nadine when she was walking to school?

❷ 🎧 Listen to the recording to find out if you were right about what happened to Nadine. What do you think happened next?

❸ 🎧 Listen to the rest of Nadine's story. Were you right about what happened next?

❹ Look at extracts 1–3 from the recording. <u>Underline</u> the verbs in the past simple (e.g. *did*) and circle the verbs in the past continuous (e.g. *was doing*). Then, answer the question that follows each extract.

1 '*Suddenly a woman appeared from nowhere and she started screaming at the dogs. The dogs ran off.*'
   • Did the three actions happen at the same time? What happened last?

2 '*The sun was shining and I was feeling good.*'
   • Do we know when the sun started shining? Do we know if the sun stopped shining?

3 '*I was walking to school when I saw a group of dogs.*'
   • Did Nadine see the dogs before she started walking to school?

❺ Look at extracts 1–3 again and complete these rules with *past simple* or *past continuous*.

<u>Past simple and past continuous rules</u>

1 We use the (1) ......*past simple*...... to talk about actions or situations in the past (often one action happened after the other).

2 We use the (2) .... to talk about an activity that was already happening at a moment in the past. We don't know if this activity finished or not.

3 We often use the (3) .... (*I did*) and the (4) .... (*I was doing*) together to show that an action happened in the middle of an activity. We can use *when, as* or *while* to introduce the activity in the (5) ...., e.g. *As/When/While I was walking to school, I saw a group of dogs* but we generally use *when* to introduce the action in the (6) ...., e.g. *I was walking to school when I saw a group of dogs.*

❻ Tommy is an exchange student from the USA. Read what he says about his first day at a Japanese school and put the verbs in brackets in the past simple or past continuous.

'This morning I (1) ....*woke up*........ (wake up) early to visit Ryukoku High School. I (2) .... (look) out of the window. It (3) .... (rain). I (4) .... (have) a quick breakfast and we (5) .... (get) ready to go. We (6) .... (drive) to school. At the school we (7) .... (change) our shoes for slippers. As I (8) .... (put) on my slippers, my Japanese friend (9) .... (start) looking at my feet. The slippers (10) .... (be) too small!'

❼ 🎧 Listen to Tommy and check your answers.

❽ Work in small groups. Use the past simple and past continuous to tell each other about:

- an unusual journey to school
- your first day at high school.

Listening Part 1

❶ Read the four Listening Part 1 questions and <u>underline</u> the important words in each.

1 What time does John have to <u>leave school today</u>?

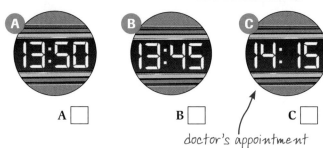

A ☐   B ☐   C ☐

doctor's appointment

2 What are the students going to do today at 11 am?

A ☐   B ☐   C ☐

3 What does Nathan have to buy?

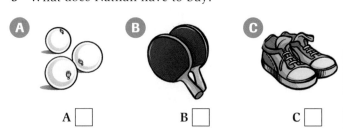

A ☐   B ☐   C ☐

4 What will the weather be like tomorrow?

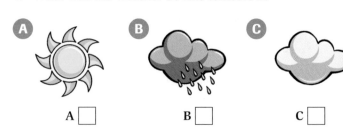

A ☐   B ☐   C ☐

② Look at the pictures for questions 1–4. What can you see in each?

③ 🔊 Listen to the recordings for questions 1–4 and make a note of the important words you hear next to the pictures. (Picture C in Question 1 has been done for you.)

④ 🔊 Listen to the recording again and choose the correct picture. Remember to put a tick (✓) in the box below it.

Grammar
Used to

▶ page 120 *Grammar reference:* Used to

① Work in pairs. *Teen* magazine has interviewed Candy about her days at primary school. Read this extract and answer the question below.

Candy: In primary school I used to have the same teacher for all my subjects and we rarely got homework. We used to have little tests but we didn't use to take exams. I always used to have lunch in the school canteen. After lunch, our teacher used to take us to a big room to play games. At the end of the day my mum or dad used to collect me from school.

- Which words does Candy use to talk about things that happened regularly in the past but don't happen now?

② Look at the extract again and answer these questions about *used to*.

1 Does *used to* change when we change the subject pronoun *(I/you/he/she, etc.)*?
2 What happens to *used to* in a negative sentence?
3 What verb form generally follows *used to*?

③ Rewrite what Candy says so that it is true for you.

In primary school I used to have the same teacher for most of my subjects …

④ Work with a partner to interview other students about their lives during the last five years. Read the rules about questions, then write at least five questions with *used to,* using the topics in the box.

| clothes | free time | friends | sport | studies |

Rules about questions

Remember that in the question form, we say *Did you use to …?* and not ~~*Did you used to …?*~~

For example: *What primary school did you use to go to? Did you use to get homework? What sports did you use to play when you were younger?*

⑤ Change pairs. Take turns to ask your questions from Exercise 4. Where possible, answer the questions using *used to.*

Reading Part 1

Exam advice

- You read five short texts (e.g. notices, signs, labels, messages, etc.).
- Each text has three explanations, A, B and C, and you have to choose the correct one.
- When you have made your choice, compare it with the text and decide if it really explains what the text says.

① Look at the text in each question. What does it say? Circle the letter next to the correct explanation – A, B or C.

1
Do you want to earn some extra cash in the school holidays?

A local petrol station needs an attendant to wash cars and fill them up with petrol.

To apply, phone Stefan on 566223

Stefan
A needs a job during the summer break.
B would like to hear from people who are interested in the job.
C is looking for someone to wash his car.

2

From: Mara

To: Natasha

Hi. If you can borrow your brother's scooter, my dad's looking for students to deliver pizzas. Let us know what you think when you come for dinner tomorrow.

Mara has written the email to

   A invite Natasha to have dinner.

   B ask Natasha if she can borrow her scooter.

   C inform Natasha about a job.

3

Zoe,

Jan Harris phoned. They want to celebrate their wedding anniversary on Saturday but need someone to look after their son from 8 to 11 pm. Can you do it? She'll ring you around 9 pm this evening.

Mum

Jan Harris

   A wants Zoe to phone her back tonight.

   B has invited Zoe to go out on Saturday night.

   C would like Zoe to take care of her child for the evening.

4

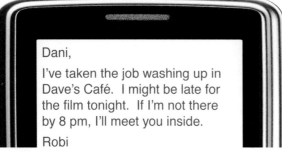

Dani,

I've taken the job washing up in Dave's Café. I might be late for the film tonight. If I'm not there by 8 pm, I'll meet you inside.

Robi

Dani should

   A meet Robi in Dave's Café.

   B go into the cinema if Robi is delayed.

   C wait inside the cinema until 8 pm.

5

● **Assistant Trainers**

Interviews for Assistant Trainers for the sports team start Friday at 4.30pm. Arrive at least 15 minutes before if you still need to fill in a form.

   A You will have an opportunity to hand in your application on Friday.

   B Everybody should get there 15 minutes before the interview starts.

   C You must complete an application form before Friday.

Vocabulary

Earn, have, make, spend and *take*

❶ ⊙ **PET candidates often make mistakes with verb + noun combinations. Use the verbs from the box to complete questions 1–5 correctly.**

earn	~~have~~	make	spend	take

In which job(s) mentioned in **Reading Part 1**:

1 can you ....*have*..... fun?

2 can you .... friends?

3 must you .... your time to do things carefully?

4 do you .... most of your time helping people?

5 can you .... a good wage?

❷ Work in small groups. Ask and answer questions 1–5. Remember to explain why.

Speaking Part 4

❶ Work in small groups. Discuss these questions.

1 Do teenagers work in your country? Why (not)?

2 Have you got a part-time job?

3 Do you think teenagers should work? Why (not)?

Marcelo

Linh

❷ 🔊 **Listen to Linh from Vietnam and Marcelo from Colombia talking about teenagers and part-time work. Make notes on how they answer the questions in Exercise 1.**

3 (11) Listen to the recording again. Linh and Marcelo take turns to speak by asking each other questions. They also show they are listening to each other. Complete the expressions in the table. (They are numbered in the order you will hear them.)

questions for taking turns	showing you are listening
What about in Vietnam?	I'm not so sure.
(1) What do you ....?	Maybe.
(2) Don't you think ....?	(4) Yes and ....
(3) Do you ....?	(6) R ....?
(5) Have you got a ....?	(8) Good ....!
(7) What do your teachers ....?	

4 Work in pairs. Try this Speaking Part 4 question. Remember to use some of the expressions from Exercise 3.

> Your photographs showed people at work. Now I'd like you to talk together about the work members of your family do and the sort of work you'd like to do in the future.

Writing Part 2

1 Read these two Writing Part 2 questions. The important information has been underlined in the first question. Now underline the important information in the second question.

1

> Your English-speaking friend has helped you study for your English exam.
> Write an email to Isabel. In your email, you should
> • thank Isabel.
> • tell Isabel about the exam.
> • invite Isabel to your house.

2

> You can't go to sports practice after school.
> Write a note to your coach. In your note, you should
> • apologise.
> • explain why.
> • suggest another time you could do this practice.

2 Work in pairs. Look at each Writing Part 2 question again and answer these questions.

1 What do you need to write? (A note, card, email, etc.)
2 Who are you writing to? Do you know their name?
3 Why are you writing?
4 What three points do you need to include?

3 Match these answers with the questions in Exercise 1.

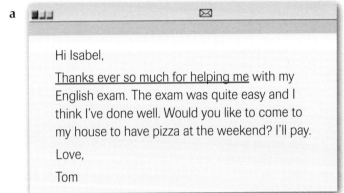

a

> Hi Isabel,
>
> Thanks ever so much for helping me with my English exam. The exam was quite easy and I think I've done well. Would you like to come to my house to have pizza at the weekend? I'll pay.
>
> Love,
>
> Tom

b

> Dear Mr Trenton,
>
> I'm sorry that I won't be able to go to football practice this afternoon because I have to go to the dentist. Why don't I train with the other team at lunchtime? I promise I'll be at football practice on Thursday.
>
> Best wishes,
>
> Sam

4 Work in pairs. Read the answers again and underline the expressions which are used to *thank, invite, suggest, explain* and *apologise.*

5 Work in pairs. Use this Writing Part 2 question to answer the questions in Exercise 2 again.

> You agreed to meet your English-speaking friend tomorrow, but now you can't go.
> Write an email to Jason. In your email, you should
> • apologise.
> • explain why you can't meet.
> • suggest meeting another day.
> Write 35–45 words.

6 Write your answer to the task in Exercise 5.

Unit 1 *Vocabulary and grammar review*

Grammar

❶ Complete the email with *at*, *in* or *on* in each gap.

Hi everybody,

Well, here I am (1) ....*in*.......... New Zealand, staying with a very friendly family (2) .... the town of Westport. It's quite a big house and my bedroom is (3) .... the second floor. I like it because there are lots of cupboards to put my things (4) .... and the bed is much bigger than the one (5) .... my room (6) .... home!

(7) .... the evenings and (8) .... weekends, the family sometimes take me out, though often we just stay (9) .... and watch TV. I usually go to bed quite early (10) .... night, and get up (11) .... about 7.30 (12) .... the morning.

I'm enjoying myself a lot here, but I'm looking forward to being home again (13) .... August 15th.

❷ Circle the correct option in *italics* in sentences 1–8.

1 I have a big family and there's always a lot of (*housework*)/ *houseworks* to do.
2 Can you lend me *a few / a little* money until Friday?
3 It's very dark and cold here in winter so I don't go out *a lot / a lot of*.
4 The living room is very big but there's only *a little / a few* furniture in it.
5 These days, Max spends a lot of *time / times* in his room.
6 I haven't got *much / many* work to do so I'll go out soon.
7 Paula isn't very well, but I think she can eat *a few / a little* food now.
8 My parents sometimes invite *a little / a few* people to have dinner with us.

❸ Correct the errors.

1 We don't eat always in the dining room.
   We don't always eat in the dining room.
2 Hello, I call to ask if you want to go out somewhere tonight.
3 Why do you stand here in the rain at this time of night?
4 Do you sleep ever all morning?
5 I'm never believing anything my brother tells me.
6 I every day make my own bed.
7 How do you often have a bath?
8 I get normally home at about half past five.

Vocabulary

❹ Complete the crossword with words from Unit 1.

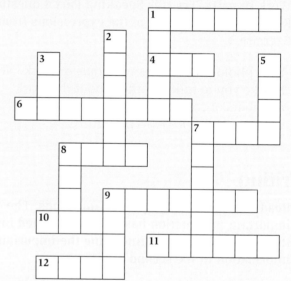

Across
1 where we keep food cool
4 have something
6 to or in a higher part of a house
7 comfortable and warm
8 where we wash the dishes
9 thick warm cover for a bed
10 hole in the side of a mountain
11 where people keep their car
12 room that leads to other rooms

Down
1 level of a building
2 stay the same
3 where water comes from
5 put things in the right place
7 what we use to make meals
8 seat for two or more people
9 it rings at the door

Unit 2 *Vocabulary and grammar review*

Vocabulary

❶ Circle the correct option in *italics* to complete these sentences.

1 Many students get part-time jobs to *take* / (earn) some extra money.
2 When I'm older, I'd like to *study* / *learn* economics at university.
3 Yesterday we went on a school trip and we *got* / *had* a lot of fun.
4 When Jack went to secondary school, he soon *did* / *made* a lot of new friends.
5 Tomorrow we're going to *pass* / *take* a maths test. I'm really nervous.
6 I was late for school so I *lost* / *missed* the first lesson.
7 I have to go to school because I'm *sitting* / *passing* my exam today.
8 We've decided to *learn* / *study* golf on holiday.

Grammar

❷ ⊙ Correct one mistake with a verb in each sentence 1–10. (Some have a spelling mistake and some have an incorrect irregular form.)

▷ **page 132** *Grammar reference: Irregular verbs*

1 Some years ago I ~~traveled~~ to England with a friend called Bruno. *travelled*
2 Yesterday I woke up very early because I was planing to go to the beach.
3 I only payed 25 euros for these boots.
4 Last weekend, I founded a very good restaurant in my town.
5 I went to the shopping centre and there I baught some new clothes.
6 While my brother was playing football, he felt and injured his leg.
7 My friend Sara bringed her dog to school one day.
8 I met Holly a very long time ago. We were studing at the same school.
9 In the first lesson our English teacher teached us some new words for sports.
10 We puted all our things in the car and we set off for the mountains.

❸ Put the verbs in brackets into the correct form of the past simple or past continuous to complete the sentences. Be careful with your spelling!

1 Carolina ....*fell*....... (fall) asleep when she ...*was doing*... (do) her homework.
2 It was a beautiful day. The sun .... (shine) and the birds .... (sing).
3 Yesterday, when I .... (have) my dinner, the phone .... (ring).
4 My parents .... (choose) this school because it .... (be) near our house.
5 I .... (see) an advertisement for a job in the supermarket while I .... (buy) some milk.
6 My rabbit .... (escape) as I .... (clean) its cage.
7 At first I .... (think) German .... (be) difficult but now I like it.
8 In our history class, we .... (read) a short article and .... (write) a short text.
9 Thanks a lot for inviting me to your party. I really .... (enjoy) myself.
10 The children .... (laugh) when the clown .... (appear).

❹ Complete these sentences with *used to* or *didn't use to*.

1 I don't play the piano now but when I was younger I ...*used to play it*... .
2 I have lunch at school now but at primary school I ....
3 I live close to school now but when we lived in Tokyo we ....
4 My brother is now a really good student but when he was younger he ....
5 Mr Puy doesn't give us much homework but when Mrs Garcia was our teacher she ....
6 Martin's never late for school but before he bought the alarm clock he ....

Unit 3 Fun time

Starting off

❶ Match the verbs in the box with a–j to form leisure activities. Which are shown in the pictures?

collecting	diving	flying	going
keeping	playing	~~sailing~~	seeing
sending	surfing		

a ....*sailing*.......... a boat
b .... friends
c .... dancing
d .... in a balloon
e .... unusual objects
f .... computer games
g .... the Internet
h .... text messages or emails
i .... fit
j .... underwater

❷ What's the best way to spend a day off? Put a–j in order, starting with the activity you most like (or would like) to do. Compare your answers with a partner.

Listening Part 2

❶ Before you hear the recording, read the instructions in the box below and look at questions 1–4 on page 27. What kind of information, e.g. *a place*, must you listen for? Match a–d with questions 1–4.

a   a reason
b   a time
c   the speaker's opinion
d   frequency

❷ 🔢 Listen to the recording and answer the questions.

- You will hear a man talking on the radio about four ways of spending a day out.
- For each question, put a tick (✓) in the correct box.

1 The train leaves Fort William at

   A 12.25. ☐

   B 10.20. ☐

   C 14.10. ☐

2 *Go Wild* adventure courses are not dangerous because

   A you have to wear safety equipment. ☐

   B somebody is always holding you. ☐

   C only adults can go on the course. ☐

3 Passengers on the boat trip in Wales nearly always see

   A sharks. ☐

   B whales. ☐

   C dolphins. ☐

4 What does the speaker say about the hot-air balloon flights?

   A The route never changes. ☐

   B They are a little too short. ☐

   C There are no flights in winter. ☐

❸ Complete questions 1–7 with expressions from the recording using these words.

advice	ahead	fee	hours
journey	~~part~~	value	

1 How old must you be to take ....part......... ?

2 What are the opening .... ?

3 How much is the admission .... ?

4 Is it good .... for money?

5 What time is the return .... ?

6 Do they give you good safety .... ?

7 Is it best to book .... ?

❹ Work in pairs. Decide which of the four activities from the recording you would most like to do. Then ask your partner about other interesting ways of spending a day out (e.g. *sightseeing, visiting a museum or art gallery*). Ask some of the questions from Exercise 3.

Exam advice

- Before you listen, look at each question and decide what kind of information you need (e.g. a date, a result, an attitude to something, etc.).
- When you first hear the recording, listen for details about this kind of information and choose the best answer.
- Listen carefully the second time to check that you are right.

Vocabulary
Negative prefixes

❶ On the recording, Spencer Watson mentions 'four *unusual* ways to have a great day out'. Make these adjectives negative by writing *im-*, *in-* or *un-* on the left.

.... fit, fair, healthy

.... correct, dependent, active

.... possible, polite, probable

❷ Add *im-*, *in-* or *un-* to these words and complete the sentences.

~~direct~~	formal	kind	patient	~~tidy~~	true

1 The express train is faster, but the ......*indirect*...... route through the hills is more beautiful.
2 I always put everything in its place, but my brother's room is very ......*untidy*...... .
3 Teenagers often use .... language when they talk to their friends.
4 It's .... to say that somebody else isn't good at sport.
5 It's completely .... that dolphins are a kind of fish.
6 When we arrived at the theme park, we were .... to start going on the rides.

❸ Complete these sentences with information that is true for you.

1 I think it's unhealthy to ...*eat a lot of cakes*... .
2 It's unusual for me to ....
3 It's impossible for me to ....
4 I think it's very unlucky to ....
5 I think it's quite unfair to ....
6 I don't want to be unfit because ....

Reading Part 4

❶ Look at the pictures in the newspaper report and answer these questions.

- Would you like to be on the boat in the first picture? Why (not)?
- How old do you think the boy in the second picture is?
- Do you think someone of that age is old enough to be out at sea on their own?

❷ Question 1 in Reading Part 4 is usually about the *purpose* of the text. Quickly read the text and complete this statement. Use your own words.

The writer's main purpose is to ...

❸ Look at options A, B, C and D. Which is closest to your answer in Exercise 2?

A To warn young people to take care at sea
B To describe a great achievement by a boy
C To encourage teenagers to take up sailing
D To explain how to become an expert sailor

The teenager who sailed across an ocean

1 To the music of a steel band and accompanied by dozens of small boats, 14-year-old Michael Perham sailed into Antigua (Jamaica) yesterday – and became the youngest person to cross the Atlantic alone. After an amazing 5,600-kilometre voyage lasting six-and-a-half weeks, Michael's achievement beat the previous record set by 15-year-old Sebastian Clover.

2 Looking smart and relaxed in a white T-shirt and baseball cap, the teenager got off his 8-metre boat – called Cheeky Monkey – and walked through the huge crowd waiting for him on the Caribbean island. 'It feels fantastic being back on dry land – really brilliant,' he said. 'I'm looking forward to a comfortable bed and a great dinner. I don't care what it is, I'll enjoy eating anything that's not out of a can!'

3 The idea for the voyage began when Michael was 11 and he saw a television film of Sebastian Clover crossing the Atlantic. Fascinated, he later attended a talk by Sebastian and told his father, an experienced sailor, that he too would like to break the record. Mr Perham agreed to teach him how to sail, and he soon realised that his son had the ability and the courage to turn his dream into reality. Three years later, Michael was ready to set out on his great adventure.

4 Read the text more carefully and think of answers to these questions. Which paragraph gives you the answer to each?

1 What did Michael say when he arrived in Jamaica?
2 Why did Michael decide to sail across the Atlantic Ocean?
3 How did Michael feel during the voyage?

5 Now look at the multiple-choice options for questions 1–3 above. For each question, decide which of A, B, C or D is closest to your understanding of the text.

1 A He preferred being at sea
  B He enjoyed sleeping on his boat
  C He wanted to have a good meal
  D He liked opening tins of food

2 A He had a conversation with Sebastian
  B His father suggested the idea to him
  C He wanted to do the same as Sebastian
  D He was already an expert sailor

3 A Occasionally he was a little frightened
  B He missed being with other people
  C The time seemed to pass very quickly
  D He was sure nothing could go wrong

4 He insisted he hadn't felt afraid while he was at sea and he'd never felt like giving up. 'The hardest thing was being away from friends and family,' said Michael. 'There were times when the trip seemed to go on forever and you are right in the middle of an empty ocean. I knew there was always danger, but I'd practised handling emergencies.' In fact, the teenager had to deal with terrible storms, sharks and problems with the boat which nearly ended the record attempt.

5 But the amazingly confident 14-year-old reminded everyone how young he really is when he said: 'My next project isn't such an adventure. After all this time away, I've got to get on with all the school work I've missed!'

Adapted from the *Daily Mail*

6 Look again at the parts of the text that gave you the correct answers to questions 1–3. Are they in the same order as the questions?

Exam advice

- Quickly read the text to get the general idea of what it is about.
- For each question, decide what the text says about it before you look at options A–D.
- Choose the option closest to your understanding of the text.

7 Discuss these questions with a partner. Give reasons for your answers. Begin your answers with the words given.

- What kind of record would you like to break?
  I'd like ...
- What difficulties would there be?
  There would be ...
- How much time would you need for training?
  I'd need ...
- How would you feel if you succeeded?
  I'd feel ...

Grammar
Verbs followed by *to* or *-ing*

▶ page 121 *Grammar reference: Verbs followed by* to *or* -ing

> We can use *-ing* or the infinitive after verbs such as *begin, start, like, love, hate, prefer* and *continue* with little difference in meaning, e.g. *It began to snow. / It began snowing*, but with other verbs only one form is possible.

1 Look at the underlined verbs from the text. Which are followed by a verb ending in *-ing*, and which are followed by an infinitive? Complete the table.

1 I'll <u>enjoy</u> eating anything
2 Mr Perham <u>agreed</u> to teach him
3 he'd never <u>felt like</u> giving up
4 the trip <u>seemed to go</u> on forever
5 I'd <u>practised</u> handling emergencies

verb + *-ing*	verb + infinitive
enjoy	*agree*

Now add these verbs to the correct column in the table.

admit	afford	avoid	decide	expect	fancy
finish	hope	learn	manage	mind	miss
promise	suggest	want	would like		

Can you add more verbs to each column?

❷ ⊙ Some of these sentences contain mistakes made by PET candidates. Tick (✓) the sentences that are correct. Rewrite the incorrect sentences.

1 I would like to learn dancing the 'Samba'.
   I would like to learn to dance the 'Samba'.
2 We decided catch the train.
3 I really enjoy to be here.
4 I'll never forget to visit the Statue of Liberty last year.
5 We hope to go to the same island again next year.
6 Do you fancy to come with us?
7 I must remember to phone Carlos tomorrow.
8 When we finished to eat I went to my house.
9 I forgot asking you about your family.
10 Do you remember sailing into Cape Town?

❸ Which two verbs in sentences 1–10 can be followed by verb + -ing and the infinitive, but with a change of meaning?

❹ Complete questions 1–6 with either the -ing or the infinitive form of the verb. Then ask your partner the questions.

1 Where do you want ....*to go*.......... (go) on holiday next summer?
2 What kind of music do you enjoy .... (listen to) at home?
3 What are you planning .... (do) at the weekend?
4 Where do you fancy .... (go) this evening?
5 Do you ever forget .... (bring) anything to the lesson?
6 What would you like .... (do) after the lesson?

❺ Tell your partner about something that you:

1 can't afford to buy
   I can't afford to buy a new computer.
2 are learning to do
3 decided to do last week
4 are planning to do on Saturday
5 want to start doing
6 must remember to do tomorrow
7 will finish doing soon
8 shouldn't forget to do next weekend
9 always hate doing
10 really love doing.

Vocabulary
Phrasal verbs

⊙ page 121 *Grammar reference: Phrasal verbs*

> **phrasal verb** *noun* [U] a phrase which consists of a verb in combination with a preposition or adverb or both, the meaning of which is different from the meaning of its separate parts: *'Look after', 'work out'* and *'make up for'* are all phrasal verbs.

❶ Read the entry from the *Cambridge Learner's Dictionary* and complete these example sentences with the three phrasal verbs given.

1 I'm trying to .... the total cost.
2 I hope this money will .... the inconvenience.
3 Could you .... the children while I'm out?

❷ In pairs, find phrasal verbs in the text about Michael Perham with these meanings, then answer the questions below.

1 leave (a train, bus, ship, etc.) [Paragraph 2] *got off*
2 feeling happy about something that is going to happen [Paragraph 2]
3 make (something) become [Paragraph 3]
4 start a journey [Paragraph 3]
5 stopping doing something before you have completed it [Paragraph 4]
6 continue [Paragraph 4]
7 take action (e.g. to solve a problem) [Paragraph 4]
8 continue doing (a job) [Paragraph 5]

• Which *three* of the phrasal verbs consist of three words?
• Which *one* is separated by other words?

❸ <u>Underline</u> the phrasal verbs in sentences 1–6, then match them with meanings a–f.

1 You can <u>catch up with</u> everyone else if you run fast.

a took part with others

2 My sister took up singing; she's got a lovely voice.

b registered to do something

3 I want to learn Chinese so I've put my name down at a language school.

c started doing a hobby

4 My friends were all playing cards so I joined in, too.

d started a journey

5 Some children enjoy stamp collecting, but go off it when they get older.

e get to the same level as others

6 We set off early and took the ten o'clock ferry.

f stop liking

❹ Work in pairs. Fill in the gaps with the correct form of phrasal verbs from Exercises 2 and 3.

Chris: Hi, Ava. Are you and Megan going away on holiday soon?
Ava: Yes, on Saturday. We want to (1) ......*set off*...... very early in the morning.
Chris: Are you going to the coast?
Ava: No, we (2) .... beach holidays last summer. There were too many people. We've decided to (3) .... skiing instead. We're off to the Alps.
Chris: Do you know how to ski?
Ava: Er, not really. That's why I'm going to (4) .... my name .... for lessons.
Chris: I tried it once but I found it really difficult. After three days I (5) .... and went home!
Ava: Well, the lessons (6) .... until late in the evening, every day, so I should improve quickly. Megan's a good skier and I've got a lot to learn, but I'm sure I can (7) .... her. I'm really (8) .... trying, anyway!
Chris: Yes, I'm sure you'll have a great time.

❺ (13) Now listen to the dialogue to check your answers.

6 Complete the table about people's hobbies with these words.

backpack	bike	brush	camera	camper	collection
collector	cook	cooker	cyclist	helmet	instrument
musician	oven	paint	painter	photographer	tent

hobby	person	equipment
chess	player	board, pieces
camping		
collecting		
cooking		
cycling		
music		
painting		
photography		

7 Work in pairs. Which other words go with the hobbies above? Make a list (e.g. chess: *indoor game, black and white squares, queen, move*).

8 Choose one of the hobbies from the table and describe it to your partner, but without saying what it is called. Your partner has to guess what it is. Then change roles.

You're outdoors, you have to find somewhere safe and dry, you put up your tent, you light a fire to cook your food or use a little gas cooker, you sleep in a sleeping bag ...

Speaking Part 2

1 🔊14 Two teenagers, Olivia and Daniel, are talking about what they could do in their free time. Look at this list of hobbies, listen to the recording and answer questions 1–3.

canoeing	fishing	water-skiing	mountain-biking	rock-climbing

1 Which hobby/hobbies does Daniel suggest?
2 Which does Olivia suggest?
3 Which do they decide to take up?

2 🔊14 Listen again, and fill in the missing words in sentences 1–8.

1 OK then, ...how.......... about going fishing?

2 Well, I think I'd .... to do something a bit more exciting.

3 Perhaps we .... try a water sport?

4 I think we .... do something cheaper.

5 All right, ... don't we go rock-climbing?

6 I think it'd be .... to do something less dangerous.

7 So .... we do that, then?

8 Yes, ... go for that one.

3 🔊15 Listen again to sentences 1, 3, 5 and 8 and answer these questions.

• Which words have the strongest stress?
• What kind of information do these words give?

Now practise asking the questions, stressing these words.

4 🔊16 Listen again to sentences 2, 4 and 6. Practise saying these, using the same polite tone to reply to suggestions.

❺ Work in pairs. Continue Olivia's and Daniel's discussion, suggesting more hobbies. Use some of expressions 1–8 and give reasons why you would or wouldn't like to do them. Remember to be polite!

❻ Do this Speaking Part 2 task with a partner. Talk for at least two minutes.

You and a friend have holidays later this year but you still don't have any firm plans for two weeks of them. Talk together about the different kinds of holiday you could have and about the things you could do. Here are some pictures with some ideas to help you.

Writing Part 1

❶ Study this example of sentence transformation and answer the questions.

> I don't have enough money for a new camera.
> I can't .... a new camera.

1 Which word(s) in the first sentence do *you* have to change?
2 Why would the answer *afford buying* be wrong?
3 What is the correct answer?

❷ Correct the mistakes in the answers to 1–5, and say what is wrong in each case. Underline the words you have to change from the first sentence to the second.

1 I want to <u>have</u> piano <u>lessons</u>.

   Answer: I want to learn ~~playing~~ *to play* the piano.

2 All the water in the lake is frozen now.
   Answer: All the water in the lake ...*has turned*... ice.

3 Let's leave the house very early in the morning.
   Answer: I suggest ....*set out*......... very early in the morning.

4 It'd be a good idea to go horse riding.
   Answer: Why ....*we don't*........ go horse riding?

5 I can't wait to go sightseeing in Rome.
   Answer: I'm looking ...*forward to go*... sightseeing in Rome.

❸ Study the first sentences in each Writing Part 1 question 1–6 below. Which word(s) do you have to change? <u>Underline</u> them.

1 I'm always happy <u>when I go</u> on holiday with my family.
   I always enjoy ......*going on*........ holiday with my family.
2 Everybody likes staying in bed late in the morning.
   Nobody wants .... up early in the morning.
3 Usually, my sister suggests going to the beach.
   My sister usually says, 'How ....to the beach?'
4 This summer I'm going to start playing beach volleyball.
   I'm going to take .... beach volleyball this summer.
5 I also want to have sailing lessons.
   I want .... sail, too.
6 Summer holidays always seem too short!
   Summer holidays never seem to go .... enough!

❹ For each question above, complete the second sentence so that it means the same as the first, *using no more than three words.*

❺ Write a paragraph about what you do in your free time. Try to use each of the following:

• three verbs followed by *-ing* and/or the infinitive
• three adjectives with negative prefixes
• three phrasal verbs from this unit.

❻ In small groups, compare what you have written. Ask other students to check for mistakes, particularly with the points suggested in Exercise 5.

Unit 4 Our world

1 .....buy souvenirs.....

2 ....

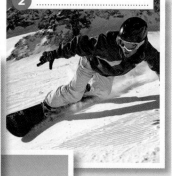
3 ....

4 ....

5 ....

6 ....

7 ....

Starting off

❶ Work in pairs. Choose some of the holiday activities in the box to label the photos.

buy souvenirs	go camping	go sightseeing
go snorkelling	go snowboarding	
go trekking	sunbathe	take photos
try new sports	visit museums	

❷ 🔊(17) Abi went to Zanzibar, an island near Tanzania, Africa. Listen to Toby asking Abi about her trip. Write down Abi's answers.

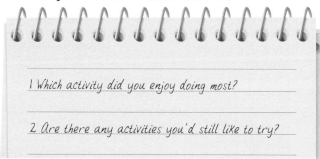

1 Which activity did you enjoy doing most?

2 Are there any activities you'd still like to try?

❸ Work in small groups. Talk to each other about your holiday activities.

Reading Part 3

Exam advice

- Underline the important information in the questions *and* the text.
- Write the question number next to the information you have underlined in the text.

❶ Work in small groups. Look at the photos with the text about an unusual holiday in Borneo and discuss which of the activities from Starting off you think you can do there.

❷ Read these ten sentences about the holiday in Borneo.

	A	B
1 Borneo is <u>larger than any other island</u> in the world.	☐	✓
2 Temperatures <u>rarely fall below</u> 20° C on Borneo.	☐	☐
3 For the first part of this trip you will sleep in the city centre.	☐	☐
4 You'll be able to try water sports in the South China Sea.	☐	☐
5 There is an airport in Sukau.	☐	☐
6 The animals in the Sepilok animal centre are all sick or injured.	☐	☐
7 It's impossible to get near an orang-utan.	☐	☐
8 Orang-utans only eat meat.	☐	☐
9 This Borneo holiday includes a free trip to Mount Kinabalu.	☐	☐
10 You will have an opportunity to buy gifts after the sightseeing tour.	☐	☐

3 Work in pairs. The important words have been underlined in the first two sentences of Exercise 2. Decide together which words you would underline in sentences 3–10, then underline them.

4 Read the text to find out whether sentences 1–10 are correct or incorrect. If the sentence is correct, tick (✓) box A. If it is not correct, tick (✓) box B. <u>Underline</u> where you find the answer in the text.

5 Check your answers with your partner. If you have a different answer, look at the text again together.

6 Work in small groups. Answer these questions.

- Would you like to go on this holiday to Borneo? Why (not)?
- Take turns to tell each other about a special holiday you have had. Decide which of you has had the best holiday.

Discover the Island of Borneo

Introduction

Borneo is one of the great islands of the world. <u>Not quite as big as its neighbour, the island of New Guinea,</u> Borneo is still an amazing island. It's famous for its jungles and wildlife, in particular the orang-utan. There are two seasons – expect heavy rain between October and March and a drier period for the rest of the year. Temperatures are generally between 24° C and 30° C all year round.

Kota Kinabalu

Fly to Kota Kinabalu, Borneo's most important city. We'll pick you up from your comfortable accommodation in the heart of this city and take you on several exciting day trips over the next few days. See your first rainforest, go trekking in the national park and spend a day on the shores of the South China Sea where you can go swimming or snorkelling in its clear blue water.

Sukau

Leaving the city behind, we fly to the airport in the north of the island. From there, the only way to continue our journey to Sukau, where you'll spend the next few days, is by bus. During this part of your trip, you will visit the Sepilok Centre, which looks after young orang-utans whose parents have died. Some of these animals arrive in very bad condition. The centre helps them to recover but this can take time.

Visitor projects

There is no age limit here. All visitors are expected to take part in research activities to understand and observe the orang-utans. Don't miss this extraordinary opportunity to get close to these creatures. Once you have spent the morning watching wild orang-utans, why not help collect the plants that are part of their diet?

Return to Kota Kinabalu

Once back in Kota Kinabalu, enjoy some free time. For a small fee, book our day trip to Mount Kinabalu. At over 4,000 metres, it is the highest mountain in South-East Asia. If you prefer to look around the city, come on our morning tour which includes a visit to the Sabah State Museum and the Tun Mustapha Tower. And when the tour is over, it's a short ride to the modern shopping centres, local stores or markets for some last-minute souvenirs.

Vocabulary

Travel, journey and *trip*

❶ ⊙ PET candidates often make mistakes with *travel, journey* and *trip*. Look at this extract from the *Cambridge Learner's Dictionary*.

> Common Learner Error
>
> travel, journey or trip?
>
> The noun **travel** is a general word which means the activity of travelling.
>
> *Air travel has become much cheaper.*
>
> ---
>
> **travel** [trævᵊl] *verb* to make a journey
> *I spent a year travelling around Asia.*
>
> Use **journey** to talk about when you travel from one place to another.
>
> *He fell asleep during the train journey.*
> *Did you have a good journey?*
> ~~*Did you have a good travel?*~~
>
> A **trip** is a journey in which you visit a place for a short time and come back again.
>
> *a business trip*
> *a 3-day trip to Spain*

❷ ⊙ Circle the correct option in *italics* in sentences 1–5 written by PET candidates.

1 My father went to Paris on a business *journey /* ⟨*trip*⟩.
2 I've won a *trip / journey* to America for two people staying in a five-star hotel.
3 We *tripped / travelled* around my country and bought some souvenirs.
4 I've just got back from Greece. It was a wonderful *travel / trip*.
5 I was really afraid of flying so I was very nervous about my *travel / journey*.

Grammar

Comparative and superlative adjectives; *(not) as … as …*

⊳ page 121 *Grammar reference: Comparative and superlative adjectives*

❶ Work in pairs. Look at these sentences about the island of Borneo and say if they are true or false.

1 Borneo is **bigger than** its neighbour New Guinea.
2 Sukau is **the most important** city in Borneo.
3 Mount Kinabalu is **the highest** mountain in South-East Asia.
4 Rain is **more common** between October and March **than** the rest of the year.

❷ Sentences 1–4 above show ways of comparing things. Look at the sentences again and complete the rules with the correct sentence number.

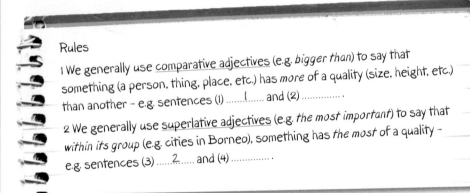

> Rules
>
> 1 We generally use <u>comparative adjectives</u> (e.g. *bigger than*) to say that something (a person, thing, place, etc.) has *more* of a quality (size, height, etc.) than another – e.g. sentences (1) ......1...... and (2) ....
>
> 2 We generally use <u>superlative adjectives</u> (e.g. *the most important*) to say that within its group (e.g. cities in Borneo), something has *the most* of a quality – e.g. sentences (3) ......2...... and (4) ....

❸ ⊙ Work in small groups. PET candidates often make mistakes with the form and spelling of comparative and superlative adjectives. Complete this table correctly.

	adjective	comparative	superlative	spelling rule
regular	deep	deep**er** (than)	(the) deep**est**	add **-er** or **-est**
	saf**e**	saf**er** (than)	(the) saf**est**	(7) ....
	nois**y**	nois**ier** (than)	(1)	**y** changes to **i**, add **-er** or **-est**
	bi**g**	big**ger** (than)	(2)	(8) ....
	beautiful	**more** beautiful (than)	(3)	(9) ....
irregular	good	better (than)	(4)	
	bad	worse (than)	(5)	
	far	farther or further (than)	(6)	

❹ ⊙ Correct one mistake made by PET candidates with the form or spelling of the comparative or superlative adjective in sentences 1–6.

1 In the centre is the ~~bigest~~ *biggest* market in Europe.
2 This town is more quiet than the town I used to live in.
3 That is the worse joke I have ever heard in all my life.
4 I was so hungry that I decided to go to the nearst restaurant.
5 Big cities are much more better than the countryside.
6 Tunisia is the hotest place I've ever been to.

5 Work in pairs. Talk about facts 1–12 below and complete each using a comparative or superlative adjective made from one of the words in brackets. (Make a guess if you don't know the answer.)

1 Asia is ....*bigger*........ than Africa. (big / small)
2 Russia is ....*the largest*.... country in the world. (large)
3 The mosquito is .... creature in the world. (dangerous)
4 Orang-utans are .... than dogs. (intelligent / stupid)
5 An African elephant is .... than a blue whale. (heavy / light)
6 The howler monkey is .... land animal. (noisy)
7 The sea horse is .... fish in the world. (slow)
8 The Great Dane is .... dog in the world. (tall)
9 Nagoya train station in Japan is .... station in the world. (big)
10 Nemo 33 in Belgium is .... pool in the world. (deep)
11 Antarctica is .... than the Arctic. (cold / warm)
12 The Amazon rainforest is .... than the rainforest in Borneo. (large / small)

6 (18) Listen to Alyssa and Fergus discussing the facts and find out how many of your answers are the same as theirs.

▶ page 122 *Grammar reference:* A bit, a little, much, far, a lot

7 How different are these places and animals? Use *a bit, a little, much, far* or *a lot* and the word in brackets as a comparative adjective to write one complete sentence for 1–5.

1 George is 2 metres tall. Fred is 1.98 metres tall. (tall)
.... *George is a bit taller than Fred* ....

2 Mount Everest, in the Himalayas, is around 8,850 metres high. K2, also in the Himalayas, is around 8,611 metres high. (high)
....

3 Arica, Chile, gets 0.76 mm of rain per year. Death Valley in Arizona, USA, gets less than 50 mm per year. (dry)
....

4 84 million people travel through Atlanta International Airport, USA each year. 67 million travel through London's Heathrow Airport. (busy)
....

5 The sperm whale's brain weighs about 78 kg. A human adult's brain weighs about 13 kg. (heavy)
....

8 Read these sentences about Borneo and orang-utans and say if you think they are true or false.

1 Borneo is **not** quite **as big as** its neighbour New Guinea.
2 Orang-utans can move more quickly in the trees, but on the ground, humans are **as fast as** orang-utans.
3 A female orang-utan can grow to be **as large as** a male orang-utan.

9 Look at the sentences in Exercise 8 again and answer these questions.

1 What expression do we use to say things are the same?
2 What word do we add to say things are different?
3 Does the form of the adjective (or adverb) change?

▶ page 122 *Grammar reference:* (Not) as … as …

10 For each sentence about animals 1–5, use *(not) as … as …* to complete the second sentence so that it means the same as the first. *Use no more than three words.*

1 Orang-utans are more intelligent than dogs.
Dogs are not as ...*intelligent as*... orang-utans.

2 African elephants have larger ears than Asian elephants.
Asian elephants' ears are not as .... African elephants' ears.

3 Goats belong to the same family as sheep but their hair is straighter.
Sheep belong to the same family as goats but their hair is not .... goats' hair.

4 The mosquito is the most dangerous creature in the world.
There is no other creature in the world .... the mosquito.

5 I'd expected dogs to be more intelligent.
Dogs aren't .... I'd expected.

Vocabulary
Buildings and places

 shopping centre

❶ Work in small groups. Use some of the words below to label the pictures.

art gallery	bridge	department store	factory
fountain	Internet café	market	monument
police station	port	river	~~shopping centre~~
stadium	tourist office	town hall	youth club

❷ Take turns to ask and answer questions about some of the places in Exercise 1.

> **A:** Is there a department store in your town?
> **B:** Yes, there's one in the shopping centre.
> **A:** How often do you go there?
> **B:** I often go there on Saturday afternoons ...

❸ These adjectives can be used to describe places. Write the opposite of each adjective. (Sometimes more than one answer is possible.)

1	crowded *empty*		8	interesting
2	narrow		9	safe
3	high		10	expensive
4	modern		11	noisy
5	dirty		12	deep
6	beautiful		13	far
7	lively		14	hilly

Grammar
Big and *enormous* (gradable and non-gradable adjectives)

▶ page 122 *Grammar reference*: Big *and* enormous

A quite big

B  very/really big

C  enormous

❶ Complete the rules about gradable and non-gradable adjectives using *quite**, *very*, *absolutely* or *really*.

Rules

Big is a <u>gradable</u> adjective – we can say something is (1) .... (2) .... or (3) .... big to talk about <u>how big</u> it is. We can also say something is *extremely* big which means that it's much bigger than usual.

Enormous is a <u>non-gradable</u> adjective and means <u>very big</u>. We can say (4) .... or (5) .... enormous but <u>not</u> normally (6) ...., (7) .... or *extremely* enormous.
---

*quite here means *a little*

▶ page 126 *for* quite *with non-gradable adjectives to mean completely*

❷ Write the gradable adjectives for these non-gradable adjectives. (More than one answer is sometimes possible.)

1	enormous *big*		5	terrible
2	tiny		6	filthy
3	boiling		7	fascinating
4	freezing		8	fantastic

❸ ⊘ PET candidates often make mistakes with gradable and non-gradable adjectives. Circle the correct option in *italics* in sentences 1–5.

1 It's a *very* / (really) wonderful place in my country.
2 It was a *quite / really* great movie. You should see it.
3 I've got a dog which is *very / absolutely* enormous.
4 The weather is *absolutely / quite* hot here, but at night it gets cold.
5 I really like this chicken dish – it's *very / absolutely* nice.

④ ⟨19⟩ Listen to Selma talking about where she lives. Note down her replies to these questions.

1 Where do you come from?
2 What do you like about living there?
3 What would you change about where you live?

⑤ Work in pairs. Ask and answer the questions in Exercise 4, trying to use *very*, *quite*, *absolutely* and *really* with gradable and non-gradable adjectives.

Listening Part 3

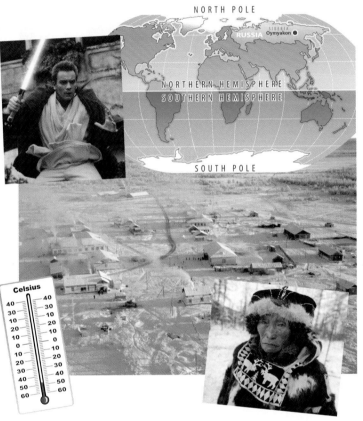

NORTH POLE

RUSSIA
SIBERIA
Oymyakon

NORTHERN HEMISPHERE
SOUTHERN HEMISPHERE

SOUTH POLE

Celsius

The **Northern Pole of Cold** is a place in the northern hemisphere where the lowest air temperature has been recorded

❶ Work in small groups. Look at the pictures and answer these questions about Oymyakon (also known as the *Northern Pole of Cold*).

1 Where is Oymyakon?
2 Which two records has this place held, do you think?
3 What do you think is the connection between Hollywood actor Ewan McGregor and Oymyakon?
4 What do you think life is like there for young people?

❷ Read these notes about Oymyakon. Decide what information you think is missing from each space (*number, date, noun, verb, adjective, etc.*).

Oymyakon, East Russia

Temperatures dropped to –71.2° C in the year
(1) ....

Winters can be **(2)** .... months long

In last 100 years, little changed in Oymyakon except for arrival of **(3)** ....

Fiodor Arnosow – **(4)** .... person to live in Oymyakon

Young people would like:

• **(5)** ....

• Internet café to meet friends

• disco with music

Ewan McGregor travelled there by **(6)** ....

Exam advice

• Before you listen, read the notes carefully and think about what *kind* of word is missing in each space.

• The notes follow the order of the recording.

• Don't worry if you don't hear the answer the first time – you will listen to the recording twice.

❸ ⟨20⟩ You are now going to listen to a radio programme about Oymyakon. For each question, fill in the missing information in the numbered space in the notes above.

❹ Work in pairs. Before you listen again, compare your answers and see if you can help each other with the missing words.

❺ ⟨20⟩ Listen to the recording again and then check your answers with your teacher.

❻ Work in small groups. Imagine you live in Oymyakon and discuss these questions.

• Do you like living in Oymyakon? Why (not)?
• What would you change about your town?
• How could you attract more tourists to your town?

Speaking Part 3

1 _Bangkok floating market, Thailand_

2 ....

3 ....

1 Work in small groups. Look at the map of the world and the five photos. Match the place names from the box below to the correct photo. Explain your choice of place.

Photo 1 must be Bangkok floating market, Thailand because I can see boats with lots of food in this photo.

> ~~Bangkok floating market, Thailand~~
> Hikkaduwa Beach, Sri Lanka   Marrakech, Morocco
> The Great Wall, China   Machu Picchu, Peru

2 Discuss these questions in your groups.

- What do you know about these places?
- What can tourists do in each place, do you think?

3 🔊 Listen to Laura describing the photo of the Bangkok floating market. Put a tick (✓) next to the things she talks about.

place ☐	weather ☐	time of day ☐
colours ☐	food ☐	transport ☐
clothes ☐	activities ☐	

4 ....

5 ....

4 🔊 Listen again. Complete Laura's expressions 1–8, then answer the question below.

1 In this photo I ......_can see_...... a lot of boats.
2 It .... a traffic jam.
3 The water .... really dirty.
4 I .... it's a market in the morning.
   It .... somewhere in Asia.
5 There .... a lot of fruit.
6 On each boat, I .... a person.
7 On one of the boats, there ....
   somebody wearing a colourful shirt.
8 I .... it will rain.

- Why do we say _look like_ in Question 2 but _look_ (without _like_) in Question 3?

5 Work in pairs. Using the expressions in Exercise 4, take turns to describe one of the other photos. The listener should close their book and not look at the photos.

Writing Part 3

❶ Read this Writing Part 3 task and answer the questions that follow.

- This is part of a letter you receive from an English-speaking friend.

> As part of a school project I have to write about an important city in your country. Which city should I choose? Can you tell me about this city?

- Now write a letter to your friend.
- Write your letter in about 100 words.

1 What do you need to write?
2 How many words do you need to write?
3 What information should you include?

❷ Work in small groups. Choose an important city in your country and decide which of the things in the box you could write about. Then think of some adjectives to describe each one.

buildings	museums	shops	streets
transport	views	weather	

❸ Kirsty lives in Durban, South Africa. Read her answer to the Writing Part 3 task.

Durban, South Africa

Dear Oscar,

As you know, I've lived in Durban all my life, so why don't you write about my city? It's one of the largest cities in South Africa. In fact over three million people live there. Durban is famous for its port. People say that it's the busiest port in Africa. Durban is on the east coast of South Africa and has the 'Golden Mile' – a group of beaches which are never too crowded and they are fantastic for surfing. There are absolutely fascinating museums, modern shopping centres and traditional markets, too. The weather is great because the sun even shines in winter. I hope this is enough information.

Lots of love,

Kirsty

❹ Work in pairs. Look at the writing checklist. Can you answer *yes* to all the questions? Why (not)?

> **Writing checklist**
> 1 Does Kirsty answer all the parts of the question?
> 2 Is her answer well organised?
> 3 Does she open and close the letter in a suitable way?
> 4 Does she connect her ideas with words like *and*, *because* and *which*?
> 5 Does she use a variety of structures (*tenses*, *comparative adjectives*, etc.) and vocabulary?
> 6 Does she write about 100 words?

❺ <u>Underline</u> the expressions in Kirsty's writing that you could use in your own letter. Then check if you have underlined the same expressions as your partner.

Exam advice
- Read the question carefully and underline the key words.
- Answer all the parts of the question.
- Make sure you can say *yes* to the questions in the writing checklist in Exercise 4.

❻ Write a rough copy of your letter, using Kirsty's letter as a model.

❼ Work in small groups. Read each other's letters to find out if you can answer *yes* to all the questions in the writing checklist.

❽ Write the final copy of your own letter.

> In preparation for the PET exam, it is useful to write rough copies of your Writing Parts 2 and 3 answers. Your teacher and other students can then help you to improve your work before you write your final copy. However, in the real exam you won't have time to write a rough copy – just write quick notes before you write your final copy.

Unit 3 *Vocabulary and grammar review*

Vocabulary

❶ Fill in the gaps by adding *im-*, *in-* or *un-* to the word in brackets.

1 It was ....*impossible*...... (possible) to see anything in the fog.
2 You can't run 20 kilometres in one day if you're .... (fit).
3 It's .... (fair) to charge children the same price as adults.
4 Petrol is very expensive now, so big cars are becoming .... (popular).
5 It's .... (healthy) to eat too much and do no exercise.
6 You shouldn't use .... (formal) expressions when you write a job application.
7 People became .... (patient) when they had to wait outside the stadium.
8 That old bicycle is .... (safe) and nobody should ride it.
9 Heavy snow is forecast, so drivers should avoid any .... (necessary) journeys.
10 In colder countries, many animals are .... (active) during the winter.

❷ Match the beginnings of sentences 1–8 with their correct endings a–h.

1 I'm going to put my name   **a** up painting as a hobby.
2 We're all really looking   **b** with any problems like that.
3 People who like art often take **c** down for swimming lessons.
4 You must work hard to catch   **d** out very early in the morning.
5 I'm sure that you can deal   **e** forward to surfing tomorrow.
6 In the next game, you can join **f** up for not winning the race.
7 It's a long walk, so I need to set **g** in and play in our team.
8 Getting second prize didn't make **h** up with the rest of the class.

Grammar

❸ Complete the text with the *-ing* or the infinitive form of the verb in brackets.

I'm planning (1) ....*to go*.......... (go) away on holiday next week, but there are still so many things I need (2) .... (do) before we leave! I want (3) .... (get) some new clothes and I feel like (4) .... (go) shopping right now, though I can't afford (5) .... (buy) everything I'd like (6) .... (have). So I've decided only (7) .... (look for) the things I really must take with me. I'm also hoping (8) .... (see) my friends before I go, so I've suggested (9) .... (spend) Sunday afternoon together. And I must remember (10) .... (buy) some more credit for my mobile this afternoon. I forgot (11) .... (do) that yesterday, and I can't imagine (12) .... (be) away from home for a month and not sending a single text message!

❹ Circle the correct option, a, b or c.

1 While I'm away, a neighbour is ....*b*..... my cat.
   a looking for   **b** looking after   **c** looking at
2 My brother has a wonderful .... of old coins.
   a collection   **b** collecting   **c** collector
3 I love going out to sea and .... deep under the water.
   a surfing   **b** sailing   **c** diving
4 My brother is a very good .... He makes some lovely meals.
   a cook   **b** cooker   **c** cooking
5 I want to learn to play the piano, or another musical ....
   a object   **b** equipment   **c** instrument
6 The castle charges a lower admission .... for children.
   a fare   **b** fee   **c** value
7 It's more fun to take .... in a game than just watch it.
   a team   **b** part   **c** practice

Unit 4   *Vocabulary and grammar review*

Vocabulary

❶ Eeva has written this letter about her home town, Helsinki. However, she has made eight mistakes with adjectives – she has used the opposites! Correct the letter by changing the <u>underlined</u> adjectives to their opposites. (More than one answer is sometimes possible.)

Hi John,

                                 biggest

I live in Helsinki which is the capital and (1) <u>smallest</u> city in Finland. Helsinki is (2) <u>terrible</u> – I love it! It's located near the Baltic Sea so the weather is not very cold for such a northern country. February is by far the (3) <u>hottest</u> month. Last February was (4) <u>boiling</u>, temperatures fell to −15° C. As for the city itself, Helsinki is extremely clean. I love shopping and there are many places to go in the city centre. Tourists love the (5) <u>calm</u> market square but I prefer Stockmanns, it's a (6) <u>tiny</u> department store. Tourists also visit the Museum of Finnish Art but I think it's a little (7) <u>interesting</u>. Helsinki has 300 islands, some of them are completely (8) <u>crowded</u>. In the summer, we often take our boat to an island and spend the day there. Why don't you come and visit me?

Hope to hear from you soon.

Lots of love,

Eeva

❷ Choose the correct option in brackets to complete these sentences about record breakers.

1 At around 3,600 metres above the sea, La Paz, Bolivia, is the world's ...... *highest* .... capital city. ((highest)/ lowest / widest)

2 The Eiffel Tower is older .... the Empire State Building but the Empire State Building is taller. (then / as / than)

3 One of Copenhagen's most popular tourist attractions is the .... small Little Mermaid statue. (absolutely / very / far)

4 Mauna Loa, Hawaii, is .... larger than any other volcano. (more / far / very)

5 The cyclist, Mark Beaumont, took just under 195 days to .... around the world by bike. (travel / trip / journey)

6 One of the world's largest .... is in Dubai, United Arab Emirates. It has over 1,200 shops. (shopping centres / department stores / markets)

Grammar

❸ **⊙** PET candidates often make mistakes with comparisons. Correct one mistake in each of these sentences.

               taller

1 He was ~~taler~~ than me and more handsome too.
2 This cinema is more better than the cinema in Enfield.
3 I don't like the countryside even if it is more safe than cities.
4 I like living in the city much more that the countryside.
5 The restaurant had bigger windows as my school sports hall.
6 The food here is much more expensive then in my country.

❹ Read these sentences about a holiday. Complete the second sentence so that it means the same as the first, *using no more than three words.*

1 I thought the journey was going to be really terrible.
   The journey wasn't as .... *bad as* .... I'd expected.

2 This year's hotel was nearer to the beach than last year's.
   Last year's hotel was .... from the beach than this year's.

3 The restaurant in our hotel was more popular than any other restaurant in town.
   The restaurant in our hotel was the ....
   .... restaurant in town.

4 Of all the activities, I liked going snorkelling best.
   I liked going snorkelling .... any of the other activities.

5 I have never visited a place as hot as this.
   This is .... place I have ever visited.

Unit 5 Feelings

1 ...*jealousy*....
2 ....
3 ....
4 ....
5 ....

Starting off

❶ Which picture shows each of these emotions?

| anger | fear | happiness | ~~jealousy~~ | sadness |

❷ Do the quiz and match an emotion from the box with questions 1–5.

❸ Look at the key on page 173. Do you agree with what it says about you? Why (not)?

Listening Part 4

❶ You are going to hear a teenager, Ben, talking to his sister, Erica, about his best friend, Liam. Look at the first part of their conversation, then answer the questions below.

Erica:	I've got a feeling you're upset about something. What is it?
Ben:	Well, Liam moved away with his family last year and I don't think things are as good now.
Erica:	Oh, I'm a bit surprised. It seems to me you spend half your time on the phone to him, or writing him emails and texts and things.
Ben:	Yes, I do. And we chat online, too. But for me it's not the same as seeing each other.

1 Which words do they use to give their opinions?
I've got a feeling ...
2 Which other words do you know for giving opinions?

HOW EMOTIONAL ARE YOU?

1 ...*sadness*.......
The film you are watching has a very sad ending. What do you do?
a cry a lot   **b** you never cry   **c** cry a little

2 ....
You are in a café when somebody spills your drink, and doesn't say 'sorry'.
What do you do?
a say nothing to them   **b** tell them it's OK
c shout at them

3 ....
You have broken a tooth, so you have to go to the dentist. What do you do?
a look a bit nervous   **b** say how afraid you are
c say you like seeing the dentist

4 ....
Your exam results are much better than you expected. What do you do?
a scream and jump around   **b** smile a little
c continue working

5 ....
Someone you don't like suddenly wins a lot of money. What do you do?
a take no notice of them   **b** say they're very lucky
c say they don't deserve it

② ㉒ Listen to the rest of the conversation. Decide if each sentence is correct or incorrect. If it is correct, put a tick (✓) in the box under A for YES. If it is not correct, put a tick (✓) in the box under B for NO.

                                         A   B

1 Erica thinks Ben should see Liam more often. ☐ ☐

2 Ben enjoys travelling by road to see Liam. ☐ ☐

3 According to Ben, the train costs too much. ☐ ☐

4 He says that Liam wants to visit him at weekends. ☐ ☐

5 Ben says that Liam and he are still good friends. ☐ ☐

6 Erica is sure that Liam knows how Ben feels. ☐ ☐

❸ Match the underlined expressions from the conversation 1–6 with their meanings a–f.

1 you're <u>upset</u> about something   **a** wants very much
2 Liam <u>moved away</u>   **b** have a good relationship
3 you and Liam actually <u>get together</u>   **c** unhappy or worried
4 I don't think he's <u>keen on</u> doing that   **d** make (someone) remember (something)
5 we <u>get on</u> really well   **e** went to a different place to live
6 you need to <u>remind</u> him   **f** meet to spend time with someone

❹ Do you think you can still be good friends with somebody when you live a long way from each other? Talk to a partner about it. Use opinion expressions and some of the expressions above.

Grammar

Can, could, might and *may* (ability and possibility)

▷ page 122 *Grammar reference:* Can, could, might, may *(ability and possibility)*

❶ <u>Underline</u> the verbs for ability and possibility (modal verbs) in these extracts from the conversation between Erica and Ben, then answer the questions below.

> *Whenever I can, Erica.*
>
> *And Liam could get one, too.*
>
> *He might not realise that*

- Which of these modal verbs is negative?
- Where does *not* go?
- What is the short form?
- What are the negatives of the other two modal verbs?

② ⊙ These sentences contain mistakes with modals made by PET candidates. Say what the errors are (e.g. *wrong word order, wrong tense*, etc.) and correct them.

1 We can ~~to~~ go to the cinema next weekend. *Modals are followed by the infinitive without 'to'.*
2 I know it may seems strange.
3 Sorry but tomorrow I'm not can go.
4 What we could do?
5 Here we can doing a lot of sports.
6 You will might see them in December.
7 It's could be quite boring for you.
8 We could met at 8 o'clock near the cinema.

❸ Read this email and complete the rules below with the underlined words.

  ■ ◢ ◢   ✉

Hi Kylie,

I'm sorry but I don't think I <u>can</u> go out on Thursday. I <u>may</u> be busy all evening on Friday, too, so Saturday <u>might</u> be better. That new film is on at the cinema and it <u>could</u> be really good – your favourite actor's in it. I <u>could</u> meet you there at about 7.30. Let me know what you think.

Bye for now,
Lauren

---

1 We use .... or .... for ability.
2 We use .... , ... or .... for possibility, with no real difference in meaning.

❹ Choose the correct modal (*can, might,* etc.) in Kylie's reply.

Hi Lauren

Thanks for your message. I (1) may / (can) see you're very busy at the moment, so perhaps it (2) can / might be better to meet another weekend. Also, I (3) couldn't / mightn't go out until later because my little brother will be here with me and I (4) can't / may not leave him alone at home.

It's a pity we (5) can't / may not see each other more often. You're my best friend and I know I (6) might / can always talk to you about anything. (7) Could / May you phone me in the next few days? I've got some interesting news and I (8) mightn't / can't wait to tell you about it!

Love,

Kylie

❺ Work in pairs. Tell your partner about things you normally *can* and *can't* do during the week. Then say what you *might* do next weekend.

In the week I can't get up late, but I can see my friends at school. At the weekend I might meet my friends in town, or I might go swimming.

Should, shouldn't, ought to, must, mustn't, have to and *don't have to* (obligation and prohibition)

▶ page 122 *Grammar reference:* Should, shouldn't, ought to, must, mustn't, have to, don't have to *(obligation and prohibition)*

A   B

❶ We use *should* or *ought to* to advise someone. In the negative, *shouldn't* is more common than *oughtn't*. Match pictures A and B with these sentences.

1 'You shouldn't go out tonight.'
2 'You ought to get a new T-shirt.'

❷ Give more advice to the people in the pictures. Use *ought to, should* and *shouldn't*.

'You should comb your hair.'

❸ Match pictures C–F with sentences 1–4.

C    D

E    F

1 'You *must* be home by 11 pm.' F
2 'You *have to* be 18 to ride this.'
3 'You *mustn't* make a noise, children.'
4 'It's Sunday – you *don't have to* get up.'

❹ Now match the modals in *italics* in sentences 1–4 above with their meanings a–d below.

a it's not necessary to do it   4

b you're not allowed to do it   ☐

c it's necessary to do it (because it's a rule or law)   ☐

d it's necessary to do it (because the speaker says so)   ☐

❺ Complete the sentences using *must, mustn't, have to* or *don't have to*.

1 'It's still early. ~~We don't have to go~~ home yet.'
2 'Your hands are dirty. You .... wash them.'
3 'It's a secret. You .... tell her what I said.'
4 'The club's free. You .... pay to get in.'
5 'You can't get married. You .... be 18.'
6 'No, I can't wait. You .... decide now!'

❻ Quickly read the text on page 47 and choose the correct ending for this sentence, A, B or C.

The purpose of the text is to:
A advertise an Internet site for young people.
B advise young people on Internet safety.
C tell young people not to use the Internet.

7 ⟨23⟩ **Circle the correct option in *italics* for 1–7 below. Then listen to the recording to check your answers.**

Internet sites like MySpace, Bebo and Facebook are a great way for young people to keep in touch with friends, but there are things you (1) (should) / ought do to stay safe. On some sites you (2) *don't have to / mustn't* use your real name if you don't want to, so invent a name for yourself. On most sites it's a rule that you (3) *ought to / have to* give an email address, but this (4) *doesn't have to / mustn't* be your normal one – you can use any address. You can write lots of interesting things on your online page, but something you (5) *must / have to* never do is put your house address or phone number. In fact, you (6) *shouldn't / don't have to* give any information that could let strangers know your identity, because on the Internet you never know who is looking. Remember, too, that you (7) *don't have to / mustn't* put your friends' personal details on your page, or you could put them in danger. So the message is: have fun, but take care.

8 **Think about your everyday life. Tell your partner about something:**

1 you have to do at school or work.
  I have to arrive on time.
2 you mustn't do at school or work.
3 you don't have to do at weekends.
4 you must do this week.
5 you shouldn't do but sometimes do.
6 you ought to do but probably won't do.

Vocabulary
Adjectives and prepositions

1 ☉ **In these correct sentences written by PET candidates, underline the preposition which comes after the adjective.**

1 My father was very angry with me.
2 I never get tired of watching this film.
3 He was very sorry about what happened.

2 **Work in groups. Complete the table with the prepositions *about*, *of* and *with*.**

afraid, ashamed, jealous, proud, fond	(1) ....
bored, disappointed, impatient, satisfied	(2) ....
sad, nervous, crazy, sure, depressed	(3) ....

3 **Can you think of any other adjectives that go with these prepositions? Add them to the table. Remember that some adjectives can be followed by different prepositions (e.g. *sure of, sure about*).**

4 **Write the correct prepositions in 1–6, then answer the questions about yourself. Say why.**

1 Is there anything you feel sad ...... *about* ......?
2 Is there anyone you sometimes get angry .... ?
3 When you were a child, what were you afraid .... ?
4 What do you sometimes get bored .... ?
5 Is there anything you sometimes feel nervous .... ?
6 What, in your life, are you most proud .... ?

Adjectives with *-ed* and *-ing*

☉ page 123 *Grammar reference: Adjectives with -ed and -ing*

1 **Quickly read the story *Love in the air* on page 48 and answer these questions.**

• Why did the man ask the airline to help?
• What happened in the end?

2 **Look at this extract from the text. What *-ing* adjective does it use? How does the spelling change from the word in brackets?**

For many people the flight to Australia is long and boring ...

3 **The extract could be rewritten like this. What *-ed* adjective does it use?**

Many people feel bored on the long flight to Australia.

4 **Answer these questions about both extracts.**

1 What is the flight to Australia often like?
2 How do people flying to Australia often feel?

5 **Fill in gaps 1–12 in the text with the correct form of the adjective. Use *-ing* if it describes something, or *-ed* if it tells us how someone feels about it.**

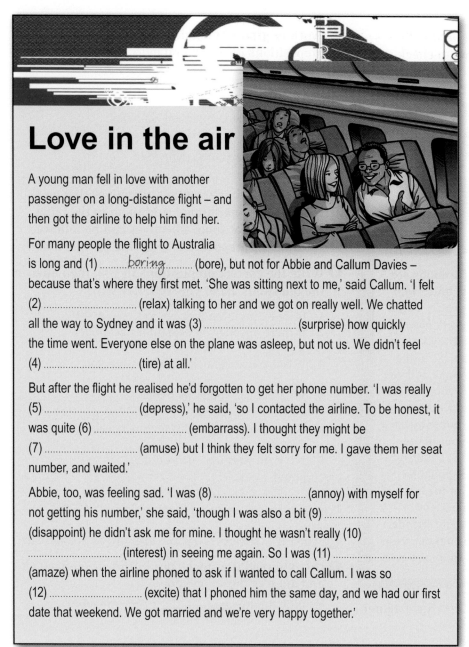

Love in the air

A young man fell in love with another passenger on a long-distance flight – and then got the airline to help him find her.

For many people the flight to Australia is long and (1) ....boring........ (bore), but not for Abbie and Callum Davies – because that's where they first met. 'She was sitting next to me,' said Callum. 'I felt (2) .... (relax) talking to her and we got on really well. We chatted all the way to Sydney and it was (3) .... (surprise) how quickly the time went. Everyone else on the plane was asleep, but not us. We didn't feel (4) .... (tire) at all.'

But after the flight he realised he'd forgotten to get her phone number. 'I was really (5) .... (depress),' he said, 'so I contacted the airline. To be honest, it was quite (6) .... (embarrass). I thought they might be (7) .... (amuse) but I think they felt sorry for me. I gave them her seat number, and waited.'

Abbie, too, was feeling sad. 'I was (8) .... (annoy) with myself for not getting his number,' she said, 'though I was also a bit (9) .... (disappoint) he didn't ask me for mine. I thought he wasn't really (10) .... (interest) in seeing me again. So I was (11) .... (amaze) when the airline phoned to ask if I wanted to call Callum. I was so (12) .... (excite) that I phoned him the same day, and we had our first date that weekend. We got married and we're very happy together.'

❻ Write three pairs of sentences using adjectives from the text.

It's <u>relaxing</u> to listen to music.
I always feel <u>relaxed</u> when I play my favourite songs.

❼ (24) You will hear four people talking. Listen and match speakers 1–4 with emotions a–d.

Speaker 1   **a** bored   Speaker 3   **c** annoyed
Speaker 2   **b** amazed   Speaker 4   **d** disappointed

❽ Tell a partner about the last time you were:

- annoyed
- tired
- surprised
- disappointed

Then ask your partner to describe situations that were:
- exciting
- embarrassing
- frightening
- amusing

Reading Part 5

❶ Read this paragraph. How would you answer the question at the end of the text? With a partner, think of some possible reasons.

In countries around the world, the number of people who say they enjoy life is going down. From the United States to China, more and more adults, teenagers and children say they are depressed, with ten times more people in the USA now experiencing depression than fifty years ago. At the same time, people in most countries have far more money than their parents' or grandparents' generations had. We're richer than ever before, so why aren't we happier?

❷ Work with a partner. Look at the pictures then answer the questions below.

- Which of these things would make you feel very happy?
- Why?
- What other things make you happy?
- Do you think we can learn how to feel happier?

❸ Quickly read the text *How to be happier*, without filling in any gaps, and answer these questions, according to the text.

1 When do we usually think about our happiness?
2 When should we think about the things that make us happy?
3 What may happen if we often do this?

❹ Look at a–d and the four possible answers (A, B, C and D) to each of 1–10 below the text. Which questions test:

a modal verbs .....2....., ..., ...
b adjectives and prepositions ...., ..., ...
c words with similar meanings ...., ..., ...
d adjectives with *-ing* .... ?

> ### Exam advice
> For each gap, decide what kind of word (e.g. *adjective, modal, adverb,* etc.) you need by looking at the four options. A, B, C and D are always the same kind of word.

❺ Read the text and choose the correct word, A, B, C or D, for each space. There is an example at the beginning (0).

How to be happier

Our happiness does not depend only (0) .....A..... what we have, say scientists. What we (1) .... we have is just as important. This is why the rich often seem miserable but people with very little (2) .... be much happier with their lives.

It is (3) .... how rarely we think about how lucky we are. Most of us have good health, homes and friends. We don't notice how good life normally is until we're feeling sad (4) .... something. But we don't (5) .... to wait for something negative to happen.

Instead, we (6) .... be grateful all the time for the good things in our lives. We can do this by writing down five of them (7) .... night. For example, something that we own, or the people we are fond (8) ....

By repeating this every day for a month it will become a (9) .... People who do this are healthier, more successful and more satisfied (10) .... their own lives.

0 A (on)	B in	C at	D by
1 A remind	B realise	C wonder	D doubt
2 A can	B shall	C do	D need
3 A amusing	B annoying	C surprising	D embarrassing
4 A about	B around	C along	D among
5 A must	B have	C would	D could
6 A ought	B may	C should	D might
7 A most	B every	C all	D some
8 A for	B of	C from	D to
9 A habit	B way	C use	D form
10 A into	B over	C under	D with

❻ Which good things in your life are you grateful for? Think of as many as you can, and write down the five most important.

Vocabulary
Adjectives and their opposites

❶ Match adjectives 1–5 with their meanings a–e.

1 miserable   a bad or harmful   *cheerful*
2 nervous   b gives a lot to other people
3 negative   c very pleased
4 delighted   d worried or afraid
5 generous   e very unhappy

❷ Now match 1–5 with their opposites from the box.

> ~~cheerful~~ depressed
> mean positive relaxed

❸ These adjectives describe experiences. Put them into pairs with opposite meanings.

> ~~awful~~ ~~fantastic~~ funny
> ordinary serious strange

awful/fantastic

❹ Now match the adjectives from the box with situations 1–6.

1 Somebody tells you the best joke you've ever heard. *funny*
2 You have a problem. You can solve it, but you must think carefully.
3 You lose your wallet or purse with all your money in it.
4 Like every day, you're standing at the bus stop.
5 You hear a noise in the dark, but you can't see anyone.
6 By chance, you meet your favourite film star.

5 Work in pairs. Tell your partner about awful, funny, fantastic and strange things that sometimes happen.

It's really <u>awful</u> when people talk about you behind your back.

Speaking Parts 3 and 4

1 Work with a partner. Choose a picture each, A or B, and say what you can see in it. Think about how the person felt while they were there.

2 (25) To see if you were right about their feelings, listen to the people in the pictures.

3 (25) Listen again and complete the questions.

1 How .... you .... ?
2 What .... in the .... ?
3 How long .... you .... to wait?
4 What .... your .... to that?

4 Work with a partner. Do the exam task together. You could choose up to five of the suggested life events below.

> *Exam advice*
>
> Make the discussion longer by asking the other candidate how they felt, what happened next, etc.

> Your photographs showed people in situations that caused **strong feelings**. Now I'd like you to talk together about **important events** in your life, and how you felt at the time.

- moving house or changing school
- making a new friend
- taking an important exam
- receiving a special present
- being frightened by something
- doing something for the first time
- being very surprised by something
- doing something very well
- being very angry about something
- hearing or seeing something funny

Writing Part 3

1 Read this sentence from a letter that a friend sent you.

> *So tell me, what's your favourite way of relaxing, and why do you like it?*

Which of these points should you put in your reply, do you think? What else should you include?

1 Where you go to relax
2 How your best friend relaxes
3 What might be a good way to relax
4 When you usually relax
5 How you relax
6 How you relaxed when you were a child

❷ Read this reply from Olivia. Which of the points from Exercise 1 does she include?

Hi Nathan,

Thanks for your letter - it was great to hear from you.

How do I like to relax? Well, what I most like to do is go into my room and read an interesting book, particularly at weekends. I really like being there because it's so warm and cosy, and I can listen to my favourite music. I put a sign outside the door saying 'Do not disturb', so nobody comes in. I don't even answer phone calls!

So that's what I do to feel relaxed. How about you? Write soon and let me know.

All the best,

Olivia

❸ Which of these expressions would you use in a letter to a friend? Where would you put them? Tick (✓) the suitable expressions and write 'B' for beginning or 'E' for end.

✓E

Lots of love,   I have received your letter dated June 15.   I look forward to hearing from you.   Dear Sir/Madam,   Well, that's all for now.   Hi Lisa
All the best,   This is just a quick letter to say …   Yours sincerely,
It was great to hear from you.   Dear Sir/Madam,   Give my love to everyone.
Don't forget to write soon.   Sorry I've taken so long to write back.   Dear George

❹ Look at Olivia's letter. Which of these, or similar, expressions does she use?

❺ When she gives reasons, Olivia uses the linking word *because*. Which other word linking cause and effect can you find in her letter?

❻ Join sentences 1–5 using the linking words in brackets. Start with the words given.

1   I can go to the sports centre quite often. It's near my house. (as)
    I can go to the sports centre quite often as it's near my house.

2   There are so many good films. I never get tired of going to the cinema. (because)
    I never …

3   I often go out in the evenings. I don't have much homework to do. (since)
    Since I …

4   Water-skiing is really exciting. I enjoy it a lot. (because)
    I enjoy water-skiing …

5   I'm on my PlayStation® every day. I've got some really good games. (so)
    I've …

❼ Read the instructions for the exam task, and follow the steps below.

- This is part of a letter you receive from an English-speaking friend.

  In your next letter, please tell me about something exciting you like to do. Why is it such good fun?

- Now write a letter, answering your friend's questions.

- Write your letter in about 100 words.

Exam advice

Make your writing more interesting by using adjectives, especially strong ones like *amazing* or *crazy* (*about*).

1 Choose an exciting activity.

2 Make notes about where, when and what.

3 Plan the order for your points. Add reasons.

4 Write your letter, using expressions like those in Exercise 3 and cause-and-effect links from Exercise 6.

5 Check your work for mistakes.

Unit 6 Leisure and fashion

1 .....cartoon.....

2 ....

3 ....

4 ....

5 ....

6 ....

Starting off

❶ Work in pairs. Use some of the words in the box to label the television screens with the type of programme.

advert	~~cartoon~~	chat show	comedy series
documentary ✓	quiz show	reality show	
sports programme	the news	the weather	

❷ (26) Listen to Lucy and Ben talking about four different programmes. Put a tick (✓) next to the *types* of programme they talk about.

❸ Work in small groups and discuss these questions.

1 How much TV do you watch? When do you watch TV?
2 What's your favourite TV programme? Why?
3 Do you prefer to watch TV or do something else? Why?

Reading Part 2

❶ Work in pairs. Look at the page from a Hong Kong entertainment guide and find one example of each of these things:

1 martial arts   *Fight Planet*   5 film
   demonstration
2 musical   6 comedy club
3 concert   7 unusual circus
4 play   8 night-club

❷ Silvie and Kat would like to go out. Read about what they want to see and don't want to see and answer the question below.

1  Best friends Silvie and Kat would like to see <u>something completely different</u>. They saw their favourite band last week so they <u>don't want to hear more music</u>. They have<u>n't got time to reserve tickets</u>. ☐

• Why have some expressions been <u>underlined</u>, do you think?

❸ Read the entertainment guide on page 53 to find out what Silvie and Kat choose to see. <u>Underline</u> where you find the information in the guide. Why do they not choose the other seven options?

A University Spotlight

We have put together a great show for Hong Kong. Come and see local university students stand up and tell jokes. Tickets are selling quickly so book early. Special discounts for students.

GetIn, Fri 21, 10 pm & Sat 22, 11 pm. Short walk from station.

B Kids Rock

Set in the year 2306. Rock and roll is not allowed and young people are told what to think and do. A band of live musicians play more than 20 pop songs. For the next month, Hong Kong audiences will have the chance to see this show.

Haynes Theatre, Tue–Fri 8 pm, Sat 2 pm & 8 pm, Sun 1 pm & 7 pm. Limited parking on site. Easy access by public transport.

C Prince of Mandavia

(English with subtitles in Cantonese)

Cartoon fun! Max does not want to be the next Prince of Mandavia. He wants to have a normal life like his friends, monkey, elephant and bear. When trouble comes to Mandavia, can the friends save their country from its enemies? Fantastic music by everyone's favourite band, *Keith's Door.*

Silver Hill Cinema Mon–Sun 2 pm, 4 pm, 6 pm, 8 pm, 10 pm & 12 pm. Free parking for every two adult tickets.

D Liala

No large tent or animals here, just a mix of gymnastics, dance, theatre and music. Liala tells the story of a young woman's journey. This show opened this week in a very special venue and has already received very positive reviews. Suitable for all ages.

The LIALA Theatre. Tues–Sun 7 pm and 10 pm. 55-min ferry ride from Hong Kong, then shuttle bus.

E Found in Hong Kong

Mostly music and definitely good fun. Listen to the sounds of a very unusual orchestra. Dressed up as strange animals, the musicians have replaced their instruments with everyday objects found in the streets, such as bottles, drink cans and boxes. Not to be taken seriously – be prepared to laugh!

Cultural Centre Sat 4 pm & 8 pm. Car park nearby. Tickets still available. Easy access by public transport. Gift Shop open during interval. Under-8s not admitted.

F Reggae Nights

Well, you've all heard of Bob Marley. Disc Jockeys Doctor Jupiter and Master Moon play their records for this reggae disco. Come on down for a great evening.

Club 999 Sat 9 pm – late. Admission free. (Over-18s only.) Short walk from public transport.

G Fight Planet

You haven't seen anything like this before. Expect some amazing action as Thai Kickboxers come to Hong Kong. Battle Fighters include Matt 'Monkey' Barr and Paul 'Tiger' Knowles. Entertainment for audiences of all ages. Souvenirs will be on sale after the show.

Star Hall. Parking for disabled customers only. No tickets for early performance. A few tickets available for 11 pm.

H Best Friends

Set in a city school, the English teacher has to teach a group of difficult students. *Best Friends* takes a serious look at the role of the modern teacher and asks whether a teacher can make friends with their students. Nothing different about this story but highly recommended for parents and their teenage children!

The Academy. Shop open during interval. Tue–Fri 7.30 pm, Sat 2.30 pm & 8 pm. No parking available until further notice.

4 Read the information about the people below and <u>underline</u> the important words.

2

Teenagers Martha and Artie are visiting the Hong Kong *Futures Show* with their parents because they all love science fiction. Martha and Artie love live music, especially reggae, but their parents want to see a musical.

3

Al and Ed are university students who want to have fun in Hong Kong tonight. They can't afford to spend very much money but they like listening to good music. ☐

4

Lily (19) and Ken (18) want to see something with their 5-year-old cousin, Mai, who is mad about animals. Lily wants to drive, but she doesn't want to pay for parking. ☐

5

Lara (16) and her mum prefer something funny to serious drama. Their flight home tomorrow is at 8 am so they need to go to bed early. Lara still wants to buy some presents before they leave. ☐

5 Read the guide again carefully and decide which event A–H would be the most suitable for each group of people 2–5. <u>Underline</u> where you find your answer in the guide.

6 Work in pairs. We learn that Martha and Artie love reggae music. The word *reggae* is used in event F – *Reggae Nights*. Why is this event *not* the correct answer for them?

7 Find *four* more examples where words in the descriptions of people are repeated in the guide *but do not* tell us the correct answer.

8 Work in small groups. Choose one event from the entertainment guide that you would all like to see. When you are ready, explain your group's choice to the rest of the class.

Vocabulary
Going out

❶ Work in pairs. The words in the box appear in the guide. Look at the guide again and try to decide what these words mean.

admission	audience	interval	live
~~performance~~	review	subtitles	venue

❷ Now match the words to their definitions 1–8 from the *Cambridge Learner's Dictionary* to see if you decided on the correct meanings in Exercise 1.

1 ...*performance*... *noun* acting, singing, dancing or playing music to entertain people
2 .... *noun* the money that you pay to enter a place
3 .... *noun* the people who sit and watch a performance at a theatre, cinema, etc.
4 .... *adj* done with an audience
5 .... *noun* a report in a newspaper, magazine or programme that gives an opinion about a new book, film, etc.
6 .... *plural noun* words shown at the bottom of a cinema or television screen to explain what is being said
7 .... *noun* UK (US *intermission*) a short period of time between the parts of a play, performance, etc.
8 .... *noun* a place where a sports game, musical performance or special event happens

❸ 🔊(27) Listen to Liam using some of the words from Exercise 1 to give his opinion on one of the events in the guide. Which event does he talk about?

❹ Work in small groups. Take turns to describe one of the events in the entertainment guide. Can the others guess which event you are describing?

Grammar
Present perfect

❶ 🔊(28) Listen to Tom and Evan planning a night out together in Hong Kong. What do they decide to do?

❷ 🔊(28) Listen again and complete these extracts from their conversation, then answer the question below.

1 Have you .... ?
2 I haven't .... the circus show *Liala* ....
3 I've .... *Liala*.
4 I've .... reading the play.

• What tense is used in all four extracts?

▶ page 123 *Grammar reference: Present perfect*; Just, already *and* yet

❸ Work in pairs. We often use the adverbs *yet*, *already* or *just* with the present perfect. Complete these rules below by writing *yet*, *already* or *just* in gaps 1–6.

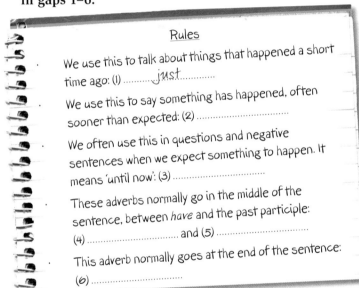

Rules

• We use this to talk about things that happened a short time ago: (1) ....*just*.........

• We use this to say something has happened, often sooner than expected: (2) ....

• We often use this in questions and negative sentences when we expect something to happen. It means 'until now': (3) ....

• These adverbs normally go in the middle of the sentence, between *have* and the past participle: (4) .... and (5) ....

• This adverb normally goes at the end of the sentence: (6) ....

❹ Harry has not been in contact with his English-speaking friend for a long time and decides to send an email. Complete Harry's email using the words given in the present perfect.

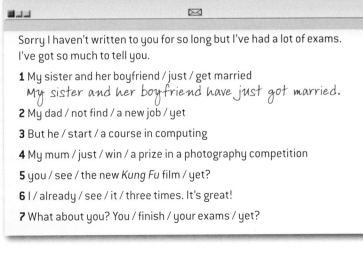

Sorry I haven't written to you for so long but I've had a lot of exams. I've got so much to tell you.

1 My sister and her boyfriend / just / get married
My sister and her boyfriend have just got married.

2 My dad / not find / a new job / yet

3 But he / start / a course in computing

4 My mum / just / win / a prize in a photography competition

5 you / see / the new *Kung Fu* film / yet?

6 I / already / see / it / three times. It's great!

7 What about you? You / finish / your exams / yet?

page 124 *Grammar reference:* Since *and* for

5 ⊙ **PET candidates sometimes make mistakes with *since* and *for*. Look at this extract from the *Cambridge Learner's Dictionary* and complete the sentences that follow so that they are true for you.**

> Common Learner Error
>
> **since** or **for**?
>
> When you talk about the beginning of a period of time, use **since**.
>
> *I have lived here since 1997.*
>
> When you talk about the whole period of time, use **for**.
>
> *I have lived here for five years.*

1 I have lived here since ....
2 I have been at my school for ....
3 I have had my watch since ....
4 .... has been my English teacher for ....
5 I have played .... since ....

6 **Work in pairs. Use *how long* to ask each other questions about the sentences in Exercise 5.**

How long have you lived here?

Present perfect or past simple?

page 124 *Grammar reference: Present perfect or past simple?*

1 **Read the Grammar reference section: *Present perfect or past simple?* on page 124, then put the verbs in brackets into the present perfect or past simple to complete sentences 1–7.**

1 It's the second time I ...*haven't done*... (not/do) my homework.
2 .... you .... (read) this month's *Surf* magazine yet?
3 I'm not going to the theatre. I .... (see) that show three months ago.
4 I'm worried about Emily. I .... (not hear) from her recently.
5 Our football team are playing better now. We only .... (win) twice last year.
6 You look tired. What time .... you .... (go) to bed last night?
7 How many exams .... you .... (take) since the beginning of this year?

2 **Work in pairs. You're going to read about DJ Jupiter or the kickboxer, Lewis Young. Write at least four questions about their lives. Use the present perfect or past simple and some of the question words in the box.**

> what   why   when   where   how
> how long   how many times

3 **Student A, turn to page 173 and read the text about DJ Jupiter. Student B, turn to page 174 and read the text about the kickboxer.**

4 **Using the questions in Exercise 2, take turns to ask each other questions about what you have read. If you don't know the answer, make a sensible guess.**

Vocabulary

been/gone, meet, get to know, know and *find out*

1 **Read these dictionary extracts.**

> Common Learner Error
>
> **go**, **gone** and **been**
>
> **Gone** is the usual past participle of the verb **go**. Sometimes you use the past participle **been** when you want to say that you have gone somewhere and come back, or to say that you have visited somewhere.
>
> *Paul has gone to the cinema this evening* (= he is still there)
>
> *Paul has been to the cinema this evening* (= he went and has come back)
>
> *Have you ever been to New York?* (= Have you ever visited New York?)
>
> ────────────────────
>
> **meet**, **get to know** and **know**
>
> When you **meet someone**, you see or speak to them for the first time. When you **get to know** someone, you learn more about them and after this you can say that you **know** them.
>
> *I met Nick on holiday.*
>
> ~~I know Nick on holiday.~~
>
> *We got to know each other and became good friends.*
>
> ~~We knew each other and became friends.~~
>
> *How long have you known Nick?*
>
> ~~How long have you got to know Nick?~~
>
> ────────────────────
>
> **know** or **find out**?
>
> To **know** something means to already have information about something.
>
> *His parents already knew about the party.*
>
> To **find out** something means to learn new information for the first time.
>
> *His parents were angry when they found out about the party.*

❷ Work in pairs. Circle the correct option(s) in *italics* for questions 1–6. Check your answers by looking at the extracts in Exercise 1 again.

1 Have you ever *been* / *gone* abroad? Where have you *been* / *gone*?
2 Have you ever made a friend on holiday? How did you first *meet* / *know* each other?
3 Have you got a best friend? How long have you *known* / *met* them?
4 Imagine all your friends have *been* / *gone* on holiday and you are on your own. What do you do?
5 Do you enjoy *knowing* / *getting to know* new people? Why (not)?
6 How often do you use the Internet to *find out* / *know* information? Have you used it this week? What for?

❸ Work in small groups. Take turns to ask and answer the questions in Exercise 2.

Listening Part 1

Lost property office

❶ Work in small groups. Look at the picture of the lost property office at a summer camp. Use the words in the box to talk about some of these items.

button	collar	cotton	fashionable	leather	long/short sleeves
old-fashioned	patterned	plastic	pocket	round neck	
sleeveless	striped	tight	V-neck	woollen	

There's a V-neck sweater on the table.

❷ ◉ PET candidates often make mistakes when describing clothes. Correct one mistake in sentences 1–6.

                   colourful
1 Most of the time, I wear a ~~colourfull~~ shirt, tight black jeans, and my favourite boots.
2 My best friend always wears beautifuls clothes.
3 The bride wore a long and white wedding dress.
4 Not long ago I bought three new fashion T-shirts.
5 At weekends, of course, I wear jeans and T-shirt.
6 Yesterday I bought some brown shoes and a blue trouser.

❸ Work in pairs. Read the questions carefully and <u>underline</u> the important words. Decide what each picture shows and what the difference is between each one.

1 Which is Mark's sweater?

A ☐   B ☐   C ☐

2 What has Mary lost?

A ☐   B ☐   C ☐

3 What has John lost?

A ☐   B ☐   C ☐

4 Which coat is Barbara talking about?

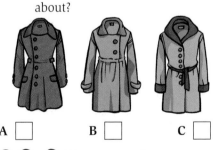

A ☐   B ☐   C ☐

❹ ㉙–㉜ Listen to each recording twice. Choose the correct picture and put a tick (✓) in the box below it.

❺ You are at the summer camp and you have lost some things. Describe two items from the lost property office picture to your partner. Can your partner find your lost items?

Speaking Part 4

❶ Read the instructions for the speaking task below. What *two* things will you need to talk about?

> Your photographs showed people going out. Now, I'd like you to talk together about what you like to do at home and what you like to do when you go out.

❷ Work in pairs. Look at statements 1–7 and decide which you should or should not do in this part of the speaking exam. Put a tick (✓) or a cross (✗) in each box in the *You* column.

	You	Jon & Ivan
1 Listen carefully to the examiner's instructions.	✓	✓
2 Talk to your partner about your likes/dislikes, opinions and experiences.	☐	☐
3 Change the topic to something completely different.	☐	☐
4 Ask your partner about their likes/dislikes, opinions and experiences.	☐	☐
5 Look at your partner and show you're interested in what they're saying.	☐	☐
6 Try to speak a lot more than your partner.	☐	☐
7 Worry if you can't think of anything more to say.	☐	☐

❸ (33) Listen to Jon and Ivan doing this task. Which of 1–7 do they do? Put a tick (✓) or a cross (✗) in each box.

❹ Look at this extract from the recording and decide if statements 1–3 below are true or false.

> **Jon:** So, Ivan, what do you like to do at home? Do you like watching TV?
>
> **Ivan:** Yes, I love watching TV. We normally switch on the TV after dinner and watch a film, a football match or a documentary. What about you? Do you like watching films?

1 Both Ivan and Jon ask questions.
2 Ivan's answer is too short.
3 Ivan completely changes the topic of the conversation.

❺ Look at more of Ivan and Jon's questions below. Write down your full answers to these questions.

1 Do you like watching films? *Yes, but I prefer watching sports to films. I find some films a little bit boring.*
2 Did you see the basketball match last night?
3 How often do you go to the cinema?
4 Have you seen the new *Batman* film yet?
5 Do you like musicals?

❻ (33) Listen to Jon and Ivan again. Are their answers to questions 1–5 similar to yours?

❼ Read this Speaking Part 4 task. What *two* things will you need to talk about?

> Your photographs showed people buying clothes. Now I'd like you to talk together about the type of clothes you wear during the week and the clothes you wear at weekends.

❽ Work in pairs. Make a list of some things you could talk about and some questions you could ask your partner.

9 Change pairs. Do the Speaking Part 4 task in Exercise 7.

Exam advice

- You will **not** have time to prepare your answer.
- Use full answers to develop the topic, **but don't** change it to something completely different.
- Take turns to speak by asking your partner questions.

Writing Part 2

1 Work in pairs. Look at the photo and imagine this is your aunt's cat. What happened to the vase?

2 Read this exam task and underline the important words.

> You looked after your aunt's cat while she was on holiday. She has sent you some money.
>
> Write an email to your Aunt Kath. In your email, you should
>
> - thank her
> - say what you are going to buy
> - describe what the cat did.
>
> Write 35–45 words.

3 Read these two answers and decide which you think is best.

1

> Dear Aunt Kath,
>
> Thank you very much for sending me some money. As you know, I love science fiction films and so I think I'm going to buy a new DVD. I haven't seen all the 'Star Wars' films yet.
>
> Yours,
>
> Bettina

2

> Dear Aunt Kath,
> Money is very nice – thank you very much. I will buy a new game from my computer. The cat is much more bad than my small brother. He break something. I have a strong headache for a week!
>
> Yours,
>
> Katia

4 Work in pairs. Look at the Writing Part 2 marking scheme on page 136 and answer this question.

- What mark do you think the examiner gave each answer? Why?

5 Now try this Writing Part 2 task.

> It's your birthday. Your cousin has sent you some money to buy some clothes.
>
> Write an email to your cousin, Dorota. In your email, you should
>
> - thank your cousin
> - say what you are going to buy
> - suggest you meet soon.
>
> Write 35–45 words.

Exam advice

- Read the question carefully and underline the important points.
- Make sure you include all three points in your answer.
- Write between 35 and 45 words. If you write less than 25 words you can only get a maximum of 2 points. If you write more than 45 words, your answer might not be so clear and you could make more mistakes.
- Open and close your answer in a suitable way, e.g. *Dear* and *Yours*.

6 Work in small groups. Read each other's answers and decide if you have all followed the exam advice.

Unit 5   *Vocabulary and grammar review*

Vocabulary

❶ Circle the correct prepositions 1–10 to complete the letter.

> Hi Fran,
>
> Sorry I've taken so long to reply. You ask about our friends here, so here's what's happening. Anna, as you know, was disappointed (1) *of / on /* (*with*) her last exam results so she's working harder now, but I think she's getting tired (2) *about / of / on* studying all the time. She usually likes to go out in the evenings, so she must be getting very bored (3) *with / on / about* life. Mike is still very keen (4) *of / on / with* football and is quite proud (5) *on / with / of* the two goals he scored last Saturday, but he can't play next week and he's sad (6) *about / of / with* that. Kay, you might remember, is crazy (7) *on / with / about* music and has always wanted to be a singer. Well, a band has asked her to sing with them at a concert next Friday. She's really nervous (8) *on / about / with* singing in front of all those people, but I don't think she should be frightened (9) *with / of / on* doing it. I've told her that some people will be quite jealous (10) *of / on / about* her! Well, that's all for now.
>
> Lots of love,
>
> Jamie

❷ This text contains a number of adjectives ending in *-ed* and *-ing*. Find and correct five mistakes.

> When I was tidying my room last Sunday, I found some surprising things. Among all the ~~bored~~ boring exercise books from my primary school days, there was something amazed: my diary, from when I was eight years old. It was really interested to read my thoughts from back then, though at times I felt a bit embarrassing, too. For example, I was still very frightening of the dark in those days. I was also amusing to read how excited I was about being nine soon – I thought I would be really grown up then.

❸ Complete the crossword with words from Unit 5.

Across	Down
3 not generous	1 unhappy
4 frightened	2 something you often do
7 feeling	5 wanting what someone else has
9 terrible	6 feeling or showing thanks
11 should	8 opposite of 'positive'
12 fortunate	10 pleased with what you have done
13 like a lot	

Grammar

❹ Complete the mini-conversations with the correct modal verb in italics.

1 **A:** Do you think Matt and Libby are at the café?
   B: They *can* / (*may*) be there, but I'm not sure.

2 **A:** Do you like going to the swimming pool?
   B: No, I *can't / mightn't* swim.

3 **A:** I've got a bit of a headache.
   B: I think you *must / should* take an aspirin.

4 **A:** *Could / Might* you run for an hour without stopping?
   B: No, I'd be too tired after 30 minutes!

5 **A:** Are the buses to the city centre expensive?
   B: No, you *mustn't / don't have to* pay if you're under 16.

6 **A:** The weather's not looking very good now.
   B: No, I think it *can / might* rain later.

7 **A:** What do I need to go to the USA?
   B: You *should / have to* take your passport.

Unit 6   *Vocabulary and grammar review*

Vocabulary

❶ Complete this text by writing a word from the box in each space.

> admission   audiences   ~~cartoons~~   interval
> live   performances   reviews

The Chinese State Circus

Are you bored of taking your younger brother to the cinema to see (1) __cartoons__? Watch out for the Chinese State Circus which arrives in town today. (2) _____ will be amazed by the acrobatics, dance and (3) _____ music. This touring show has already received very good (4) _____ in other parts of the country. There are two (5) _____ each day: one at 2.30 and the other at 7.30. Tickets are still available for many dates with half-price (6) _____ for under-18s. The show lasts about two hours with a short (7) _____ when you'll be able to buy snacks and souvenirs.

❷ Circle the correct word, A, B or C, for each space in these sentences.

1 When I go out with my friends, I like wearing __fashionable__ clothes.
  A fashion   B (fashionable)   C fashioned

2 In my country, rock stars wear _____ jeans.
  A a tight   B tights   C tight

3 My best friend often wears bright shirts and _____ skirts.
  A colourful   B colourfull   C colour

4 I first _____ my best friend when I started primary school.
  A met   B knew   C got to know

5 We're going to Casablanca to get to _____ the city.
  A find out   B know   C meet

6 I've visited Paris but I haven't _____ EuroDisney.
  A gone to   B been to   C known

Grammar

❸ ⊙ PET candidates often make mistakes with the present perfect and the past simple and their common adverbs. Correct the mistakes in sentences 1–12.

1 ~~I've~~ *I* bought some clothes last week.
2 My cousin has lived with us since three years ago.
3 I haven't seen him for ages because he's gone to Dubai a few years ago.
4 We've gone to the cinema three times this month. Let's do something else.
5 Already I've been to a few shops to look for new shoes.
6 I still can't find my watch. I looked for it everywhere in my room.
7 Paris is the best place I've never been to for clothes.
8 I lost a beautiful pair of gloves which my mother has given me for my birthday.
9 With the money you sent me, I will buy the World Cup T-shirt which just came into the shops.
10 We're planning to see a film tonight, but we didn't decide which film yet.
11 We also have a wonderful cinema in my town. It has opened six months ago.
12 Write soon and tell me what happened to you recently.

❹ Read these sentences about living in a big city. Complete the second sentence so that it means the same as the first, *using no more than three words.*

1 I started living here about three years ago.
  I've lived here ___for___ about three years.

2 This is the first time I've lived in such a big city.
  I _____ in such a big city before.

3 I joined the local gym in June.
  I've been a member of the local gym _____ June.

4 I met my best friend Farrah when I joined the local gym.
  I _____ my best friend Farrah since I joined the local gym.

5 We saw the new *X-men* film on Saturday and again on Thursday.
  We've already _____ the new *X-men* film twice (on Saturday and again on Thursday).

Unit 7 Out and about

Starting off

1 Work in pairs. Describe the pictures using the words *fog/foggy, ice/icy, wind/windy, clouds/cloudy, sunshine/sunny* and *storm/stormy.*

How do you think the people in each situation feel?

2 Complete the weather forecast for pictures 1–6 with these expressions.

blowing	centigrade	~~cold~~	degrees	~~foggy~~	
freezing	frost	gale	get wet	hot	lightning
showers	snowfall	temperature	thunderstorm		

1 It's so ....foggy........ that planes can't take off. It's also quite ....cold...........: only 3°C.
2 The .... is already high. It's going to be a very .... day with a maximum of 40 ....
3 There are probably going to be .... soon. Some people are going to ....
4 There is a .... at sea, with strong winds .... from the west, causing high waves.
5 There's a noisy .... in the mountains, with .... briefly turning night into day.
6 It's .... this morning, –5°C, with .... on the ground. A heavy .... is forecast for later.

3 Which of the weather conditions above do you think are *extreme*? Which are *mild*?

Choose two different kinds of weather from pictures 1–6. Tell your partner how each makes you feel and why.

I don't like thunderstorms because they make me feel nervous.

Listening Part 2

1 With a partner, look at the exam instructions in Exercise 2 on the next page and multiple-choice questions 1–6, then answer questions a–e.

a What is the main speaker's name?
b Who is the other person?
c What is the topic?
d What do the questions ask about the speaker?
e What kinds of weather are mentioned in the questions?

❷ 🔊(34) **Follow the exam instructions.**

> • You will hear a woman called Chloe talking to an interviewer about her hobby of photographing extreme weather conditions.
> • For each question put a tick (✓) in the correct box.

Exam advice

• Before you listen, quickly read the instructions and the questions to get an idea of what you will hear.

• When the recording is played, listen for reasons why one option is correct – and for reasons why the other two are wrong.

1 What does Chloe say about the weather in her country?

A ☐ It's cold in the north.
B ☐ It changes quite often.
C ☐ It's always sunny.

2 She started taking photos of bad weather when she was

A ☐ working.
B ☐ a child.
C ☐ at university.

3 To photograph lightning, she uses

A ☐ a digital camera.
B ☐ an expensive camera.
C ☐ an old camera.

4 Where does she take photos during thunderstorms?

A ☐ standing on a hill
B ☐ from her apartment
C ☐ sitting in her car

5 These days, which does she most like photographing in winter?

A ☐ frozen rivers and streams
B ☐ scenes with lots of snow
C ☐ patterns formed by frost

6 What does she often photograph when it's windy?

A ☐ trees
B ☐ the sea
C ☐ clouds

❸ **In pairs, study this extract from the recording and answer these questions.**

• Which of questions 1–6 does this extract answer?
• How do you know?
• Underline the parts of the text that tell you why one option is correct, and why the others are wrong.
• Are these all close together in the extract?
• Are they in the same order as options A, B and C?

Chloe:	… but I still love photographing lightning.
Interviewer:	That must be quite difficult. How do you get good pictures?
Chloe:	Well, the first thing is the right camera. It doesn't have to be expensive, or particularly modern – I've had mine for many years – and I avoid using digital ones.

❹ **Would you like to study extreme weather conditions close up? Tell your partner why or why not.**

Vocabulary

Extremely, fairly, quite, rather, really and very

❶ **Study these extracts from the recording, then complete the rules about adverbs of degree (*extremely, fairly*, etc.) with the underlined words.**

it can be <u>quite</u> different

it's <u>really</u> fascinating

that must be <u>quite</u> difficult

is <u>rather</u> dangerous

Rules

1 Adverbs of degree such as *very, extremely* and .... make an adjective stronger.

2 The adverbs *fairly* and .... make it weaker.

3 The adverb .... usually makes it weaker, but with adjectives like *sure, true* and *different*, it can mean 'completely'.

2 Talk to your partner about your country's weather in different seasons. Use adverbs of degree with words like *wet*, *warm* and *windy*.

In winter it's fairly sunny, but it's extremely cold.

Too and *enough*

 page 126 *Grammar reference:* Too *and* enough

1 Look at examples a–d with *too* and *enough*, then circle the correct underlined option to complete rules 1–5.

a *it's often too dark to photograph them when it's stormy*

b *I had enough time to buy an umbrella before the bus arrived.*

c *It was a hot July day. There were too many cars and there was too much noise.*

d *It was autumn, but the weather was mild enough for us to have a picnic.*

Rules

1 In the examples above, *too* means <u>as much as</u> / <u>more than</u> you need or want. It does not mean the same as *very*.

2 We put *too* <u>after</u> / <u>before</u> an adjective, often followed by the <u>-ing</u> / <u>to infinitive</u> form of the verb.

3 We use *too much* before <u>countable</u> / <u>uncountable</u> nouns and *too many* before <u>countable</u> / <u>uncountable</u> nouns.

4 In the examples above, *enough* means <u>as much as</u> / <u>more than</u> you need or want.

5 We usually put *enough* <u>after</u> / <u>before</u> a noun but <u>after</u> / <u>before</u> an adjective, often followed by the <u>-ing</u> / <u>to infinitive</u> form of the verb.

---

2 ☉ *Too* and *enough* can be difficult for students. Tick (✓) the sentences 1–8 written by PET candidates which are right. Correct the sentences which are wrong.

1 That's the way I like it: not too hot and not too cold. ✓

2 We didn't have enough money for to buy new instruments.

3 I like it too much because it's a nice place.

4 I gave her enough money for get not only one, but two ice-creams.

5 I can't buy it because it's too much expensive.

6 It was hot enough to spend the whole day in the water.

7 In the summer I like wearing a T-shirt and a skirt, because it's too hot for wearing trousers.

8 Spring has begun but it is not enough warm yet to walk in the hills.

Grammar

The future: *Will, going to,* present continuous and present simple

 page 125 *Grammar reference: Ways of expressing the future*

1 (35) Listen to this conversation between Mia and Owen and fill in the missing verbs. You can use short forms like *'s* (*is*), *'ll* (*will*) and *'m* (*am*).

Mia:	It's getting a bit late, Owen.
Owen:	Yes, but look at the rain! I'm hoping it (1) ......*'ll stop*...... soon, though I don't think there's much chance of that.
Mia:	No, the weather forecast said it's a big storm so it (2) .... for hours. What time do you have to be at the station?
Owen:	I (3) .... Jason and Mark there at 8.30, in the café near the main entrance. The train (4) .... at 8.45.
Mia:	It's quite a long walk to the station, isn't it? And it's 8.15 already. Look, I (5) .... you in the car.
Owen:	Thanks!

2 In pairs, match the verb forms in 1–5 above with uses a–e.

a for timetables and future dates *leaves*

b for decisions at the moment of speaking

c for things that aren't certain, e.g. after *I think*

d for future arrangements between people

e for predictions based on evidence, and plans

③ Put the words in the right order in questions 1–7. Then answer the questions in complete sentences.

1 will / think / cloudy / it / do / tomorrow / you / be ?
Do you think it will be cloudy tomorrow?
No, I think it'll be sunny.

2 your friends / next week / you / when / seeing / are ?

3 this evening / are / where / go / going / you / to ?

4 your holidays / begin / do / this summer / date / what ?

5 a job / think / get / you / when / do / will / you ?

6 the Earth / get hotter / scientists / going / say / is / to / do ?

7 a text message / will / next send / you / when ?

④ Complete the replies to 1–7 using *will, going to*, the present simple or the present continuous.

1 Which colour jacket do you want to buy?
I've already decided. I'm *going to buy a black one.*

2 Have you arranged to go to the dentist's?
Yes, I've got an appointment. I ....

3 This suitcase is too heavy for me.
Give it to me. I ....

4 Can't you stay a few minutes longer?
No, I must go. It's half past ten and the last train .... at eleven.

5 Would you like something to drink?
Yes, please. I ....

6 Would you like to come out this evening?
I'm sorry, but I've already got plans. I ....

7 Do you think it'll be dry later on?
No, look at those black clouds. It ....

⑤ What would you say in each of these situations? Tell your partner.

1 A friend invites you to a party but you already have a ticket for a concert. *I'm sorry but I'm going to a concert with friends.*

2 Your friend is having trouble with their computer and you want to help.

3 Someone asks you about the departure time of your flight to New York.

4 You're in a small boat and you notice the wind is getting stronger.

5 You see an accident and you're the only person there with a mobile phone.

6 Someone asks you what subject you want to study at university.

Reading Part 1

① Look quickly at 1–5 below. What *kind* of text is each?

1
Vancouver College Ⓥ Ⓒ
MAIN ENTRANCE
no parking

..........*road sign*..........

2
To: Dan Watkins
From: unknown sender

Register with us to receive regular updates by email on our special offers: flights to New York, Hong Kong and Sydney!

....

3
Passenger ferry
strong winds
take care when boarding

....

4
Check-in
All international flights
Closes 30 minutes before departure

....

5
OCT 11–18
ROAD WORKS
WHEN RED LIGHT SHOWS WAIT HERE

....

② Study texts 1–5 more carefully and match them with purposes a–e below. Underline the words in the texts which tell you the purpose.

a to advertise something   `2`

b to warn you of danger   `☐`

c to say what you must do   `☐`

d to say what you must not do   `☐`

e to inform and advise you   `☐`

❸ Look at the first question in Reading Part 1 below and decide:

1 what kind of text it is
2 what its purpose is.

Now do the same with each of questions 2–6.

❹ Follow these exam instructions.

> • Look at the text in each question.
> • What does it say?
> • Mark the letter next to the correct explanation – A, B or C.

Exam advice

Look at the information around the text. There may be (a) picture(s) which will help you to understand why the text was written and who it was written for.

1
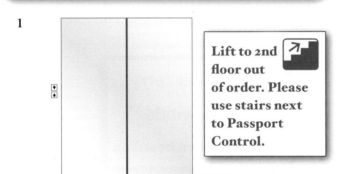

Lift to 2nd floor out of order. Please use stairs next to Passport Control.

(A) You will need to walk upstairs to get to the second floor.
B You must go through Passport Control on the second floor.
C You can use the stairs or take the lift to the second floor.

2

Tony – Ticket agency phoned. Rock concert at exhibition centre instead of sports hall. At same time, I think – but call them to check.
Joe

A The time that the concert starts has changed.
B The concert will take place somewhere else.
C Joe will call the agency for details of the concert.

3

Description:
Mountain bike for sale

End time: **54 mins**
Item location: **North-west**

• for age 13+
• ridden only twice
• buyer must collect

A The seller will deliver the bicycle to the buyer.
B The bicycle is suitable for teenagers or adults.
C The owner of the bicycle has never used it.

4

Do not take these tablets for more than three days without your doctor's advice.

A You should take the tablets every day until you feel much better.
B You must not take the tablets without speaking to the doctor first.
C You must ask the doctor if you want to take the tablets for a week.

5

Path for the use of horse riders, cyclists and pedestrians only

A Motor vehicles are not allowed on this path.
B All people using this path must go on foot.
C Riders are requested to go slowly on this path.

6

To: Monica

From: Carmen

Just to let you know that our bus leaves at 7.50 tomorrow morning, not 7.20. So how about calling for me here at 7.30 instead of 7.00?

Carmen wants to
A meet Monica at a different place.
B go on a later bus with Monica.
C change the time they are meeting.

Vocabulary
Compound words

❶ **Match the words in A with the words in B to form compound words. Then match these with definitions 1–10.**

A | ~~back~~ cross guest guide hitch
over rail sight sign suit

B | book case hike house night
~~pack~~ post road roads seeing

1 book that gives information about a place
2 bag with a handle for carrying clothes, etc.
3 place where two roads meet and cross each other
4 get free rides by standing next to the road
5 tracks that trains travel on
6 bag that you carry on your back   *backpack*
7 sign by the road that gives information
8 during the night and until the morning
9 small, cheap hotel
10 visiting interesting places

❷ **Complete the letter with compound words from Exercise 1.**

Next week I'm going on a fantastic journey: across Australia! I'm flying to Darwin, in the north of the country, and I'm going to stay (1) ...... *overnight* ...... there. My (2) .... says it's quite an interesting city, so I think I'll spend the morning doing some (3) .... I love travelling by train, so then I'm going to take the new (4) .... to Alice Springs, right in the middle of the country. I'll find a hotel or (5) .... for the night and the next day I'm going to (6) .... down the main road. I'm taking all my things in a (7) .... so that I don't have to carry a heavy (8) .... in my hand. About 200 kilometres south of Alice I'll reach a (9) .... where there's a (10) .... that says 'Uluru 247 km'. Uluru is also known as 'Ayers Rock' – one of the most amazing sights in the world.

Prepositions of movement

▶ page 125 *Grammar reference: Prepositions of movement*

❶ 🔊 **Read this telephone message about travelling around a city and fill in the missing prepositions (*in*, *off*, etc.). Then listen to check your answers.**

> Hi Leon; Toby here. I'm really pleased you're coming to our new house next week. The quickest way here is (1) ..*by*.. train to the city centre, which takes an hour and is usually (2) .... time. Then you can get (3) .... the number 64 bus to Edge Hill, getting (4) .... by the stadium. From there it's about fifteen minutes (5) .... foot. Or, if you don't feel like walking, you could jump (6) .... a taxi and ask the driver to take you to the new flats in Valley Road. When you get (7) .... (8) .... the taxi, you'll see the main entrance in front of you. See you soon!

❷ **Use words from the message above to complete these rules.**

Rules

1 For buses, trams, trains, planes or boats we use .... or *onto* when we board them, and .... when we leave them. We use the same prepositions for bicycles, motorbikes and horses.

2 For cars and similar vehicles we use .... or *into*, and .... when we leave them.

3 With the prepositions in rules 1 and 2 we often use the verb ...., but sometimes we use others like .... or *climb*.

4 We travel .... bus, train, plane or boat, or in other words, ... road, rail, air, land or sea, but we go somewhere .... foot. We also say we are *on board* a train, plane or ship, or *at sea*.

5 If you arrive neither late nor early, you say you are (or the bus, train, plane, etc. is) .... time.

❸ 💿 Tick (✓) the sentences 1–8 written by PET candidates which are right. Correct the sentences which are wrong.

1   I jumped into my car. ✓
2   I got into the train.
3   Could you come at time, please?
4   She said 'Come with me'. I followed her and we got on the car.
5   I'm going to start lessons this Monday, but I can't go on bus.
6   We just wanted to get off the plane.
7   Then we headed back home by foot.
8   She finally got into the plane.

Speaking Part 2

❶ (37) Listen to students Ingrid and Mikel discussing the best way to get across the city, and answer the questions.

1   Tick (✓) the means of transport they talk about.

bus	helicopter
taxi	bike
boat	tram
metro	scooter

2   Which *two* do they decide to use?

❷ Look at expressions 1–8 from the recording and complete them with these words.

about	another	because	~~keen~~	like	not	one	rather

1   why are you ....Keen........ on … ? | a |
2   well, ... it … | |
3   I think I'd .... go … | |
4   why .... ? | |
5   for .... thing, … | |
6   for ...., it … | |
7   so what .... going …? | |
8   what I'd most .... to do is … | |

❸ (37) Listen again to check your answers, then match expressions 1–8 with a–d below by writing a letter in each box.

a   asking for reasons   b   giving reasons
c   asking about preferences   d   stating preferences

❹ (38) Listen and repeat these extracts from the recording. What do you notice about the pronunciation of the underlined words?

1   why <u>are</u> you keen   4   sail down <u>the</u> river
2   well, <u>for</u> one thing   5   we <u>can</u> ride to the harbour
3   it's going <u>to</u> be really hot   6   half <u>an</u> hour

❺ Talk to your partner about the different ways of getting across your town, and decide on one or two means of transport to travel from one side to the other. Use language from Exercises 1 and 2.

❻ Do this Speaking Part 2 exam question with a partner. Talk for at least two minutes.

You and a **friend** have decided to spend a month of the summer holidays seeing as much as possible of **your country**. Talk together about the different **means of transport** you could use and **decide which** you are going to use.

Here is a picture with some ideas to help you.

Writing Part 1

When you are writing, try to think of **different ways of saying the same thing**. For instance, instead of *sail down the river* we can say *go down the river by boat*. We call these **parallel expressions**.

1 🔊(39) **Read this discussion and rewrite the underlined expressions 1–7 using the words in brackets. Then listen to check your answers.**

Pat: Do you think people in 2020 will still (1) ~~go everywhere by car~~ drive everywhere (go)?

Kelly: No, I don't. For one thing, the traffic will be (2) <u>so awful that it'll be impossible</u> .... (too) for us to go anywhere.

Pat: Actually, we're (3) <u>not very far from</u> .... (quite) that situation already.

Kelly: Yes, I agree. And cars cause (4) <u>extremely high levels of</u> .... (so) pollution, especially in cities. I think a lot of countries (5) <u>plan</u> .... (going) to reduce the number of vehicles.

Pat: So do you think most of us will end up (6) <u>walking everywhere</u> .... (foot)?

Kelly: Yes, I think we probably will, and I wouldn't mind that at all. In fact, (7) <u>I'd prefer to</u> .... (rather) do that.

2 **Study the first sentences in each Writing Part 1 question 1–6 on the right. Which word or phrase has a common parallel expression? Underline the word or phrase.**

Exam advice

- Look for a word or words in the first sentence with a parallel expression.
- Then look at the second sentence to see if this parallel expression fits the grammar.
- You may want to write it in pencil first to check that the completed sentence means the same as the first sentence.

3 **Now do this Writing Part 1 exam task.**

- Here are some sentences about the future climate.
- For each question, complete the second sentence so that it means the same as the first, *using no more than three words*.

1 It will be <u>too</u> warm to live in some parts of the world.
It won't be .... to live in some parts of the world.

2 In some countries, temperatures will rise a lot.
Temperatures will be .... in some countries.

3 In those places, it will be sunny nearly all the time.
In those places, the sun .... almost all the time.

4 Even in the mountains it will be so warm that it won't snow.
Even in the mountains it will be .... for snow.

5 However, the weather will be even wetter in Britain.
However, it .... even more in Britain.

6 Also, Antarctica will still be the coldest place in the world.
Also, Antarctica will still be .... than any other place in the world.

4 **Think about the future climate in your country. Which parts of it will most feel the effects of climate change and in what ways? Write four sentences.**

Unit 8 This is me!

Starting off

❶ Work in small groups. What do you know about the famous people in the pictures and their families?

❷ Circle the correct answers in the quiz, then check your answers on page 174. Are you surprised by any of the answers?

All in the family!

1 Whose stepmother and stepsisters were not very kind to her?
   A Cinderella   B Sleeping Beauty   C Goldilocks

2 Benjamin Aguero's father is Argentinean football player Sergio 'Kun' Aguero. Who is Benjamin's famous grandfather?
   A Maradona   B Pele   C Zico

3 His uncle Toni is his coach. Another uncle played football for Barcelona and the Spanish national team. Who is this famous tennis player?
   A Fernando Verdasco   B David Ferrer   C Rafa Nadal

4 Which famous couple was paid around $14 million for photos of their new-born twins in 2008?
   A Brad Pitt & Angelina Jolie   B Tom Cruise & Katie Holmes   C David & Victoria Beckham

5 In the cartoon series *The Simpsons*, who is Abraham Simpson?
   A Homer Simpson's nephew   B Bart Simpson's grandfather   C Marge Simpson's uncle

Reading Part 3

❶ Work in pairs. Read this extract from the *Cambridge Learner's Dictionary*.

> coach [kəʊtʃ] *noun* someone whose job is to teach people to improve at a sport, skill, or school subject

❷ Maradona is a football coach. Who is the other sports coach in the quiz?

❸ Look at the text title and photo on page 71. What do you think a *life coach* is?

❹ Check your ideas by reading paragraph B *What is a life coach?*

⑤ Read sentences 1–10 about the text. <u>Underline</u> the most important words in each sentence.

1 Sylvana has <u>a very good relationship with</u> her daughter, Irina. ⬚ A

2 Life coaching was <u>first</u> used to <u>help children decide on their futures</u>. ⬚

3 Simone Waltz used to work in radio. ⬚

4 Jem wants to do a degree before going to Africa. ⬚

5 Jem's parents would like him to do his degree in another country. ⬚

6 One teenager used singing to help her study and she got nearly perfect marks in science. ⬚

7 Irina would be happy to go to any university. ⬚

8 Irina has always been keen on keeping fit. ⬚

9 Mo Ahmed has worked with children younger than six. ⬚

10 Some of Regina's friends in her new school play basketball. ⬚

⑥ Work in pairs. Look at the paragraph headings in the text. In which paragraph do you think you will find information about each sentence? Write the correct letter (A–E) in each box.

⑦ Read the text to decide if each sentence is correct or incorrect. <u>Underline</u> where you find the answer in the text. When you are ready, compare your answers with your partner.

> In Unit 7 we looked at *parallel expressions*. In this part of the PET reading paper, the sentence and the text often use different words and expressions which have *similar meanings*.

⑧ Work in pairs. Look at the words and expressions you have underlined in the sentences and the text and find four more parallel expressions.

1 have a good relationship → get on well
2 decide → make decisions

Life coaches find success with young people

A 'I've seen a huge difference in Irina since she started talking to a life coach,' says her mother Sylvana. '<u>I get on very well with Irina</u>, but you can't always talk to your mother about everything. Talking to someone who listens but is not a close family member is very important.'

B What is a life coach?

An athlete improves because he trains with a coach. A life coach can also guide you to success. A life coach encourages you to think not only about what you want, but also about how you are going to get it. Until now, life coaches have helped adults, for example business executives who need to make decisions or parents who want some advice on bringing up their children. Now it's the turn of our young people.

C Life coach Simone Waltz

Simone Waltz, a former radio producer, set up her life coaching company five years ago. 'I offer teenagers a place to talk, to decide on their future plans and to sort out problems,' says Waltz. Jem's parents are delighted with what Waltz has done. Jem has got a place at university to study medicine but he has decided to take part in a volunteer project in central Africa first. 'Yes, we were surprised, but Jem is still very young. This experience abroad will help him grow up before he goes to university here.'

D Life coach Tara Newhouse

Tara tells the story of a 15-year-old who was failing in science, until they found out she learnt best through music. Once she made up songs to learn by, she achieved 99 per cent in her tests. Tara has also helped Sylvana's daughter, Irina, who was not sure she wanted to go to university. Now she hopes to get into a top university. Irina now feels more confident about everything. She has even taken up exercise for the first time in years.

E Life coach Mo Ahmed

Mo Ahmed has coached children as young as five years old. 'It could be something as simple as learning multiplication tables – asking them how they're going to do it, how are they going to make it fun?' Mo has also helped teenager Regina who was having problems making friends when she moved to a new school. They talked together about the things Regina really enjoyed doing. By joining the school basketball team Regina has made several new friends.

Vocabulary

Phrasal verbs

1 Work in pairs. The eight phrasal verbs in the box below appear in the text, sometimes in a different form (e.g. *bringing up*). <u>Underline</u> them in the text and try to decide what each verb means by looking at the complete sentence.

bring up	find out	~~get on with~~	grow up
make up	set up	sort out	take up

2 Work in pairs. Replace each expression in *italics* in sentences 1–8 with a phrasal verb from the box, so that the meaning stays the same. Remember to use the correct form of the verb.

▶ page 121 *Grammar reference: Phrasal verbs*

1 I moved to Athens when I began my degree but
   grew up
   I ~~became older~~ in a small village near Thessaloniki with my parents and two brothers.
2 When I was very young, my aunt *looked after me* until I was old enough to look after myself.
3 I would like to have a life coach to help me *deal with* my problems.
4 When I'm older, I'd like to *start* my own fashion design company.
5 If I had to choose another sport, I would *start playing* basketball.
6 I *have a good relationship with* my older sister. We often go out together.
7 If I didn't know an answer in an exam, I would never *invent* an answer.
8 If I *discovered* that my parents were reading my emails, I wouldn't get angry.

3 Rewrite the sentences in Exercise 2, where necessary, so that they are true for you.

1 *I was born in Naples but I grew up in Rome, the capital city of Italy.*

4 Work in small groups. Compare your sentences. Find at least three things that you have all got in common.

Grammar

Zero, first and second conditionals

▶ page 126 *Grammar reference: Zero, first and second conditionals*

1 Work in pairs. Kristian is fifteen. He would like to go to drama school to train to be an actor but his parents want him to stay at school. What advice would you give to Kristian?

2 (40) Kristian is talking to his life coach, Mo. Listen to the recording and answer these questions.

1 Why has Kristian's dad contacted Mo?
2 What two pieces of advice does Mo give?
3 In your opinion, will Kristian become an actor?

3 (40) Listen to the recording again and complete sentences 1–5 with the verb in brackets in the correct form. Use short forms (*I'll*, *won't*, etc.) where possible.

1 I .....*'ll need*..... (need) my parents' permission if I .... (want) to go to drama school.
2 If I .... (stay) at school until I'm eighteen, it .... (be) too late.
3 If you .... (want) to be an actor, you .... (have) to start your training at an early age.
4 I .... (have) to give up football if I .... (go) to classes after school.
5 If I .... (study) at drama school, I .... (have) enough time for everything.

4 Work in pairs. Look at this conversation between Kristian and his friend Josh, then answer the questions that follow.

> **Kristian:** I'm thinking about joining the drama club.
> **Josh:** What? **(6)** <u>If you join the club, you'll have to give up football</u> and you're our best player.
> **Kristian:** I know. **(7)** <u>If the drama club met on Wednesdays, I could do both</u>.
> **Josh:** But the club doesn't meet on Wednesdays. What are you going to do?

1 Does Josh want Kristian to join the drama club in sentence (6)? Why (not)?
2 Does the drama club meet on Wednesdays according to Kristian in sentence (7)?
3 Do both Josh and Kristian talk about a real possibility in (6) and (7)?

5 Sentences (1–7) in Exercises 3 and 4 are all examples of conditionals. Conditionals are often divided into three types. Match sentences 1–7 with the types of conditional a–c below.

a Type 0 (Zero conditional): [3]

This expresses things which are *always* or *generally true*.

If it <u>snows</u>, our dog <u>gets</u> very excited.

b Type 1 (First conditional): [1] [ ] [ ]

This expresses a real possibility in the future.

If it snows on Saturday, I'll make a snowman.

c Type 2 (Second conditional): [ ] [ ] [ ]

This is used when the speaker is not thinking about a real possibility but is imagining a situation that will probably not happen.

If it snowed in July, I would go skiing on the beach.

6 <u>Underline</u> the verbs in each example in Exercise 5. What form of the verb do we use in each conditional type?

7 When do we use (and *not* use) a comma in conditional sentences? Look at the examples in Exercise 3 again to help you.

8 Work in pairs. Look at this example situation and answer the questions below.

> rain at the weekend
> *If it rains at the weekend, I'll go to the cinema.*

1 Why have we used the first conditional here?
2 When would we use the second conditional to talk about rain?

9 Now look at situations 1–6 and write one sentence for each, *using the first or second conditional*. You will need to think about whether each situation is a real possibility or not for you.

You:
1 lose your mobile phone
2 see a friend cheating in an exam
3 get good marks at school
4 find a lot of money in a rubbish bin
5 get lost in a foreign country
6 get a lot of homework from your teacher

If I lose my mobile, I'll get very annoyed.

10 Work in pairs. Write a question for each of the situations in Exercise 9, then change pairs and take turns to ask and answer the questions.

What will you do if it rains at the weekend?
I won't play football in the park.

When, if, unless + present, future

▶ page 126 *Grammar reference:* When, if, unless + *present, future*

1 Work in pairs. Look at the pictures below and say if each teenager will definitely call home.

2 Complete these rules about sentences with *if, unless* or *when*.

> Rules
> · we use (1) .... for things we are sure will happen
> · we use (2) .... for things that may happen
> · (3) .... generally has the meaning of *if ... not*.

3 Read sentences 1–6 and circle the correct option in *italics*.

1 I'll write again soon *if* /(when) I finish my exams.
2 I wouldn't be able to write very well *if / when* I broke my right hand.
3 We'll miss the bus *if / unless* we run.
4 Paula'll play tennis tomorrow *if / unless* it rains.
5 My uncle can't hear *when / unless* you shout.
6 They'll come to your party *if / unless* their parents say they can't.

This is me! (73)

Listening Part 3

1 Work in small groups and answer these questions.

1 Where are the *extras* in the photos?
2 Have you or anyone you know ever been an extra?
3 Would you like to be an extra? Why (not)?

2 You will hear Vanessa from *Extras Agency* talking about being an extra. Before you listen, read through the information below. What information do you think is missing in each space (e.g. *number, date, noun, verb, adjective*, etc.)?

Extras Agency

Extras:
• appear in crowds
• buy things in (1) ....
• support sports events, etc.

Are films made in my area?
Find out by looking at the (2) ....

What about age?
No limit. Ask parents for permission if under
(3) ....

What are directors looking for at the moment?
• look 16 years old
• maximum 1.7 m
• have interesting (4) ....

What can I expect?
Usually 16 hours a day, 6 days a week, day off on (5) ....

Where can I get more information?
Phone Vanessa (6) .... or visit
www.extrasextras.com

Exam advice
• Be careful with spelling, especially if you are given the spelling of the word in the recording or if it is a very common word, e.g. *Monday*.

3 🔊⁴¹ Listen to the recording twice and for each question, fill in the missing information in the numbered space.

Vocabulary
Describing people

1 🔊⁴² Film director, Darrilus Hassi, is looking for an actor for his latest film. His assistant Marti telephones an agency and speaks to Harry. Look at the pictures and listen to the recording. Put a tick (✓) next to the actor Marti chooses.

2 Work in pairs to complete the mind map on page 75 with these words.

attractive	bald	beard	beautiful	~~blond(e)~~
broad shoulders	curly	dark	fair	
good-looking	grey	long	medium height	
moustache	pale	plain	red	scar	short
slim	straight	~~wavy~~		

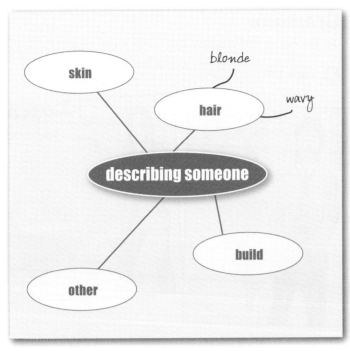

③ Harry from the agency describes one of the actors as *honest* and *reliable*. Write the opposites of these character adjectives.

1 hard-working *lazy*   5 rude
2 smart   6 calm
3 noisy   7 confident
4 mean   8 warm

④ Add *un-*, *im-* or *dis-* to make these character adjectives negative.

....*un*.... friendly   .... patient
.... pleasant   .... honest   .... reliable

⑤ Add *-ful* or *-less* to these nouns to make adjectives. Watch your spelling!

wonder ....   cheer ....
beauty ....   hope ....

• Is *hopeful* the opposite of hope*less*?

⑥ Add *-ish* to these nouns to make adjectives. Be careful with your spelling.

Nationality: Finn .... Turk .... Brit ....
Swede .... Scot ....

Behaviour: self .... child .... fool ....
baby ....

⑦ ⊙ PET candidates often make mistakes with adjective order. Read the rules at the top of the page and correct one mistake in each of the examples a–f that follow.

Rules

1 Adjectives generally go <u>before</u> the noun and we don't normally use more than two adjectives before each noun:
    very nice
  a *In my youth club, there are four ∧ girls very nice.*
  b *My best friend has hair and eyes black.*
2 When there are two adjectives together, we generally put the opinion adjective before the fact adjective:
  c *At the beginning of the film, a young handsome man is sitting in a café.*
  d *He talks to a woman who is wearing a white beautiful dress.*
3 When there are two fact adjectives together, we generally put those that describe shape or size before those describing colour:
  e *I've made a new friend with black short hair.*
  f *He lives in a house with a green big garden.*

Speaking Part 1

❶ Work in pairs. Add the other letters of the English alphabet in the correct place in this pronunciation table.

eɪ	iː	e	aɪ	əʊ	uː	ɑː
A	B, C, D	F	I	O	Q	R

❷ ⟨43⟩ Listen to the recording and check your answers.

❸ ⟨44⟩ ⊙ PET candidates often make spelling mistakes. Listen to the first part of the recording. You will hear a single word followed by a sentence including this word. Think carefully about spelling and write down the single word you hear. For example:

Recording: For. I've bought a present for you.
You write: *for*

Recording: Four. My dog is four years old.
You write: *four*

❹ ⟨45⟩ Listen to the second part of the recording and check your spelling of each word.

❺ Work in pairs. Student A says the words on page 173 to Student B who writes them down. Then Student B says the words on page 174 for Student A to write down.

6 (46) Listen to three extracts from a PET speaking test and complete the table below. Be careful with the spelling of the students' surnames.

1 What's your name?		
Angela	Eduard	Yuji
2 What's your surname?		
Tedesco	(1)	(2) ....
3 Where do you live / come from?		
Italy	(3)	(4) ....
4 Do you study English? Do you like it? Why (not)?		
Likes travelling and meeting people	Prefers (5)	Useful for me and it's a (6) .... language
5 What other questions does the examiner ask?		
Do you think English will be useful for you in the (7) future ?	What did you do (8) .... ?	What do you enjoy doing in your (9) .... ?

7 (46) Listen to the recording again and answer these questions.

1 Do you think the candidates answer their last questions well? Why (not)?
2 What does Eduard say when he doesn't understand the examiner's question?
3 Does the examiner repeat the *same* question to Eduard?

8 Work in groups of three. Take turns to be the examiner. The examiner asks each student the first four questions from the table and chooses one Question 5 for each student.

Grammar
So do I and nor/neither do I

▶ page 127 *Grammar reference:* So do I *and* nor/neither do I

1 (47) Listen to and read what Ken says and circle the answer on the right which is true for you. Complete the phrase where necessary.

'My name's Ken.'	'So is mine.'	'My name's ...'
'I'm 15 years old.'	'So am I.'	'Really? I'm ...'
'I've got two brothers.'	'So have I.'	'Oh! I've got ..'
'I live in Taipei.'	'So do I.'	'Do you? I live'
'I don't like football.'	'Neither/Nor do I.'	'I really like ..'
'I went to the cinema.'	'So did I.'	'I went ...'
'I haven't been to Paris.'	'Neither/Nor have I.'	'I have. I went'

2 (48) Zosia is from Krakow, Poland. Listen to Zosia and answer appropriately using one of the phrases on the right from Exercise 1. Be careful! Zosia does not always use the same verb as Ken and her sentences do not follow the same order.

'My name's Zosia.'   'My name's David.'
'I'm from Krakow.'   'I'm not. I'm from Málaga, Spain.'

3 Work in pairs. Take turns to say a sentence about you. Your partner should answer using a suitable phrase.

Writing Part 2

1 **Work in small groups. Read the extract from the *Cambridge Learner's Dictionary* about punctuation and answer this question.**

- Which of the *uses* are the same in your language?

	uses
capital letter	• the first letter of a sentence: *Football is very popular in Britain.* • for countries, nationalities, languages, religions, names of people, places, events, organisations, trademarks, days, months, titles: *Portugal, Africa, Russia,* etc. • for titles of books, films, etc.: *Matrix Reloaded* • for abbreviations: *OPEC, AIDS, WWF*
full stop UK/ period US	• the end of a sentence: *I'm going for a walk.* • sometimes after an abbreviation: *Marton Rd. / Mrs. White / Dr. Evans*
comma	• between items in a list: *I need some peas, butter, sugar and eggs.* • to show a pause in a long sentence: *They didn't want to eat before I'd arrived, but I was an hour late.* • when you want to add extra information: *The woman, who I'd met last week, waved as she went past.*
apostrophe	• for missing letters: *don't, I'll, it's (it is)* • for possessives: *Paul's bike* • Note: words ending in 's' don't need another 's' added: *James' house*
hyphen	• to join two words together: *blue-black*

> Remember: we also use a capital letter for the personal pronoun *I*, e.g. *I love skiing* (not ~~i love skiing~~).

2 ⊙ **PET candidates often make mistakes with punctuation. There is no punctuation in sentences 1–5. Rewrite them to be correct.**

1 i am keen on tshirts trousers and jackets
2 ill send a present to marina i hope she likes it
3 say hi to your sister see you soon gari
4 i cant come to your english lesson on monday
5 my blanket is like a penguins skin its black and white

3 **Work in pairs. Read this Writing Part 2 question and <u>underline</u> the important words.**

> You are going to meet your cousin Myra at the station but you have never met her before.
>
> **Write an email to Myra. In your email, you should**
> - **describe yourself**
> - **ask Myra to describe herself**
> - **suggest a place to meet in the station.**
>
> **Write 35–45 words.**

4 **Read Pablo's answer (he is Myra's cousin). Do you think his teacher gave him full marks? Why (not)?**

> *Hi Myra,*
>
> *I am very happy becouse you are coming. Im tallish with short hair blue eyes an i always wear my favorit blue cap. what do you look like? Lets meet outside the resturant wich is in the station*
>
> *Pablo*

5 **Now read what Pablo's teacher wrote about his answer.**

> *You have included all three points and you have connected these points together well. However, I can't give you full marks because you have made several mistakes with spelling and punctuation.*

6 **<u>Underline</u> the three points in Pablo's answer and circle the words Pablo uses to connect these points. Correct Pablo's five spelling mistakes and his five mistakes with punctuation.**

7 **Write your own reply to the exam question in Exercise 3.**

8 **Work in small groups. Read each other's answers to see if you have included the three points and if you have made any mistakes with spelling or punctuation.**

This is me! 77

Unit 7 Vocabulary and grammar review

Grammar

❶ Complete sentences 1–8 using *too* or *enough* and these adjectives.

> big   cold   ~~dark~~   expensive   old
> sleepy   thick   warm

1 It was nearly midnight and it was ....*too dark*........ to see anything.
2 I'd like to wear those shoes but they aren't .... for me. I'm size 44.
3 Put the heating on, please. It's not .... in this room.
4 You can't skate on the lake. The ice isn't .... to be safe.
5 I must go to bed. I'm .... to stay awake any longer.
6 You're only 16 so you're not .... to drive a car on the road.
7 Put a sweater on. It's .... to go outside in just a T-shirt and jeans.
8 I really liked that computer but it was .... for me to buy.

❷ Circle the correct option in *italics* for each conversation 1–6.

1 **A:** How's Andrea these days?
  B: She *'ll* / *'s going* to have a baby.
2 **A:** Have you got any plans for tonight?
  B: Yes, I *meet* / *'m meeting* Ryan at 9 o'clock.
3 **A:** You look rather tired.
  B: Yes, I think I *'m going* / *'ll go* to bed early.
4 **A:** What time do you have to go home?
  B: The timetable says the last bus *leaves* / *is leaving* at midnight.
5 **A:** My computer has just crashed!
  B: Don't worry. I *'m going to* / *'ll* fix it.
6 **A:** The score's now England 0, Brazil 5!
  B: Brazil *will* / *are going* to win.

Vocabulary

❸ Match the beginnings and endings of these sentences.

1 It's much healthier to go on
2 We left the terminal and got onto
3 The driver and passenger got into
4 In big cities, many people go by
5 You should let other people get off
6 The police told the men to get out of

a the car and drove to the airport.
b train instead of taking the car.
c the train before you get on.
d foot than to sit in a car or a bus.
e the car and put their hands up.
f the plane, after a six-hour delay.

❹ Complete the crossword with words from Unit 7.

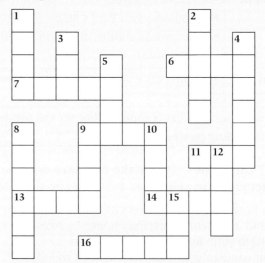

Across
6 go by boat
7 underground railway
9 what winds do
11 opposite of wet
13 very strong wind
14 opposite of extreme
16 boat for passengers

Down
1 like a bus, but on rails
2 get onto a plane
3 rainy
4 when the sky is covered
5 between cold and warm
8 trip in a plane
9 bicycle
10 between hot and cool
12 go by bicycle or horse
15 very cold, frozen solid

Unit 8   *Vocabulary and grammar review*

Vocabulary

❶ **Read this text and choose the correct word for each space.**

ANGELIQUE KIDJO

Angelique, also (1) ....*known*.......... as The African Queen, is one of the greatest female singers (2) .... the world. She was born in Cotonou, Benin, West Africa, and she (3) .... in Cotonou with eight brothers and sisters. Her uncles, aunts and grandparents come from Ouidah, a small village. She was (4) .... in a very open family. Angelique took (5) .... singing when she was six years old. Angelique is good (6) .... languages and sings in French, English and two African languages: Fon and Yoruba.

By the 1980s Angelique realised, 'Unless I (7) ....

Benin, I'll have problems.' In 1983 she left for Paris, France, where she studied both Jazz and Law. She couldn't decide between being a lawyer or a musician but thought, 'I will make a bigger difference to the world (8) .... I become a musician' and so she developed her music career. She first (9) .... her future husband, who is musician and producer Jean Hebrail, at Le CIM, a jazz school in Paris. Now they both live in New York with their teenage daughter. She has also been a Goodwill Ambassador for UNICEF (10) .... 2002, helping to bring education to children all over the world, in particular in Africa.

1	A	told	B called	C named	D	(known)
2	A	of	B in	C on	D	at
3	A	grew up	B got on with	C grew	D	born
4	A	set up	B sorted out	C brought up	D	grown up
5	A	on	B off	C out	D	up
6	A	in	B at	C on	D	of
7	A	leave	B don't leave	C will leave	D	won't leave
8	A	when	B unless	C if	D	so
9	A	knew	B found out	C made up	D	met
10	A	for	B in	C since	D	ago

❷ ◎ **PET candidates often make mistakes with punctuation and spelling. Correct one mistake in each of the following sentences.**

1 I'm busy all week except ~~friday~~. *F*
2 I only go shopping if I have to becouse most of the shops are expensive.
3 When I woke up, I did'nt have breakfast because it was late.
4 We had a party for my sisters birthday last Sunday.
5 My favourite place to eat is a typical italian restaurant near here.
6 I've just received your letter. You ask wich films I like best.
7 When I'm at home, I often were an old T-shirt and jeans.
8 I am so surprised by what he has done. I cannot belive it.

Grammar

❸ **Complete these conditional sentences, using your own ideas.**

1 If I didn't have to go to school, *I'd play football all day.*
2 I'd be extremely angry if …
3 If I go to bed late, …
4 If I found a dog, …
5 I often get embarrassed if …
6 Unless it rains, …
7 I'll have a party if …
8 If I don't help at home, …

❹ **Read these sentences about Rebecca's cousin, Tobias. Complete the second sentence so that it means the same as the first, *using no more than three words.***

1 My cousin Tobias lived in Innsbruck, Austria until he was 18 years old.
   My cousin Tobias ....*grew*............ up in Innsbruck, Austria.

2 He's rather short and his hair is curly and red.
   He's rather short and he .... curly red hair.

3 He loves playing chess and I do, too.
   He loves playing chess and .... do I.

4 He'll come and visit me this summer if he doesn't have to work in his dad's café.
   He'll come and visit me this summer .... he has to work in his dad's café.

5 He doesn't have enough money, so he won't travel by plane.
   If he had more money, he .... by plane.

Unit 9 Fit and healthy

Starting off

① Answer questions 1–8 in the quiz.

How fit and active are you?

Take this short and simple test to find out ...

1 How much exercise do you think you should do every day?

A Some, but I don't know how much I should do.
B At least 30 minutes a day – more if I have time.
C As little as possible.

2 What's your perfect way to spend a free afternoon?

A shopping with friends
B watching TV
C rollerblading, playing football, or doing another sport

3 How many times a week do you actually exercise? You can include things like dancing, or tidying your room ...

A never
B 3–4 times
C most days

4 You're in the park with your friends and someone suggests a game. What do you do?

A You join in and run the furthest and fastest – you don't like to lose.
B After a minute or two you sit on the grass again for a well-deserved rest.
C You say 'No way!' You really dislike running around.

5 You're bored and need to find something to do. What's your first choice?

A Go for a ride on your bike, or go out for a walk.
B Chat on the computer with your friends.
C Text your friends to suggest meeting up in a café.

6 You're on the ground floor of a building and you have to go to the 5th floor. What do you do?

A walk up the stairs
B run up the stairs
C wait for the lift

7 If you have to run for the bus, how do you feel afterwards?

A I'm exhausted.
B I'm fit so I feel fine.
C I am a bit out of breath.

8 Which would you describe yourself as?

A slow and tired all the time
B fine, but I'd love to have a bit more energy
C full of energy all the time

❷ Look at your score on page 174. Do you think you should make any changes to the way you live?

Listening Part 4

❶ 🔊(49) You are going to hear two young people talking about health. Read the first part of their conversation, then listen and fill in the missing words which show agreement or disagreement.

Kelly:	They keep saying on TV things like 'today's teenagers are unfit and unhealthy', and I just don't believe it.
Jason:	(1) .... There's all this stuff about us not getting enough exercise because we're watching TV or playing computer games all the time, when in fact nowadays everyone is mad about sports.
Kelly:	Well, (2) ...., but certainly a lot of young people are doing active things. Perhaps more than older generations did.

❷ In pairs or groups, think of other expressions that show we agree or disagree with somebody. Which are polite, and which show strong disagreement?

❸ 🔊(50) Look at sentences 1–6, then listen to the rest of Kelly and Jason's conversation. Decide if each sentence is correct or incorrect. If it is correct, put a tick (✓) in the box under A for YES. If it is not correct, put a tick (✓) in the box under B for NO.

		A YES	B NO
1	Kelly thinks that people's diets now are less healthy than in the past.	☐	☐
2	Jason and Kelly share the same opinion about people not sleeping enough.	☐	☐
3	Kelly believes that cycling to school is becoming more popular.	☐	☐
4	Kelly says that air pollution in the cities is getting worse.	☐	☐
5	Jason says that Kelly is often ill.	☐	☐
6	In the end, Jason and Kelly agree about young people's health.	☐	☐

Vocabulary
Illnesses and accidents

❶ 🔊(51) Listen to this extract from Listening Part 4 and answer the questions.
'coughs and colds and sore throats; perhaps a headache or a stomach ache'

- How do you say the underlined words?
- What do they mean?

❷ In pairs or groups, put these words under the three headings.

aspirin	bandage	bruise	cut	disease	earache
flu	fracture	high temperature	injection	~~injury~~	
medicine	operation	pill	plaster	plaster cast	
sprain	tablet	wound	X-ray		

accidents	illnesses	treatments
injury		

❸ In pairs, write ten short sentences with words from the table, using the points below to help you. Remember that we normally use *my, your, their,* etc. with parts of the body.

- We form verbs from the 'accident' nouns (e.g. She *injured* her leg; I've *cut* my thumb).
- We use *have* or *have got* with the 'illnesses' (e.g. He's *got* flu; She's *got* a high temperature).
- We use *have, take* or *put on* with the 'treatments' (e.g. I've *had* an operation; Joe *took* a pill for his headache; A nurse *put* a bandage *on* my arm).

❹ Tell your partner about any illnesses or injuries you have had (for instance when doing sports), then say what treatment you had, using expressions from Exercise 3 and the words in the table.

Grammar

Which, that, who, whose, when and *where* clauses (defining and non-defining)

page 127 *Grammar reference:* Which, that, who, whose, when, where *clauses (defining and non-defining)*

1 With a partner, read this text about sports injuries and circle the correct relative pronoun in *italics* for options 1–8.

Most people (1) *which* / *that* do regular sport are healthier, and often feel happier, than those (2) *who* / *whose* do little or no exercise. Care must be taken, though, to avoid the injuries (3) *when* / *which* sport can sometimes cause. People (4) *whose* / *that* favourite sports are running or jumping, for instance, may injure their ankles or knees. Training (5) *where* / *that* involves doing the same exercise again and again can do serious damage, particularly to athletes in their early teens, (6) *when* / *which* their bodies are still developing. It is important not to do too much too soon. Everyone should 'warm up' before they begin – if possible in the place (7) *who* / *where* they are going to exercise. It is essential, too, to follow any safety advice (8) *when* / *that* they receive.

2 (52) Listen to check your answers.

3 Complete the rules with the correct relative pronouns, then answer the question below.

Rules

Defining relative clauses

We use **defining** relative clauses to give **essential information** about someone or something.

We use:

- (1) ......that...... and (2) .... for people
- (3) .... and (4) .... for things
- (5) .... for time
- (6) .... for places
- (7) .... for possession.

We can leave out a relative pronoun (except *whose*) if it is the object of the clause:

the injuries (which) sport can sometimes cause

- Which other relative pronouns in the text are the object of the clause and could be left out?

4 Quickly read this text and answer the questions.

1 What is the problem?
2 What solution does the speaker recommend?

People (1) ....who / that.... work very hard, and individuals (2) .... lives are busy in other ways, may suffer from a kind of stress (3) .... can actually damage their health. One way (4) .... they can reduce stress levels is to find a time, every day, (5) .... they can relax. They should find something (6) .... they enjoy doing, such as reading, in a place (7) .... they feel comfortable and unlikely to be disturbed.

5 Complete spaces 1–7 with relative pronouns.

6 (53) Listen to check your answers.

7 Look at the text again and decide which of relative pronouns 1–7 we could leave out.

8 Correct sentences 1–6 by adding a relative pronoun, if necessary.

1 The TV series ^which/that starts tonight is about doctors.
2 People swim a lot are usually quite fit.
3 That road is a place accidents are common.
4 Lucy has recovered from the illness she had.
5 The boy tooth hurt went to the dentist.
6 Winter is the time many people catch flu.

9 Work in pairs. Make as many sentences as you can beginning with these words.

1 Going to the dentist is something which frightens me. / I don't like.
2 My room is the place where …
3 Watching sport on TV is something that …
4 Sunday is the day when …
5 A good friend is someone who …
6 A lucky person is somebody whose …

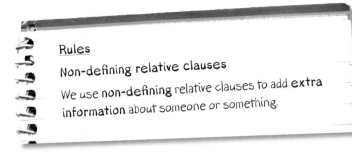

Rules

Non-defining relative clauses

We use non-defining relative clauses to add extra information about someone or something.

10 In pairs, look at this example of a non-defining relative clause and answer questions 1–6.

Cycling to school, which is very healthy, is more and more common.

1   What is the relative pronoun?
2   What is the relative clause?
3   What do the commas do to the relative clause?
4   Does the sentence make sense <u>without</u> the relative clause?
5   Can we leave out the relative pronoun?
6   Can we use *that* to begin a non-defining relative clause, do you think?

11 Make one sentence from 1–6, using non-defining relative clauses.

1   My arm is better now. I hurt it last week.
    My arm, which I *hurt last week, is better now.*
2   My aunt works in the hospital. She's a doctor.
    My aunt, who is …
3   The lake was very cold. I went there for a swim.
    The lake, where …
4   Ricky is my best friend. His sister is a nurse.
    Ricky, whose …
5   In 2010 the sports centre opened. I was 12 then.
    In 2010, when I …
6   Surfing is popular in my country. I really enjoy it.
    Surfing, which I …

12 ⊙ Defining and non-defining relative clauses can be difficult for students. Correct one mistake in each of sentences 1–10 written by PET candidates. (Sometimes the mistake is with punctuation.)

1   Her farm has a swimming pool ~~that~~ *where* we can swim.
    Or 'Her farm has a swimming pool that we can swim in.'
2   I am visiting my mother who is ill.
3   He has a son, that is about my age.
4   The last book that I read it was 'The Lord of the Rings'.
5   I've met a guy, who's name is Daniel.
6   I'm in Brazil, that is a beautiful country.
7   That is all what I can tell you.
8   There are many places are very beautiful.
9   I'll tell everyone whose I know.
10 I have to go to the airport which it is quite far from the city.

Vocabulary
Sports

1 Match comments 1–3 with pictures A–C, then answer the question below.

1   'Doing gymnastics can be hard work, but I want to be the best.'
2   'I really enjoy playing basketball – it's so fast-moving.'
3   'I always look forward to going paragliding in the summer.'

•   Would you like to do, or watch, any of these sports? Why (not)?

❷ Look at comments 1–3 again. Which verb – *do*, *go* or *play* – do we use with each sport? Write the sports in the table.

do	go	play

❸ Add these sports to the table.

athletics   baseball   boxing   climbing   cycling
football   golf   ice hockey   jogging   running
skiing   squash   surfing   swimming   tennis   volleyball

❹ In pairs, look for patterns for which kinds of sports often go with which verbs.

❺ ⊙ PET candidates often find it difficult to put the right verb and the right sport together. Correct the mistakes in sentences 1–6.

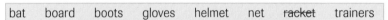

1 I practise horse riding twice a week. *(go written above "practise")*
2 You can make a lot of sports and activities.
3 In winter you can make snowboarding.
4 We have done table tennis.
5 At first, we made aerobics.
6 We played windsurfing.

❻ With a partner, note down as many sports as you can that are played in these places.

court   gym   pitch   ring   stadium   track

❼ Look at the words in the box and decide if they are *clothes* or *equipment*.
Then think about which sports they are used in and complete the mind map as for *racket*.

bat   board   boots   gloves   helmet   net   ~~racket~~   trainers

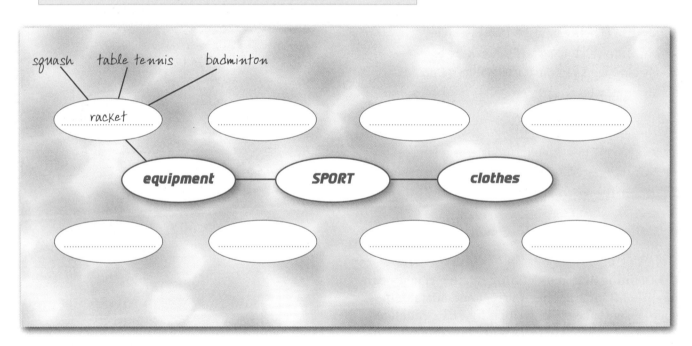

❽ Complete expressions 1–3 by matching the verbs from the box with the right nouns.

~~beat~~   draw   lose   score   win

1 ....*beat*.......... a player or team
2 .... a goal
3 ...., ... or .... a match or game

Reading Part 5

1 ice hockey

2 squash

3 aerobics

4 scuba diving

① Which of these words would you use to describe the sports in the pictures?

competitive   individual   non-competitive   team

② Work in pairs. Discuss which kinds of sports you prefer to take part in and why.

③ Read the text *Choose your sport*. Try to fill in gaps 1–10 without looking at any of options A, B, C or D. Use these clues to help you.

1   Which verb often goes with the adjective *fit*?
2   Which phrasal verb means *start doing* a sport or hobby?
3   Which relative pronoun can we use with things?
4   Which relative pronoun can we use with people?
5   Which noun do we use for a number of people who play a sport?
6   Which verb goes with *jogging* and *swimming*?
7   What does a tennis player use to hit the ball?
8   Which verb means *doing better than all the others*?
9   Which noun means *something that tests your ability*?
10 Where do people play tennis?

④ Read the text again and choose the correct word, A, B, C or D, for each space.

Choose your sport

Everyone knows that exercise is good (0) .....B..... the body and the mind. We all want to (1) .... fit and look good, but too many of us take (2) .... the wrong sport and quickly lose interest. So now fitness experts are advising people to choose an activity (3) .... matches their character.

For instance, those (4) .... like to be with other people often enjoy golf or squash, or playing for a basketball, football or hockey (5) .... If, though, you're happier on your own, you may prefer to (6) .... jogging or swimming.

Do you like competition? Then try something like running, or a (7) .... sport such as tennis. If, on the other hand, (8) .... isn't important to you, then activities like dancing can be an enjoyable (9) .... without the need to show you're better than everyone else.

Finally, think about whether you find it easy to make yourself do exercise. If so, sports like weight training at home and cycling are fine. If not, book a skiing holiday, Taekwondo lessons, or a tennis (10) .... You're much more likely to do something you've already paid for!

0 A	to	B	for	C	with	D	by
1 A	keep	B	have	C	last	D	hold
2 A	in	B	down	C	out	D	up
3 A	when	B	that	C	how	D	where
4 A	which	B	who	C	whose	D	what
5 A	team	B	group	C	band	D	crew
6 A	play	B	do	C	make	D	go
7 A	bat	B	board	C	stick	D	racket
8 A	beating	B	gaining	C	winning	D	knocking
9 A	defeat	B	challenge	C	victory	D	score
10 A	track	B	ring	C	court	D	gym

Speaking Part 2

❶ (54) **Listen and complete these expressions that show agreement or disagreement.**

1 You may be ....*right*.........., but …
2 I'm not really .... about that.
3 Yes, I .... agree with you.
4 I don't think .... because …
5 That's not the .... I see it.
6 I don't agree at ....
7 That's ....
8 I think so ....

❷ **Which of expressions 1–8 do we use to do the following? Write the numbers in the boxes.**

a agree?   3 ☐ ☐
b disagree strongly?   ☐ ☐
c disagree politely?   ☐ ☐ ☐

❸ (54) **Listen again. Underline the stressed word(s) in each expression from Exercise 1.**

You <u>may</u> be right, but …

❹ (54) **Listen again and repeat, stressing the same words as in the recording.**

❺ **In these final parts of conversations, the speakers make a decision. Complete the sentences with words from the box.**

| agreed | both | glad | ~~idea~~ |
| so | then | thing | what |

A: Yes, that's a good (1) ....*idea*.......... . Let's do
that, (2) ....
B: Right, we're (3) .... That's
(4) .... we'll do.

A: OK, we (5) .... like the idea.
(6) .... shall we do that?
B: Yes, that's the best (7) .... to do. I'm
(8) .... we agree.

❻ (55) **Listen to the recording to check your answers.**

❼ (55) **Listen again and underline the words which are stressed.**

❽ **Do this Speaking Part 2 task with a partner. Read the instructions, then think about these things:**

- which kind of sport would suit your personality
- which you would enjoy most
- which would be best for your fitness and health

Talk together for at least two minutes.

Your **friend** and you would like to start doing a **sport**, but you are **not sure** which to choose. Talk together about the **different sports** you could do and decide **which** you are going to take up.

Here is a picture with some ideas to help you.

Writing Part 3

❶ **In Writing Part 3 you have to write a story *or* a letter. Look at these instructions and answer questions 1–4.**

- Your English teacher has asked you to write a story.
- Your story must have the following title:
  The most frightening experience of my life

1 Do you have to write a letter, or a story?
2 Do the instructions give you a title, or the first line?
3 Should you write in the first person (*I*) or the third person (*he/she/it*)?
4 Which are the key words?

1 Last month I went snowboarding in Canada with my friend Lucy, who is a champion snowboarder. I was feeling nervous when we reached the top because it had started to snow heavily and I couldn't see much.

2 Lucy set off first, but by the time I followed she had disappeared. I went down faster and faster and I thought I saw her go off to the right, so I turned right, too. But soon I came to some cliffs and had to stop. I was terrified. Had she gone over the edge?

3 I waited and shouted, and suddenly Lucy was there. I'd gone the wrong way but she'd heard me calling and eventually she'd found me. I felt safe at last.

2 The story on this page has three paragraphs. Read it and decide which paragraph:

a describes the main events ⬜ 2
b sets the scene for the action ⬜
c states the writer's feelings afterwards ⬜
d tells us about the final event ⬜
e explains what really happened ⬜
f introduces the story, saying who did what, where and when ⬜

Past perfect

🔊 **page 128** *Grammar reference: Past perfect*

3 We use the past perfect when we are already talking about the past and we want to say something happened earlier. In pairs, look at this example from the text. Then do questions 1–3.

*I was feeling nervous when we reached the top because it **had started** to snow heavily.*

1 Find five more examples of the past perfect in the text.
2 What is the question form of the past perfect?
3 What is the short form of the past perfect?

4 We often use the past perfect to form longer sentences in stories. Join the sentences using the words given and the past perfect.

1 I sprained my ankle. I didn't go for fitness training.
   I didn't go to fitness training because *I'd sprained my ankle.*
2 I walked all the way home. I felt tired.
   I felt tired because …
3 The match started. I arrived at the stadium.
   By the time I …
4 I left my trainers at home. I couldn't run in the race.
   As I …
5 I decided to get fit. I took up squash.
   After I …

5 With a partner, look at these instructions for Writing Part 3. Ask and answer the four questions in Exercise 1.

• Your English teacher has asked you to write a story.
• Your story must begin with this sentence:
  I felt nervous when the game began.

Exam advice

Try to use a range of past tenses to tell your story, including the past simple, the past perfect and the past continuous.

6 Write your story in about 100 words. Use three or four paragraphs and include similar points to those in a–f in Exercise 2.

Unit 10 A question of taste

Starting off

❶ Work in small groups. Talk about how the types of food and drink have been organised. Then add three more types of food or drink to each.

❷ Discuss these questions.

1 What are your favourite types of food and drink?
2 Are there any types of food you don't eat? Which? Why not?

Reading Part 2

❶ Work in pairs. Look at the title of the guide on page 89, the headings and the pictures. What do you think you will have to do in this Reading Part 2 task?

❷ The following five groups of people would like to have a meal in a restaurant. Read the descriptions of the people and <u>underline</u> what the people would like and what they wouldn't like.

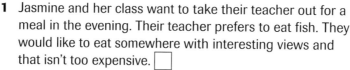

1 Jasmine and her class want to take their teacher out for a meal in the evening. Their teacher prefers to eat fish. They would like to eat somewhere with interesting views and that isn't too expensive. ☐

2 Jack's parents want to celebrate their summer wedding anniversary with the family next Tuesday. They hate being with other groups of people. The family normally orders steak, but Jack would like to try something different. ☐

3 Sara and her friends ate in *Spider-Man's Web* last week. They would like to try another character restaurant this Thursday. They aren't keen on fish and can't afford anywhere expensive. ☐

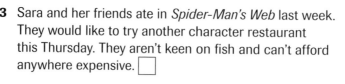

4 Jon is staying with an English-speaking friend and his family. The family would like to take their visitor to a restaurant with special views on Sunday. Jon would prefer to eat meat rather than fish or vegetarian food. ☐

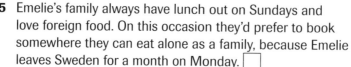

5 Emelie's family always have lunch out on Sundays and love foreign food. On this occasion they'd prefer to book somewhere they can eat alone as a family, because Emelie leaves Sweden for a month on Monday. ☐

Eight unusual restaurants

❸ Before you read the text, think about *how* the details you have underlined in the descriptions of the people might appear in the text. To help you do this, answer questions 1–5 below, *without reading the text*.

1 Jasmine is looking for a restaurant that *isn't too expensive* and Sara *can't afford anywhere expensive*. What words do you expect to read in the description of their most suitable restaurant?

2 Jack's family *hate being with other groups of people* in a restaurant and Emelie's family want to *eat alone as a family*. Can you think of a solution for them?

3 Sara and her friends would like to try *another character restaurant*. Can you think of another two possible characters for a restaurant?

4 Jon's English-speaking family and Jasmine's class are looking for a restaurant with *views*. Do you think a restaurant in the basement or inside a shopping centre will have *special* or *interesting* views?

5 Emelie's family love foreign food. Where are they from?

❹ Read the text and decide which restaurant (A–H) would be the most suitable for each group of people (1–5).

A Top Secret

Don't expect great views here, as this restaurant is a hiding place for spies. You'll need the password to get into our large dining room where you will share long tables with other spies. Reasonable prices for a range of chicken, meat or fish dishes.

B Undersea Restaurant

Located 5m under the sea, the **Undersea Restaurant** is the world's only aquarium restaurant where you and our other guests can see life under the ocean from your chair. Enjoy our special range of fresh food from the sea! Celebrate our first anniversary with great discounts. Not open for lunch on Monday.

C The Ninja Castle

Discover the world of the ninja warrior in our restaurant which has been designed as a ninja castle. It's conveniently located inside the shopping centre with private rooms for small groups. Not cheap but you can enjoy Japanese fish or meat dishes. Closed all day Tuesday.

D The Ice Room

Situated in the basement of the Winter Palace, **The Ice Room** is a very special restaurant. The tables, chairs and walls are made of ice. Enjoy our Swedish fish dishes with a cup of hot soup. Open in winter only. Reserve our smaller rooms for private parties. Dress warmly!

E Food for all

The dining room is arranged around an open kitchen so you can chat to the many guests and watch our chefs as they prepare a variety of vegetarian dishes. There's no list of prices, just pay what you can. And if you find you don't have enough money, you can wash up. Closed Thursdays.

F Floor 100

Enjoy amazing sunsets over the city from the 100th floor at the top of the Star Building as world-famous chef, Marco Louis, prepares food for all tastes. We have two private dining rooms for small groups. At **Floor 100**, expect top food for top prices! Open Monday to Saturday.

G Lights Off

At Lights Off, you and our other guests sit in a completely black dining room where you are guided and served by blind individuals who have been specially trained to serve meals in the dark. Your three-course menu includes a starter, fish or vegetarian main course and a dessert. Price range: mid–high.

H The Enormous Steak

You are the chef at the **Enormous Steak** in Marshes Wildlife Park. Choose a steak and cook it yourself on the huge indoor grill. You don't have to worry about the weather to enjoy this barbecue or to watch the animals from the windows. Expensive but recommended.

Grammar
Commands

▶ page 128 *Grammar reference: Commands*

❶ ⟨2⟩ In Reading Part 2, you read about some unusual restaurants. Listen to three short recordings. In each recording, a waiter is giving instructions to some guests. Where is the waiter? Write 1, 2 or 3 next to the correct restaurant A–H.

A Top Secret ☐ E Food for all ☐
B Undersea Restaurant ☐ F Floor 100 ☐
C The Ninja Castle ☐ G Lights Off ☐
D The Ice Room ☐ H The Enormous Steak ☐

❷ ⟨2⟩ Listen to the recordings again. Complete the waiters' instructions 1–6 with a verb, then answer the questions that follow.

1 ...Put... on these gloves.
2 Children, ... the walls please!
3 .... your friends with you next time.
4 But .... your enemies.
5 .... your steak to the barbecue.
6 .... the grill!

• What form of the verb do we use when we tell someone
   a what to do
   b what **not** to do?
• Does the form of the verb change when we talk to more than one person?

❸ Work in small groups. Imagine you are waiters at *Lights Off*. Remember that your guests eat in a dark dining room and can't see anything. Write six instructions to guide them.

Come in through this door. Don't worry, I'll guide you to your table.

❹ Change groups. Take turns to give your instructions to each other. Keep your eyes shut when you are the guests.

Vocabulary
Course, dish, food, meal and *plate*

❶ ⊙ PET candidates often make mistakes with the words *course*, *dish*, *food*, *meal* and *plate*. Read these extracts from the *Cambridge Learner's Dictionary*.

> **course** [kɔːs] *noun* [C] a part of a meal: *a three-course dinner*

> **dish** [dɪʃ] *noun* [C] food that is prepared in a particular way as part of a meal: *a chicken/vegetarian dish*

> **food** [fuːd] *noun* [C, U] something that people and animals eat to keep them alive: *His favourite food is pizza*

> **meal** [mɪːl] *noun* [C] when you eat, or the food that you eat at that time: *a three-course meal*

> **plate** [pleɪt] *noun* [C] a flat, round object which is used for putting food on: *a plate of biscuits*

❷ Alicia wrote a letter to her friend, Lee, about the food in her country. Complete Alicia's letter using *courses, dish, food, meals* and *plate*.

Dear Lee,

I'm from Quito, Ecuador. There are many different types of (1) ....food........... in Ecuador – for example: meat, fish, vegetables, etc. We eat three (2) .... a day: breakfast, lunch and dinner. In the morning, my mum often leaves different cakes or bread on a (3) .... on the table. Lunch and dinner are usually a little heavier than breakfast. Lunch is three (4) ....: a starter, which is often soup, a main course and a dessert. My favourite (5) .... is 'Fanesca', which is a fish soup, often made with cod.

Fanesca

Listening Part 1

1 How much do you remember about Listening Part 1? Circle the correct option in *italics* in sentences 1–5 in the Exam round-up box.

> ### Exam round-up
>
> In Listening Part 1:
> 1 There are *five /* (*seven*) questions.
> 2 You must read each question carefully and look at the *three / four* accompanying pictures.
> 3 You listen to a *short / long* recording for each question and put a tick (✓) in the box under the correct picture.
> 4 You will listen to each recording *once / twice*.
> 5 The first time you hear the recording, *don't write anything / try to tick (✓) the correct box*. Then, as you listen for the second time, check your answer.

2 Work in pairs. Read this first question from Listening Part 1 and look at the three accompanying pictures.

1 What did Jamie buy?

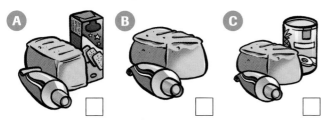

3 What do we know about Jamie's shopping trip? Complete these sentences.

- We know that Jamie buys a (1) ....*tube of* ....*toothpaste*..... **and** a (2) .... (Pictures A, B and C).
- We don't know if Jamie buys a (3) .... (Picture A) or a (4) .... (Picture C) **or** neither of them (Picture B).

4 🎧3 Listen to the first part of the recording and put a tick (✓) next to the correct picture.

5 🎧4 Listen to the second part of the recording. Is your answer still correct?

6 Work in pairs. Read the rest of the questions from Listening Part 1. Underline the key words in the questions, then look at the accompanying pictures and think about what information you will need to listen for.

---

2 What will they take to the party?

3 What time is the boy's appointment?

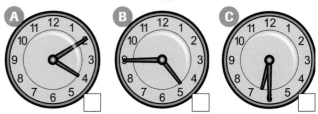

4 What did the girl buy online?

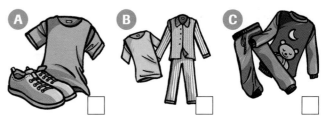

5 What is the free gift today?

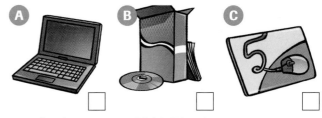

6 What is nearest to Rick's Diner?

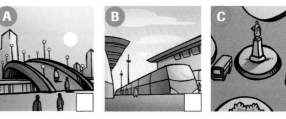

7 Where has the mother been?

7 🎧5–🎧10 Listen to each recording twice and choose the correct picture by putting a tick (✓) in the box below it.

Vocabulary
Shops and services

❶ Read this extract from the *Cambridge Learner's Dictionary* and answer the question below.

> **hairdresser** [heədresə] *noun* [C] 1 someone whose job is to wash, cut, colour etc people's hair 2 **hairdresser's** the place where you go to have your hair washed, cut, coloured etc.

- Can we use an apostrophe s (*'s*) with both people *and* places of work?

❷ Work in small groups. Label each picture 1–8 with the correct word from the box.

butcher	dentist	dry cleaner	garage
~~hairdresser~~	library	post office	travel agent

..hairdresser.. ....

....

❸ Which of the words 1–8 in Exercise 2 can also add *'s* when used for the place?

❹ In which place from Exercise 2 can you do these things? (More than one answer is sometimes possible.)

1 make an appointment
2 buy something
3 borrow something
4 book something
5 have something repaired
6 complain and ask for your money back

❺ 🔊(11) Listen to three short conversations and write down where the people have been.

1 .... 2 .... 3 ....

❻ 🔊(11) Listen to each conversation again. In small groups discuss what you think Layla, Lewis and Callum should do next.

 Unit 10

Grammar
Have something done

🔘 page 128 *Grammar reference:* Have something done

❶ Work in pairs. Look at these extracts from the recording and the rules about *have something done*.

Layla:	I normally have my hair cut at Gabrielle's.
Lewis:	We're having the scooter repaired.
Vicki:	We had this dress cleaned last week.

> **Rules**
>
> When we talk about an action somebody does for us, we can use *have something done*. For example:
>
> Layla does not cut her own hair, she <u>has</u> her <u>hair</u> cut.
>
> <u>Get</u> something done (e.g. *She <u>gets</u> her hair cut*) is also possible, but usually in informal situations only.

❷ Read this extract from the *Cambridge Learner's Dictionary* and the sentences about Vinnie and Ginny, then answer this question.

- Who is the slob?

> **slob** [slɒb] *noun* [C] *informal* a lazy or dirty person

My cousin Vinnie

He never has his hair cut.

He has his meals cooked for him.

He's cleaning his nails with a fork.

He had his flat cleaned last year.

He had his car washed three years ago.

My neighbour Ginny

She has her hair cut every three weeks.

She always cooks her own meals.

She's having her nails done today.

She cleaned her flat before lunch.

She washed her scooter this morning.

3 Use the sentences from Exercise 2 to complete the table.

	I do it myself	someone does it for me
present simple	Ginny cooks her own meals	(1) Vinnie ....
present continuous	Vinnie's cleaning his nails with a fork	(2) Ginny ....
past simple	Ginny cleaned her flat before lunch	(3) Vinnie ....

4 Here are some more situations where people *have something done*. Look at the illustrations and write a sentence with the words given. Check you have used the correct form of the verb *have* by looking at the time adverb (*now, two weeks ago*, etc.).

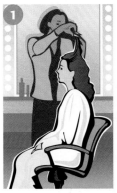     

1 Sophie / hair / cut / at the moment
   Sophie is having her hair cut at the moment
2 I / bike / repair / two weeks ago
3 John / bedroom / paint / now

4 We / photo / take / once a year
5 Our grandma / hair / colour / every three weeks
6 I can't send an email because we / our computer / mend / at the moment

5 Work in small groups. Ask and answer questions about the things people do for you.

How often do you		your photo taken?
		your hair cut?
	have	your teeth checked?
When did you last		your computer mended?
		your bedroom painted?

How often do you have your hair cut?
I have my hair cut every six weeks.

6 Read this short article about Jack Blenkharn and <u>underline</u> five examples of *have something done*.

7 Work in pairs. Read the extract from the *Cambridge Learner's Dictionary* and discuss this question.

• Do you think Jack and his mum have good taste? Why (not)?

> taste [teɪst] *noun* [U] the ability to judge what is attractive or suitable, especially in things related to art, style, beauty, etc.

A BOY of 11 has been told he can't go to school after he had his hair cut. Jack Blenkharn's mum, Carol, paid £20 for Jack to have his head decorated with the Nike logo, eight stripes and a star.

The teachers at Sale High School have ordered Jack to go home. He will only be allowed back at school when Jack has his head shaved again. Mrs Blenkharn said: 'To send an 11-year-old boy home because of his hair is crazy. Some of the girls at the school have pink hair and some of the teachers have their hair coloured regularly as well.' Dave Williams, the hairdresser, says 'Styles like this are very popular, especially as a lot of footballers have their hair shaved like this.'

Adapted from *Manchester Evening News*

A question of taste (93)

Speaking Part 3

❶ (12) **Listen to three short conversations. Ekaterina, Mateos and Ruben are staying with English-speaking families. Circle the everyday objects they ask for.**

❷ **Work in pairs. Take turns to describe one of the objects in the pictures using expressions from the table. Can your partner guess which object you are describing?**

describing everyday objects		
What is it?	**What is it made of?**	**What is it used for?**
It's a kind of ... It's something like a ...	It's made of ... (metal/plastic/wood/ glass, etc.)	It's used for ... *ing*

❸ **Answer the questions in the Exam round-up box.**

Exam round-up

How much do you remember about Speaking Part 3? Are the following sentences true or false? If you think a sentence is false, write what you think is correct.

1 The examiner will ask you to talk on your own about a colour photograph for about a minute.

2 It's a good idea to imagine you are describing the picture to someone who can't see it.

3 You should describe the places, weather, people, everyday objects, etc.

4 You should also talk about how the people are feeling, why they are doing the activities and what they might do afterwards.

5 If you don't know the word for an object, you should point at it.

❹ (13) **Listen to Natalie describing one of these three photos. Which photo is she describing?**

❺ **Put a tick (✓) next to the things Natalie describes.**
1 the place
2 the weather
3 what the people are doing
4 what the people are wearing
5 everyday objects

❻ **Work in pairs. Take turns to describe one of the other photos. Listen to your partner and put a tick (✓) next to the things your partner describes.**

Writing Part 2

❶ Before doing Writing Part 2, answer the questions in the Exam round-up box.

❷ Work in small groups. Look at the following three Writing Part 2 questions and underline the important information in each.

1

> You are going to have pizza with your class to celebrate the end of the year but you have forgotten to ask Ryan to come too.
>
> Write an email to Ryan. In your email, you should
> - apologise for the late invitation
> - invite Ryan
> - explain where you are going to eat.
>
> Write 35–45 words.

2

> You plan to go to a shopping centre in a nearby city during the school holidays.
>
> Write an email to your friend Paula. In your email, you should
> - invite her to go with you
> - explain why you want to go there
> - suggest a place to meet.
>
> Write 35–45 words.

3

> You stayed at your cousin's home over the weekend and you've just realised you left something behind.
>
> Write an email to Alex. In your email, you should
> - thank him
> - describe what you left behind
> - suggest how you can get the object back.
>
> Write 35–45 words.

❸ Remember in Writing Part 2 you may have to *thank someone, explain, invite, apologise* or *suggest*. For questions 1–5, complete the second sentence so that it means the same as the first. Be careful with verb forms.

1 <u>I'm very sorry</u> that I forgot to invite you before.
   I'm so sorry for....*forgetting*..... to invite you before.
2 I want to have my hair cut. That's why I'd like to go to the shopping centre.
   I'd like to go to the shopping centre .... I want to have my hair cut.
3 How about coming too? We'll have a great time.
   Would you like .... too? We'll have a great time.
4 Why don't we meet outside the station?
   Let's .... outside the station.
5 It was very kind of you to invite me to stay. I had a lot of fun.
   Thank you very much for .... me to stay. I had a lot of fun.

❹ Underline the words in Exercise 3 which are used to *thank someone, explain, invite, apologise* and *suggest*.

❺ Choose *one* of the Writing Part 2 questions and write your answer. When you have finished, make sure you can answer *yes* to these five questions.

1 Have you included all three points?
2 Have you connected your ideas with *and*, *but*, etc.?
3 Have you checked for mistakes with spelling or punctuation?
4 Have you opened and closed the email?
5 Have you written 35–45 words?

❻ Work in small groups. Read each other's emails. Can you answer *yes* to the five questions above?

Unit 9 *Vocabulary and grammar review*

Grammar

❶ Match these beginnings (1–6) and endings (a–f), then add relative pronouns from the box to form complete sentences.

that	~~when~~	when	where	who	whose

Sunday is the day when I relax at home.

1 Sunday is the day ⌐   **a** cut his hand.
2 All the races   **b** tennis is played.
3 Winter is the time └   **c** I relax at home.
4 James is the boy   **d** took place were exciting.
5 A court is a place   **e** husband is very ill.
6 That's the woman   **f** people catch flu.

❷ Put the words in the correct order, starting with the word that has a capital letter. Add commas to form non-defining relative clauses.

1 a swimming champion / is / Zara / only 14 / is / who *Zara, who is only 14, is a swimming champion.*
2 we play tennis / the weather / good / In summer / when / is
3 won / the best player of all / was / whose / Stevie / team
4 we live / a lot of pollution / is / where / In the city centre / there
5 better now / who / My brother / an accident / is feeling / had
6 a team sport / on a court / which / is / Volleyball / is played

❸ Complete the text using the past simple or the past perfect of the verbs in brackets.

My first tennis match

At ten o'clock last Saturday morning, I (1) ...was... (be) ready to play my first real match at the tennis club. I (2) .... (practise) all the previous week and I really (3) .... (feel) good, especially as I (4) .... (bring) my lucky trainers.

When I (5) .... (put) them on, I walked onto the court. I noticed that the grass (6) .... (be) very wet, as it (7) .... (rain) a lot the night before, but that (8) .... (not seem) important.

Jack, the other player, (9) .... (be) a little late because he (10) .... (leave) his racket at

home, but as soon as he arrived we (11) .... (start) the match. I quickly (12) .... (realise) that in the past I (13) .... (play) against stronger players than him, and I (14) .... (be) sure that I could win.

Suddenly, though, I (15) .... (slip) on the wet grass and (16) .... (fall). I (17) .... (know) immediately that I (18) .... (twist) my ankle quite badly, so that was the end of the game. I (19) .... (go) to hospital for an X-ray, and fortunately I (20) .... (not broke) it. But after that I never (21) .... (wear) my 'lucky' trainers again!

Vocabulary

❹ Circle the correct option in *italics* in each of these sentences.

1 Skiers have to wear good (gloves) / *boots* / *trainers* to keep their hands warm.
2 Last week I was coughing and I had a really *hurt* / *sore* / *injured* throat.
3 In last night's football match, Brazil *won* / *beat* / *drew* the United States 6–0.
4 I'd cut my arm quite badly, so the *medicine* / *nurse* / *patient* at the hospital put a bandage on it.
5 Nowadays, many people *take* / *have* / *have got* an injection to stop them catching flu.
6 I was practising hitting the ball with a baseball *racket* / *bat* / *board*.
7 Lydia is good at *jogging* / *gymnastics* / *athletics*, particularly the long jump and 100 metres.
8 If I have a headache, I usually take a *medicine* / *pill* / *treatment* with a glass of water.
9 After I fell off my bike, I had a big black *bruise* / *flu* / *disease* on my leg.
10 The two boxers walked into the *ring* / *pitch* / *court*, both hoping to become World Champion.

Unit 10 *Vocabulary and grammar review*

Vocabulary

❶ Complete sentences 1–5 with a suitable verb, then answer the question below.

1 You should ......*make/book*...... an appointment to see the dentist if you have toothache.
2 If you are not happy with something in a restaurant, you should .... to your waiter.
3 If you are organising a meal for a group of friends, you should remember to .... a table in the restaurant.
4 You don't need to buy books, you can .... them from the library.
5 You will save time and money if you learn how to .... broken things yourself.

• Do you agree with this advice?

❷ Wei is a student from China. He has written a letter to his English-speaking friend, Freddy, about restaurants. Correct nine more mistakes in the letter. Then write a suitable reply.

Dear Freddy,
             receive
I was pleased to ~~received~~ your letter. I am really interesting in resturants. You know I'm Chinese and I like Chinese food. Chinese food are very kind. My favourite food is chicken and all kind of chicken food. I think chicken are quite good in a Chinese restaurant. That is what my think. I hope you enjoy with your meal next Saturday. Please write and tell me all about it.

Yours,

Wei

Grammar

❸ Complete these sentences using the correct form of *have something done*. Use the correct tense and an object, as in the example (*his car*).

1 My uncle didn't have time to wash his car before my cousin's wedding, so he *had his car washed* at the garage.
2 My sister tried to cut her own hair but it looked terrible. Now she .... at the hairdresser.
3 I wanted to have a nice photo for my passport so I .... by a professional photographer.
4 We live on the ninth floor and we can't clean the windows ourselves because it's dangerous. Once a month, we .... by a window cleaner.
5 When the car broke down, my dad tried to repair it but he couldn't. In the end he .... at the garage.
6 When I was a baby I drew all over my bedroom walls. My parents were both working and couldn't paint the walls themselves. So they .... by a painter.

❹ Here are some sentences about Bella's party. Complete the second sentence so that it means the same as the first, *using no more than three words*.

1 The hairdresser cut my hair before I went to the party.
I ...*had my hair*... cut before I went to the party.
2 When I got to the party, Bella told me to put my coat in her bedroom.
When I got to the party, Bella said, '................................. your coat in my bedroom!'
3 I stayed until the party finished.
I .... leave until the party finished.
4 I really enjoyed Bella's party.
I .... a really good time at Bella's party.
5 You should go to her next party.
If I were you, ... go to her next party.

Unit 11 Conserving nature

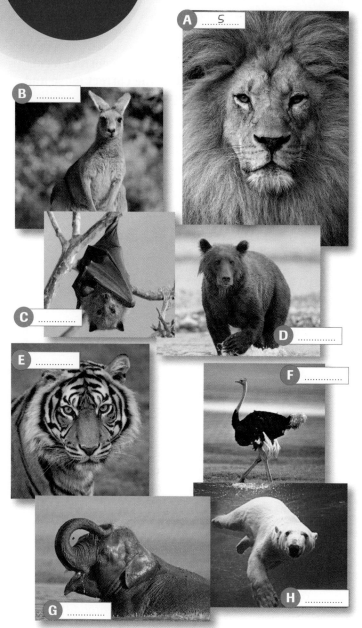

A ....S....

B ....

C ....

D ....

E ....

F ....

G ....

H ....

❷ In which continents, countries or parts of the world do these creatures live naturally?

❸ Think of two more statements about animals and ask your group if they are true or false.

Snakes are completely deaf.   T

Listening Part 2

❶ What do you know about India? What kinds of wildlife is it famous for?

❷ Before doing Listening Part 2, answer the questions in the Exam round-up box.

Exam round-up

How much do you remember about Listening Part 2? Complete the following information with these words and phrases.

~~instructions~~	key	kind	one or two	own
second	similar	six	three	twice

Begin Listening Part 2 by studying the
(1) ...*instructions*... to get an idea of the topic.
There will be (2) .... speakers and you
will hear the recording (3) .... There
are (4) .... questions or unfinished
statements and you must choose one of
(5) .... possible answers. Before the
recording is played, look at each question and
decide what (6) .... of information is
needed. Also underline the (7) ....
words in the question or unfinished statement and
options A, B and C. Then listen for expressions with
(8) .... or opposite meanings to these.
Try to think of your (9) .... answer for
each question, then decide which option is most
like it. Check your answers the (10) ....
time you listen.

Starting off

❶ Work in small groups. Match the animals in *italics* with pictures A–H, then decide whether statements 1–8 are true (T) or false (F).

1 *Tigers* can swim very well.   T
2 *Polar bears* are left-handed.
3 *Kangaroos* can't walk backwards.
4 *Ostriches* bury their heads in sand.
5 *Lions* sleep up to 20 hours a day.
6 *Elephants* are afraid of mice.
7 *Bats* can't see anything.
8 *Bears* can run as fast as horses.

❸ Study questions 1–6 for Listening Part 2 below. For each question or unfinished statement, underline the key word(s). Then do the same for each of options A, B and C.

❹ (14) Follow the exam instructions. Listen for expressions with similar or opposite meanings to the words you underlined to help you choose your answers.

> • You will hear a young woman called Lucy talking about her trip to India to see wildlife.
> • For each question put a tick (✓) in the correct box.

1 What does Lucy say about the hotel?
   A ☐ The bed was very uncomfortable.
   B ☐ Her room had a wonderful view.
   C ☐ It was a long way from the park.

2 The guide knew where the tiger was because
   A ☐ he had seen it from the car.
   B ☐ another guide was watching it.
   C ☐ other animals had noticed it.

3 Lucy got on the elephant by climbing
   A ☐ up a ladder.
   B ☐ a nearby tree.
   C ☐ onto the car.

4 When they first saw the tiger, it was
   A ☐ resting after a meal.
   B ☐ sleeping on the ground.
   C ☐ looking for food.

5 Lucy felt safe because she believed that
   A ☐ tigers in India never attack humans.
   B ☐ the tiger would not attack the elephant.
   C ☐ this tiger was too old to be dangerous.

6 The tourists were allowed to
   A ☐ get out of the car.
   B ☐ feed the monkeys.
   C ☐ photograph the tiger.

Vocabulary

Suffixes: *-ion, -ation, -ment*

❶ Look at these nouns in *italics* from the recording and answer the questions.

> … as the *advertisement* said …
> … after some *preparations* …
> … in our *direction* …

1 What is the verb form of each noun?
2 Which suffix does each noun have? Which noun is plural?
3 Which noun drops the letter 'e' from the verb form? Why?

❷ Work in pairs. Write the noun forms of the verbs in the box and then put them into three groups with the endings *-ment*, *-ation* or *-ion*. Be careful with any spelling changes.

> admire   announce   attract   celebrate   collect
> complete   confirm   connect   create   develop
> disappoint   discuss   educate   enjoy   entertain
> examine   excite   improve   inform   invent
> invite   move   pollute   prevent   protect
> relax   replace   reserve   translate

-ment	-ation	-ion
	admiration	

❸ Underline the stressed syllable in all the nouns you wrote in Exercise 2, then decide if you can see any patterns.

admiration   announcement

❹ Complete the newspaper story on page 100 with the noun form of these verbs.

> attract   celebrate   connect   direct   disappoint
> inform   invent   invite   move   translate

❺ (15) Listen to the recording to check your answers to Exercise 4.

❻ (16) Listen to the answers and repeat them with the correct word stress.

Scientists use rubber ducks in Arctic experiment

NASA scientists are aiming to get useful
(1) ...*information*... about global warming from
their latest (2) .... : Arctic rubber
ducks. They have put 90 of the toys into holes in
a Greenland glacier, a huge mass of ice moving in
the (3) .... of the sea. They hope that
icebergs and pieces of ice with the ducks inside will
melt and then be found by local people. This will
tell the scientists a lot about the (4) ....
of this glacier, why this is faster in summer, and its
(5) .... with global warming. Each duck has
the words 'science experiment' and 'reward' on it, with
a (6) .... into two other languages. There
is also an email address and an (7) .... to
write to NASA. So far, to the (8) .... of the
scientists, nobody has emailed. But they believe the
(9) .... of a big reward will bring results.
So, if you find a NASA rubber duck on a beach near you,
it could be a cause for (10) ....

Grammar

The passive: present and past simple

▶ page 128 *Grammar reference: The passive: present and past simple*

❶ With a partner, look at sentences A–D and answer questions 1–6.

  A Tigers very rarely **attack** people.
  B People **are** very rarely **attacked** by tigers.
  C The guides **allowed** the tourists to take photos.
  D The tourists **were allowed** to take photos.

1 Which two sentences are active and which two are passive?
2 Which two sentences describe an event in the past?
3 Which two sentences use a form of *be* and the past participle of the verb?
4 What is the subject and what is the object in A? How is B different?
5 What is the subject and what is the object in C? How is D different?
6 What information is in sentence C, but not in sentence D?

❷ Now decide which of these rules describe active sentences and which describe passive sentences. Write 'A' for active or 'P' for passive next to rules 1–5 on the right.

Rules

1 We often see this in formal texts (e.g. newspaper reports, textbooks, etc.). P

2 We use this a lot when we are speaking, or writing informal letters, stories, etc.

3 We use this when we are more interested in the *action* than who or what did it.

4 We use this when we say who or what did the action.

5 We can add *by* + noun if it is important to say who or what did it, but we often leave this out.

❸ Complete sentences 1–6 using the words in brackets and the correct passive form of the present simple or the past simple.

1 The mountain road ...*is not used*... (not / use) in winter.
2 When was ...*the island discovered*... (the island / discover)?
3 Sometimes, birds .... (see) flying as high as aeroplanes.
4 The young zebra .... (chase) by a hungry lion, but it escaped.
5 What time .... (crocodiles / feed) today?
6 The shark .... (not / notice) until it was very close to the boat.

❹ ⒄ In the passive, we normally use the 'weak' forms of the words *are*, *was* and *were*. Listen and practise saying sentences 1–3.

    /ə/
1 These *are* known as the 'Spring Gardens'.
    /wə/
2 The flowers *were* planted in March.
    /wəz/
3 The grass *was* cut in April and May.

⑤ Rewrite these sentences to make them passive. Do not use *by* in any of the sentences.

1 They catch a lot of fish here.
A lot of fish are caught here.
2 People saw two giraffes near the trees.
3 Somebody wrote a poem about this waterfall.
4 They grow rice in the east of the country.
5 One small cloud hid the moon.
6 They don't allow cars in the National Park.
7 Fire partly destroyed the forest.
8 Nobody told us about the crocodiles in the river.

⑥ 🔊18 Listen to the recording to check your answers. Then repeat the sentences, paying special attention to the pronunciation of *are*, *was* and *were*.

Reading Part 4

❶ Read this essay written by a Geography student and match meanings a–h with underlined expressions 1–8.

a fuel that is used in cars   2
b vehicles used by everyone
c things that are thrown away
d using less electricity, gas, etc.
e changes in the Earth's weather
f big container where empty bottles are put
g power from the sun
h using materials again

The whole world feels the effects of (1) climate change, so we all need to do what we can to prevent things getting worse. The rise in temperatures is partly caused by the use of coal and (2) petrol, so (3) energy conservation is important. We can do this, for instance, by using (4) public transport instead of the car, keeping the heating turned down, and making sure the lights are switched off when we go out. (5) Recycling, too, is essential, so glass containers should be taken to the (6) bottle bank, old newspapers and magazines collected, and different kinds of (7) rubbish placed in separate bags. We can also help by using less water around the house, and - particularly in sunny countries - using (8) solar energy to heat our water. Most of these are quite small things, but if everyone does them, they might make a difference!

2 Quickly read the text *International Climate Champions* and answer Question 1 (on the right) only.

3 Read the second paragraph of the text again and think of a possible answer to Question 2. Then find the <u>underlined</u> words that share ideas with each option A–D, and write A, B, C or D next to each. Then answer these questions.

- Which option is correct?
- Why are the others wrong?

4 Read the third and fourth paragraphs and <u>underline</u> the words that match each option A–D in Questions 3 and 4. Then decide which is correct.

5 Quickly read the whole text again and decide your answer for Question 5. Why are the other options wrong?

Exam round-up

What do you know about Reading Part 4? Answer these questions.

1 Does Question 1 always focus on the writer's purpose?

2 Do Questions 2, 3 and 4 usually focus on fact, or on opinion and attitude?

3 Does Question 5 normally focus on detail, or on the general meaning?

4 Should you begin by reading quickly through the text, or the questions?

5 Is it best to think of your own answer to each question before you look at options A–D?

6 For Questions 2–4, is the information you need for each answer usually in one paragraph, or in different parts of the text?

---

1 What is the writer's main purpose in this text?

   A to give details about how to become a Climate Champion

   B to explain why the Earth's climate is changing so quickly

   C to say what some people are doing about climate change

   D to tell readers what they can do to prevent climate change

2 What does Irene say about the sea?

   A The water near the island is now dirty.

   B Many types of fish have disappeared.

   C There is oil and gas under the water.

   D It can provide power for the island.

3 What does Ding believe about climate change?

   A It is certain to get much worse.

   B Air pollution does not cause it.

   C It is wrong to blame China for it.

   D It is caused only by rich countries.

4 Sophia thinks that young people should

   A publish their own newspapers.

   B change older people's habits.

   C follow the example of their parents.

   D avoid talking about politics.

5 What would one of these Climate Champions say to a friend?

   A It's great being a Champion! I'm the only one from our country, but we all want to do something about climate change.

   B I've made speeches about climate change and met Champions from the 12 other countries. I've even been to a meeting in Japan!

   C We are the Champions! There are already three of us from every country in the world, and we have a lot to say about climate change.

   D I work with other Champions, telling the world about the dangers of climate change. Some of us are teenagers, but people really listen to us!

6 Work in small groups and answer these questions.

- Would you like to be a Climate Champion? Why (not)?
- Do you agree with Sophia that teenagers can change older people's attitudes? If you agree – in what ways can they be changed?

International Climate Champions

The International Climate Champions (ICC) project began in 2007. It gives young people of school age a chance to speak publicly on climate change and to encourage action to reduce its effects. Each country involved selects three teenagers to be Climate Champions, who take part in local and international activities.

Climate Champion Irene Sanna lives on the Italian island of Sardinia. Irene is interested in solar energy, and also believes that Sardinia should (1) .... <u>use the waves around its coast to produce electricity</u>. That would reduce (2) .... <u>the need to import oil and gas</u> for lighting, heating and cooking. 'Energy conservation is our future. We must make plans to save (3) .... <u>our coast, which still has no pollution</u>. We must protect the (4) .... <u>animals, birds and fish in danger</u> from global warming. And we must recycle.'

Chinese student Ding Yinghan is the Beijing Climate Champion. Ding feels it is unfair to say that just one country – his own – is causing climate change. He says the air pollution that leads to global warming comes from many parts of the world, including poorer countries that are now growing more quickly. He believes the only way to prevent the situation getting even worse is for rich and poor countries to work together.

ICC in Kobe

Sophia Angelis, a junior student in Lake Arrowhead, California, is a US Champion. She's against young people's general lack of interest in politics and feels they need to discuss the problems that really matter to their generation. She has written about the need for action on world poverty and her articles have been published in her local newspaper. Sophia strongly believes that climate change is an important issue for her generation. For her, changes in the way teenagers behave are an important way of influencing choices that are made by parents.

In 2008, the Climate Champions attended the International Conference of Environment Ministers in the Japanese city of Kobe. At present, 13 countries are involved in the ICC, and more countries are expected to join soon.

Grammar
Comparative and superlative adverbs

🔊 page 129 *Grammar reference: Comparative and superlative adverbs*

> To compare how things are done at different times, or how they are done by someone or something else, we use a *comparative* or *superlative* adverb.

❶ **With a partner, study examples a–d, then answer questions 1–5.**

a countries are now growing more quickly

b these buses use energy more efficiently than the old ones did

c the only way to prevent the situation getting even worse than it is already

d of all the light bulbs, this one shines most brightly

1 <u>Underline</u> three examples of comparative adverbs and one example of a superlative adverb.
2 How do we usually form comparative adverbs?
3 Which comparative adverb in a–d doesn't follow this rule?
4 When we compare two actions, which word normally follows the adverb?
5 How do we usually form superlative adverbs?

❷ **In small groups, complete the table.**

adverb	comparative	superlative
	more quietly	
		(the) most carefully
slowly		
		(the) most easily
	faster	
badly		
		(the) hardest
	better	

③ Complete sentences 1–6 using the comparative or superlative adverb form of the words in brackets.

1 To save petrol, people should drive
   ...*more slowly*... . (slow)

2 Young people are working the .... to stop global warming. (hard)

3 You can buy food .... in small shops than in supermarkets. (cheap)

4 Of all the fuels we use, coal pollutes the air the .... (bad)

5 Wind power makes electricity .... than oil or gas. (clean)

6 Because of climate change, it now rains .... than it used to. (heavy)

④ Work in pairs. Do you agree with statements 1–6 in Exercise 3? Discuss your opinions with your partner.

Speaking Part 4

① With a partner, look at the people in pictures A and B and discuss these questions.

- In what ways are they wasting water?
- How could they reduce this waste, do you think?

② ⟨19⟩ Listen to Jake and Lily talking about this topic. What three suggestions do they make for saving water?

③ ⟨19⟩ Listen again and write the exact words Jake and Lily use to give examples. Write one or two words in each space.

1 In the garden, ...*for instance*..., it's best
2 if you water them at two o'clock, ...
3 a bucket of water and a sponge, ...
4 All those things .... dishwashers and washing machines
5 if you don't have much to wash, ... a few plates

④ What other ways can you save water in the home? Tell your partner about them. Use expressions from Exercise 3 to introduce your examples.

> *Exam round-up*
>
> What do you remember about Speaking Part 4? Circle the correct option 1–8 in *italics*.
>
> Part 4 of the Speaking test usually lasts about (1) (three)/ *five* minutes and the topic is (2) *connected with / different from* the subject of the photos in Part 3. When you speak, you should (3) *keep to this topic / change to another topic* and talk about your own experiences, as well as things you like and don't like. Try to use (4) *only the present tense / a range of tenses*. It is important when you are talking to your partner to (5) *interrupt a lot / take turns*, and when they're speaking, you should show you are (6) *listening to / not interested in* what they're saying. Help them to keep talking by (7) *asking for more details and their opinions / commenting on their grammar and pronunciation*, and when it's your turn (8) *repeat everything you say / give reasons and examples* to support what you say and feel.

⑤ Work with a different partner. Do this exam task, talking for about three minutes and giving plenty of examples. The advice sheet for young people below may help you.

Your photographs showed people doing things that affect the environment. Now I'd like you to talk together about how you can use less electricity at home.

Saving energy: what *you* can do

1 **Don't** leave things on stand-by: turn them off.

2 **Use** solar-powered chargers for your phone and MP3 player.

3 **Use** a laptop instead of a PC.

4 **Don't** leave the fridge door open.

5 **Try not** to use the air-conditioning.

6 **Instead** of turning up the heating, put a sweater on.

7 **Use** energy-efficient light bulbs.

8 **Turn off** the lights when you go out!

Writing Part 3

1 Look at this Writing Part 3 task, read the letter below it, then answer these questions.

1 Which paragraph deals with each part of the task?
2 Ana has written a good letter, but she has made one mistake in each paragraph. Can you find and correct each mistake?

- This is part of a letter you receive from an English-speaking friend.

  > *In your next letter, please tell me about the wildlife in your country.*
  > *Which is your favourite animal? Are there many of them?*

- Now write a letter, answering your penfriend's questions.
- Write your letter in about 100 words.

A *Thanks for your letter. We have some fantastic animals here, such as deer, foxes and wolves. Sometimes bears seen in the mountains, and up in the sky there are eagles and storks.*

B *The animal I like better of all, though, is the wildcat. It's a beautiful creature. In some ways it's like an ordinary cat, but bigger and with a bushy tail that's black at the end.*

C *I remember seeing one when I was a child. I was so excited! In those days you could find them more easyly, but now the countryside where they used to live is covered in holiday homes, roads and supermarkets. I think that's very sad.*

---

2 ⊙ Sentences and phrases 1–6 each contain one mistake made by PET candidates. Decide what kind of error each is, and write *G* for grammar, *V* for vocabulary, *WO* for word order, or *Sp* for spelling. Then rewrite the sentences so they are correct.

1 It was a day very cold.
   WO   *It was a very cold day.*

2 I really enjoy to be here.
3 ... a new film about animals which called 'The life of animals' ...
4 ... a film with plenty of exitement ...
5 I don't know what is the name of the mountain.
6 I hope I haven't got a lot of mistakes.

---

3 Read the advice in the Exam round-up box and decide if statements 1–8 are true or false.

Exam round-up

In Writing Part 3 you can choose to write a story or a letter. How much do you remember about PET letter-writing?

1 You must write an address at the top. *False*
2 You should use a wide range of structures and vocabulary.
3 You should use mostly formal language.
4 You should use linking words like *so* and *because* to make more complicated sentences.
5 You only need to write about one part of the question.
6 You should try to give reasons and examples where possible.
7 You can write a lot less than 100 words and still get good marks.
8 You should leave time to check your completed letter for mistakes.

---

4 Follow the instructions for the exam task below. Try to include some passive forms and a comparative or superlative adverb in your letter.

- This is part of a letter you receive from your English-speaking friend, Justin.

  > In your next letter, please tell me about the kinds of pet that are popular in your country. Why do people have them? Which do you think is the best pet to have?

- Now write a letter to Justin, answering his questions.
- Write your letter in about 100 words.

---

5 Work in pairs and give your letter to your partner. Read and check your partner's letter. Where you think there are mistakes, write *G*, *V*, *WO* or *Sp* in pencil. Then discuss your corrections together.

Unit 12 What did you say?

Martians from the planet Mars.

GRAFFITI "CAN'T BE STOPPED!"

Starting off

❶ **Work in pairs. These pictures show different ways of communicating a message. Talk together about what you can see in each one.**

❷ **Work in small groups. Discuss these questions.**

1 How often do you text your friends? Or do you prefer to phone them?
2 What do you think of graffiti?
3 Do you believe in life on other planets?

Reading *Part 3*

❶ **Work in pairs. Read these extracts about types of people, then complete sentences 1–3 with *dork*, *dude* or *geek*.**

dork [dɔːk] *noun* [C] *mainly US informal* a stupid or silly person

dude [duːd] *noun* [C] *mainly US very informal* a man

geek [giːk] *noun* [C] *informal* a man who is boring and not fashionable

1 Seth's always using his laptop. He's such a computer ....

2 Miko's such a good skater. He's a real ....

3 My uncle often drops food on himself, walks into walls and he can't use his mobile. He's a ....

❷ **Read this definition, then think of some examples of slang that you use in your own language.**

slang [slæŋ] *noun* [U] informal language, often language that is only used by people who belong to a particular group

❸ **Read the text title and look at the pictures. What do you think the text is about?**

❹ **Read the ten sentences about *Martian*, the language from Mars. <u>Underline</u> the most important words in each sentence.**

1 <u>Most older teenagers</u> in <u>China write in Martian</u> on the <u>Internet</u>.
2 Young people first started using Martian in Taiwan.
3 In the film *Shaolin Soccer*, Zhao Wei comes from Mars.
4 Teenagers who use the Internet in South-East Asia are called Martians.
5 Software companies are now selling programs to help people write in Martian.
6 Ms Li has never tried to read messages on Mei's computer.

7 When Mei starts writing things in Martian, she uses other people's work.

8 Wang Haiyong allows his students to write their homework in Martian.

9 Teenager Bei Bei Song considers herself to be up to date.

10 Bei Bei Song approves of Martian.

⑤ The sentence which is <u>underlined</u> in the text *Can you speak Martian?* tells us if one of the sentences in Exercise 4 is correct or incorrect. Which one?

Do you need to understand the word *spread* to know if the sentence is correct or incorrect?

⑥ Read the whole text and decide if the ten sentences are correct or incorrect. <u>Underline</u> where you find your answers in the text.

⑦ Write one word to complete the sentences about Reading Part 3 in the Exam round-up box on page 108.

Can you speak Martian?

Do you know what '3Q', '= =' or 'Orz' means? Perhaps you don't! This is Martian. People say that 80% of teenagers aged between 15 and 19 in China use this language when they send messages or chat with each other online. This crazy language didn't start in China, though. <u>It became popular in Taiwan in 2004 and three years later, it *spread* to mainland China.</u>

But where did the name *Martian* come from? Well, in the comedy film *Shaolin Soccer*, which was made in Hong Kong, an actor, Stephen Chow, says to actress Zhao Wei, 'Go back to your planet Mars!' Stephen says this because Zhao is a rather strange person. She isn't really a visitor from Mars, but Stephen thinks she is so strange and different that he calls Zhao a *Martian*. Stephen's words 'Go back to ... Mars!' are now so well known in South-East Asia that anyone who acts strangely there is known as a *Martian*. Similarly, the language which teenagers in China enjoy creating is also known as *Martian* because it is so strange.

Why do so many teenagers in China use Martian? The answer is quite easy, really. Teenagers can chat on the Internet for hours without being understood by their teachers or parents. In fact this very strange language has become so popular that people are buying special software to translate between Chinese and Martian.

Ms Li, mother of teenager, Mei, was worried when she switched on Mei's laptop because she could not understand the emails from Mei's friends. Mei explained, 'Those messages are in Martian because they're for me and not my mum.' Mei continued, 'Martian's not an easy language. At first, I just copy words from texts which my friends have already written in Martian. Then, I begin to create some words by myself. I take pieces from Chinese characters, add some English, Japanese or Korean words and that makes the new language.'

Wang Haiyong, a teacher, warned that although this new language can help develop the imagination, this Internet slang was not suitable for use in other situations, such as school exams or homework. 'I refuse to mark my students' work when they use this language. They know they shouldn't use it.'

Bei Bei Song is 15 years old. She doesn't use *Martian* but she doesn't think she's old-fashioned. She explains that although she spends hours on the Internet chatting to her friends, she thinks that this language is really silly. 'We're not computer geeks who need to mix three different languages with crazy pictures just to be dudes. Martian is for dorks.'

Vocabulary

Speak, talk, say, tell and *ask for*

❶ **Read these extracts from the *Cambridge Learner's Dictionary*.**

Common Learner Error

speak or **talk**?

Remember that you **speak** a language: You do not 'talk' it.

She speaks French. She talks French.

say or **tell**?

Say can refer to any type of speech.

She said she was unhappy.

Tell is used to report that someone has given information or an order. The verb **tell** is always followed by the person that the information or order is given to.

Simon told me about his new job.

Say is never followed by the person that the information or order is given to.

He told us to stay here. He said us to stay here.

ask for

When you use **ask** with the meaning of saying you want someone to give you something, remember to use the preposition **for** before the thing that is wanted.

I asked the teacher for the answers to the homework I missed.

Note:
- We also use *say* with greetings, e.g. *hello, goodbye, goodnight,* etc.
- We also use *tell* with the following nouns: the *truth,* a *lie,* a *joke,* a *story.*

❷ ⊙ **PET candidates often make mistakes with these verbs. Read sentences 1–6 and circle the correct option in *italics.***

1 Olga knows how to (speak)/ *talk* English well.
2 He *said / told* me to come to 6th Avenue.
3 My new friend can *talk / speak* several languages.

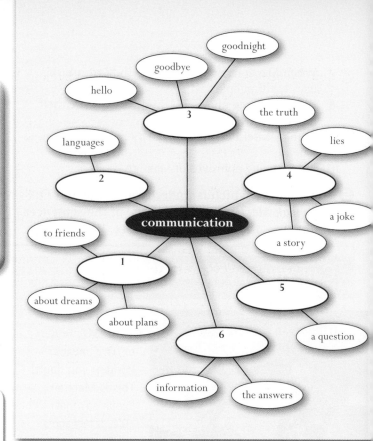

4 My new English teacher asked me to *say / tell* something about my life.
5 It was Pelr who *said / told* me about this club.
6 I'll *ask / ask for* more information about the new pool.

❸ **Write *speak, talk, say, tell, ask* or *ask for* in the correct space in the mind map above. Add at least one more expression to each verb.**

❹ **Work in pairs. Write five questions using some of the verb + noun combinations. Change pairs. Ask and answer your questions.**

Do you always tell the truth?

Grammar

Reported speech and reported commands

raise money *verb* to collect money from other people: *They're raising money for charity.*

❶ **Work in small groups. Sandford School has joined *Schools for All* which helps build new schools in East Africa. List things the students could do to raise money (e.g. *sell old clothes*).**

❷ ⟨20⟩ **Listen to some students talking about how they can raise money for this project. What events do Scott, William and Gina suggest?**

❸ Rewrite Scott's, William's and Gina's words in reported speech.

1 SCOTT: **Last year** we organised a disco to collect money.

Scott said that they .... **the year before**.

> You can leave out *that* and say: *Scott said they had organised a disco to collect money the year before.* The meaning stays the same.

2 SCOTT: **We** can organise a similar event again.

Scott said **they** ....

3 WILLIAM: We've thought about organising a football match.

William said they ....

4 WILLIAM: In **my** sister's school, the students are going to play against the teachers.

William said in **his** sister's school, the students ....

5 WILLIAM: It doesn't have to be just teachers.

William also said ....

6 GINA: **Today we**'re all wearing school uniform.

Gina said **we** .... **that day**.

7 GINA: We'll pay to wear what we want.

Gina said we .... what we wanted.

● page 129 *Grammar reference: Reported speech*

❹ (21) Listen to Tania telling Nina about the meeting and check your answers to Exercise 3.

❺ Use your answers to Exercise 3 to help you complete this table.

direct speech	reported speech
present simple	(1) *past simple*
present continuous	(2)
present perfect	(3)
past simple	(4)
will + infinitive	(5)
is/are going to	(6)
can	(7)

❻ Use the words in bold in Exercise 3 to help you complete this table.

direct speech	reported speech
today	(1) *that day*
last year	(2)
my	(3)
we	(4)

● page 130 *Grammar reference: Reported speech: other changes*

❼ Work in pairs. What do you say in situations 1–4? Complete the sentences.

1 Ana says: 'I can't play tennis; I've hurt my arm.' Later you see her playing basketball.

'You said *you couldn't play tennis because you had hurt your arm.*'

2 Thalia says: 'Someone left their MP3 player in the kitchen after the party.' Later your cousin tells you that she has lost her MP3 player.

'Thalia said …'

3 Your brother is studying abroad. He phones you and says: 'I'm having a great time here.' Later his teacher asks you if you've spoken to your brother.

'My brother said …'

4 Lukas says: 'I want to sell my bike so I can buy a new one.' Later your sister tells you she wants to buy a cheap bicycle.

'Lukas said …'

❽ Choose two situations from Exercise 7 and write the complete story in reported speech. You will need to add some extra information to the story.

Last week I wanted to play tennis with Ana but she told me she couldn't play because …

● page 130 *Grammar reference: Reported commands*

9 In the meeting about the *Schools for All* project, Ruby told the other students to do four things. Complete the reported commands.

1 'Be quiet!'
Ruby told them _to be quiet_ .

2 'Close the door, Paul!'
Ruby told Paul ....

3 'Think about the suggestions!'
Ruby told them ....

4 'Don't forget the meeting!'
Ruby told them not ....

10 Rewrite each instruction 1–4 as a reported command.

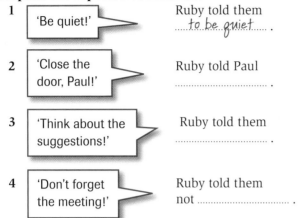
'Turn the music down!'

1 She told her brother _to turn the music down._

'Don't worry!'

2 The dentist told the boy ....

'Don't touch anything!'

3 Charlie's mum told him ....

'Don't forget to phone!'

4 Chloe's family told her ....

Listening Part 3

1 Work in pairs and answer the questions in the Exam round-up box.

> *Exam round-up*
>
> How much do you remember about Listening Part 3? Are the following statements true or false?
>
> 1 Read the notes and focus on the missing words.
> 2 You need to understand every word in the recording to be able to complete the task.
> 3 The gaps follow the order of the recording.
> 4 You will usually need to write one word, so don't waste time writing a lot more.
> 5 If you complete all the gaps when you listen for the first time, don't listen a second time.
> 6 If you don't hear the answer, leave a gap.

2 Work in small groups. Your headteacher has asked Gerry Tremain to talk to you about Web Challenge – a website design competition. What would you like to know about the competition? Write at least five questions.

3 Read Rahid's notes below quickly. Does he want to find out the same things as you?

Web Challenge

The website: in English

The teams: each team: one adult known as the (1) .... and 3–6 members

Members: must be at school

Age limit: between 9 and (2) .... years old

Website content: e.g. a favourite (3) .... or free-time activity

Prizes: digital equipment and money for schools

Entries will be displayed on the 'Web Challenge' (4) ....

First prize for teams – a week in (5) ....

Dates: competition registration closes 30th (6) ....

WEB CHALLENGE

4 Listen to the recording twice and complete the gaps.

Grammar

Reported questions

❶ Work in small groups. Write at least three more questions you would like to ask Gerry about the *Web Challenge* competition.

How will I know if I win?

❷ (23) Listen to the recording. Does Gerry answer all your questions?

❸ (23) Listen to the recording again. Write the correct student's name: *Julian, Haley, Nadia, Hamad* or *Jade* next to their question 1–5.

1 .....*Nadia*..... asked if she could enter the competition on her own.
   Can I enter the competition on my own?

2 .... asked if their coach had to work in their school.
   ....

3 .... asked how they registered for the competition.
   ....

4 .... asked what they did if they had technical problems.
   ....

5 .... asked what they would see in Australia.
   ....

❹ Write the students' actual words in the spaces above. If necessary, listen to the recording again to check your answers.

▷ page 130 *Grammar reference: Reported questions*

❺ Look at the reported questions 1–5 above, then circle the correct option in CAPITALS for a–e below, to complete these rules about reported questions.

Rules

In reported questions:

a the normal question order STAYS THE SAME / (CHANGES)

b the tense STAYS THE SAME / USUALLY CHANGES LIKE IN REPORTED SPEECH

c we ALWAYS / NEVER use *do, does* or *did* as an auxiliary verb

d we use *if* when there IS / ISN'T a question word (*what/when/where*, etc.)

e we USE / DON'T USE a question mark at the end of the sentence.

❻ Nadia's team wins the competition. Here are some sentences about Nadia's trip to Australia. For each question 1–5, complete the second sentence so that it means the same as the first, *using no more than three words*.

1 A reporter asked Nadia if she was nervous about flying to Australia.
   A reporter asked Nadia, '.....*Are you*..... nervous about flying to Australia?'

2 Nadia asked Shaila, 'Where are you from?'
   Nadia asked Shaila where .... from.

3 Nadia asked Shaila if she wanted to share a room in the hotel.
   Nadia asked Shaila, '........................... to share a room in the hotel?'

4 Nadia asked the tour guide, 'What are we going to do after breakfast?'
   Nadia asked the tour guide what ....
   .... to do after breakfast.

5 The tour guide asked the group, 'Have you enjoyed your trip?'
   The tour guide asked the group ....
   enjoyed their trip.

Indirect questions

▷ page 131 *Grammar reference: Indirect questions*

❶ (24) When Nadia returned from her trip to Australia, a local newspaper journalist interviewed her. Listen to the beginning of the interview. What does Nadia say about Sydney harbour?

❷ (24) Listen to the recording again and complete the journalist's questions below.

1 I was wondering if I could ....*ask you*....... some questions about your trip.

2 I'd like to know what you .... of Sydney.

3 I can't remember where .... in Sydney.

4 Could you tell me where ....?

5 Tell me what .... in Australia.

Plan

❸ Work in pairs. When we ask for information, we sometimes use *indirect questions* to sound more polite. Write the *direct* question for the journalist's questions from Exercise 2.

1 Could I *ask you some questions about your trip* ?
2 What did .... ?
3 Where did .... ?
4 Where was .... ?
5 What did .... ?

❹ Circle the correct option in CAPITALS to complete these rules.

Rules

When a direct question becomes part of a longer indirect question:

1 the normal question order STAYS THE SAME / (CHANGES.)

2 the tense CHANGES / STAYS THE SAME.

3 we ALWAYS / NEVER use *do, does* or *did* as an auxiliary verb, etc.

4 we use *if* or *whether* (more formal), if there IS / ISN'T a question word (*what?, when?, where?,* etc.)

5 we SOMETIMES / NEVER use a question mark at the end of the question.

❺ Compare the rules for *indirect questions* with the rules for *reported questions* on page 111. Which two rules are different?

Vocabulary
Prepositions of place

❶ 25 Listen to the recording and answer questions 1–3 by drawing a picture. If necessary, listen to the recording again.

1 Where are Todd's keys?
2 Where's the sports shop?
3 Where's Elen, Imogen's cousin?

❷ Work in small groups. Compare your pictures with the pictures on page 173.

❸ Label the pictures you drew in Exercise 1 with the words in the box.

on the right	between	opposite	on	inside
in	next to	behind	in front of	over	

❹ Work in pairs. Student A turns to page 173 and Student B turns to page 174.

❺ When you are ready, take turns to describe the position of your objects to your partner. Your partner draws the object on their plan. At the end, compare plans.

Speaking Part 3

❶ Read the examiner's instructions below and look at the photos (but don't talk about the photos yet).

Now I'd like each of you to talk on your own about something. I'm going to give each of you a photograph of people communicating with others. Please tell us what you can see in your photographs.

❷ Answer the questions in the Exam round-up box.

Exam round-up

How much do you remember about Speaking Part 3? Choose the correct option in *italics* in these sentences.

1 The examiner will ask you to describe a colour photograph *on your own / with your partner* for about *one minute / two minutes.*

2 You should *describe what you can see / use your imagination.*

3 If you don't know the word for something in the picture, *point / use one of the expressions from Unit 10.*

4 If you want to describe where something is, *point / use a suitable preposition.*

❸ Take turns to describe one of the photos on page 112. Does your partner follow the advice in the Exam round-up box?

Writing Part 3

❶ Work in small groups. Look at these pictures and sentences. What do you think happened next?

I realised that I hadn't locked the door.

The message began, 'Congratulations! You've won first prize!'

I was in class when my mobile phone rang.

As I got on the train, I saw an empty seat next to my favourite actor.

❷ Read these two Writing Part 3 questions and answer questions 1–5 below.

1

> • You have to write a story for your English teacher.
> • Your story must begin with this sentence:
>   *I was in class when my mobile phone rang.*
> • Write your **story** in about 100 words.

2

> • You have to write a story for your English teacher.
> • Your story must have this title:
>   *Winning first prize*
> • Write your **story** in about 100 words.

1 What do you have to write in each question?
2 Who do you have to write it for?
3 How many words do you have to write?
4 What's the difference between the two questions?
5 Do you *have to* write a story in Writing Part 3?

❸ Now read this story, then answer the questions that follow. Don't correct the student's mistakes for the moment.

> I was in class when my mobile phone rang. I couldn't believed it. I had forgot to switch the phone off. I didn't know what to do because the phone was still ringing. Should I answer the phone? The teacher stopped talking and she looked directly at me. She asked all the student what the noise was and we answered that it was a mobile phone. Suddenly she looked embarrassed. She told us that she had to left the classroom for a minute. She picked up her bag and left the room. As soon as the teacher closed the door, the ringing noise stoped.

1 Which question does it answer?
2 Why did the phone stop ringing when the teacher closed the door?

❹ Work in pairs. Discuss whether the following sentences are correct (✓) or incorrect (✗).

1 The student has written about 100 words. ☐
2 The answer is well organised. ☐
3 There is a clear ending to the story. ☐
4 The ideas are connected using *and*, *because*, etc. ☐
5 The student has used different tenses. ☐
6 The student has used reported speech and reported questions. ☐
7 I can understand the answer although there are some mistakes. ☐

❺ Read the answer again and correct the five mistakes. This student has made two different *types* of mistake. What are they?

❻ Write a story using one of the situations in Exercise 1 as the first line. Write about 100 words. Remember to make sure the sentences in Exercise 4 are correct for your answer.

❼ Work in small groups. Read each other's answers. If all the sentences in Exercise 4 are correct for the answer you are reading, it is probably a good answer.

Unit 11   *Vocabulary and grammar review*

Grammar

❶ Circle the correct option in *italics*.

My family and I (1) *are lived* / (live) in an old house on the coast. When it (2) *built* / *was built* in the 19th century, it was over 500 metres from the sea, but now the water (3) *seems* / *is seemed* to be getting closer all the time. The sea level (4) *is risen* / *rises* every year, and the soil (5) *washes* / *is washed* away by the waves. Sometimes, when there is a storm, the water (6) *is reached* / *reaches* the house. Last February, for instance, the basement (7) *completely flooded* / *was completely flooded* by sea water, and a small building near our house (8) *disappeared* / *was disappeared* overnight. Unless something (9) *does* / *is done* immediately, we (10) *are known* / *know* that our home will be next. Some other houses along the coast (11) *saved* / *were saved* when a barrier (12) *put up* / *was put up* in front of them, and we want the same here.

❷ Complete sentences 1–8 with the comparative or superlative adverb form of the words in the box.

bad	careful	~~early~~	frequent
good	hard	quick	strong

1 To see wild animals in the countryside, you should get up ....*earlier*........ in the morning.
2 The ice melted .... as the temperature increased.
3 Of all the people at the meeting, Lauren spoke .... She made a great speech.
4 Buses stop here .... now: every ten minutes.
5 We must try .... to find solutions to environmental problems.
6 They're all bad musicians in that band, and the guitarist plays .... of all.
7 The wind began to blow .... as the storm approached.
8 If we all use energy .... , we can reduce the amount of pollution we cause.

Vocabulary

❸ For questions 1–6, complete the second sentence so that it means the same as the first, *using no more than three words*. Include a noun with a suffix in your answer.

1 My parents were educated at the local school.
My parents' ..*education was*.. at the local school.
2 Everyone was very excited when the match began.
There was .... when the match began.
3 I'd like to reserve a room at the hotel, please.
I'd like to make .... for a room at the hotel, please.
4 The doctor quickly examined the patient and said she was fine.
The doctor gave the patient .... and said she was fine.
5 We often celebrate New Year all night.
Our New Year .... go on all night.
6 The airline did not inform us about the delay.
We were given .... about the delay.

❹ Complete the crossword with words from Unit 11.

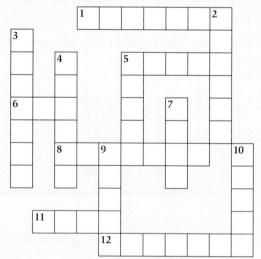

Across
1 big animal with long neck
5 long creature with no legs
6 small flying animal
8 big bird that cannot fly
11 use less of something
12 use something again

Down
2 power from gas, wind, etc.
3 things that are thrown away
4 fuel for cars and trucks
5 from the sun
7 bird that lives near water
9 big, meat-eating animal
10 use too much of something

Unit 12 *Vocabulary and grammar review*

Vocabulary

❶ ⊙ PET candidates often make mistakes when they describe *where* something is. Correct one mistake in each of these sentences.

1 In my living room, ~~in opposite of~~ *opposite* the back wall there is my TV and my hi-fi.
2 My bed is infront of the right window, opposite the door.
3 At the right there are two armchairs and a sofa.
4 I often meet my friends in the Saman café next the cinema.
5 There is a club and a park in the street where I live.
6 In the park, there's a big tree behind of a small lake.
7 I like going to the Odeon cinema because it is inside of the shopping centre.
8 Isfahan, as you know, has a lot of historic bridges on the river.

❷ Rewrite the sentences above so that they are true for you/your town.

In my living room, the TV is in front of the sofa.

❸ Complete these sentences with the verbs from the box in the correct form. You will need to use some verbs more than once.

ask	ask for	say	~~speak~~	tell

1 Some of my friends can ....*speak*.......... several languages really well.
2 In your letter you .... me about your plans to visit my country.
3 I .... 'goodnight' to everyone and went to bed.
4 I'm going to .... some new trainers for my birthday.
5 My friend started laughing and .... me why I was only wearing one earring.
6 There's a boy in my class who likes .... jokes all the time.
7 I became very nervous and decided to .... the teacher the truth.

Grammar

❹ ⊙ Frederique has written to her English-speaking friend to tell her what people have asked her this week. Correct the mistake in each sentence.

1 When I arrived at training, the coach came up to me and asked me what ~~was my name~~. *my name was*
2 My friend asked me what was the team called.
3 The next day, the phone rang at 7.30 in the morning. It was Paula. She asked me why didn't I go to the exam.
4 My mum asked me why was I crying.
5 Paula asked me what was I going to do.
6 Paula also asked me where should she go in the summer.
7 Anyway I imagine you are wondering when am I going to visit you.

❺ Kate's talking about how she spends her free time. Rewrite her statements in reported speech.

1 'I love going to the cinema on Sunday afternoons.' She said *she loved going* to the cinema on Sunday afternoons.
2 'I'm not very keen on thrillers but ...' She said .... on thrillers but ...
3 '... I love comedies.' She said ....
4 'I didn't go to the cinema last week because ...' She said .... to the cinema last week because ...
5 '... we've just finished our exams.' She said .... their exams.
6 'I'll go to the cinema today if I can.' She said ....

❻ Imagine you are interviewing Kate. Write the questions for her statements.

What do you like doing on Sunday afternoons?

❼ Rewrite your direct questions from Exercise 6 as reported questions.

I asked you what you liked doing on Sunday afternoons.

Grammar reference

Contents

Unit 1

Prepositions of time

The prepositions *at*, *on* and *in* tell us when something happens.

- We use *at* for times of the day: *at ten o'clock, at 8.15, at lunchtime*, etc. and with expressions such as *at the weekend, at night, at New Year*, etc.

- We use *on* for days and dates: *on Monday, on Saturday morning, on February 5th, on the last day of the month*, etc.

- We use *in* for years, seasons, months, long periods, and parts of the day: *in 2010, in winter, in July, in the holidays, in the afternoon*, etc.

Frequency adverbs

We use frequency adverbs to say how often something happens.

- We can use a word, e.g. *sometimes, always* or a phrase like *most afternoons* or *every night*.

- We usually put one-word frequency adverbs (and *hardly ever*) **before** the main verb: *We sometimes watch a film in the evening. I don't usually go out until 8 o'clock. It hardly ever rains in July.*

- With *am, are, is, was* or *were*, etc. they come **after** the verb: *They are always late! Nowadays my grandmother is often ill.*

- They also come **after** auxiliary and modal verbs: *It has often happened. I can never understand him.*

- If we want to, we can put *usually, often, sometimes* and *occasionally* at the beginning or end of a sentence: *Occasionally, we eat in the garden. I feel tired sometimes.*

- We cannot put *always* or *never* at the beginning or end: ~~Always I work hard. I play table tennis never.~~

- We put phrases at the beginning or end: *I have piano lessons once a week. Most evenings I stay at home.*

- We can form questions using: *How often do you, Do you ever, Do you always*, etc.: *How often do you swim? Do you ever drink tea? Do you always walk to school?*

Present simple and present continuous

Present simple

		work	
I/you/we/they He/she/it		work works	
I/you/we/they He/she/it	don't doesn't	work	on Sundays (?)
Do Does	I/you/we/they he/she/it	work	

Present continuous

I You/we/they He/she/it	'm 're 's		
I You/we/they He/she/it	'm not aren't / 're not isn't / 's not	working	this afternoon (?)
Am Are Is	I you/we/they he/she/it		

The present simple is used to describe:

- a permanent state or situation: *I live in the town where I was born.*

- a fact or something which is always true: *The earth goes around the sun.*

- an activity which happens regularly or occasionally: *He gets up at six o'clock every day.*

The present continuous is used to describe:

- a temporary situation: *I'm living with my uncle while they are painting our house.*

- an activity happening at the present moment: *I'm sorry you can't talk to her at the moment. She's having a shower.*

- an activity in progress but not exactly at the present moment: *I'm studying three foreign languages, so I'm quite busy nowadays.*

- a situation which is changing or developing: *Lots of people are coming to live here, so the town is growing quickly.*

- things the speaker finds strange or annoying, with *always*. (This is a way of complaining): *You're always using the telephone. Our phone bill will be enormous!*

- something which happens frequently, with *always*: *My girlfriend is always cooking me special meals!*

State verbs

Verbs which describe states, not actions, are not usually used in the continuous. These verbs describe:

thoughts: *believe know remember forget think* (meaning *believe*) *feel* (meaning *believe*) *guess* (meaning *believe*) *suppose understand*, etc.

feelings: *like hate want need prefer*, etc.

senses: *smell taste hear see*

possession: *have belong own contain include*, etc.

existence: *exist remain consist seem mean matter*, etc.

the verb *be*

Some state verbs can be used in the continuous when they describe actions:

I'm thinking about what you said. (I'm considering it.) *She's feeling unhappy.* (How she is at the moment.) *The shop assistant is weighing the fruit for us.* (He's measuring the number of kilos.) Other verbs like this include *see, taste, smell* and *be*.

Countable and uncountable nouns

Nouns can be either countable [C] or uncountable [U].

Some nouns can be both countable [C] and uncountable [U], but with a difference in meaning:
They say it's healthy to drink tea. [U] (tea in general) *Would you like a tea?* [C] (a cup of tea) *Living in a large house is a lot of work.* [U] *That picture is a work of art.* [C]

The grammar for countable nouns is different from the grammar for uncountable nouns.

A few, a little, many, much, a lot of, lots of

We often use different quantifiers (*a few, many*, etc.) with countable and uncountable nouns.

- For small quantities of countable nouns, we use *a few*: *a few students*.
- For small quantities of uncountable nouns, we use *a little*: *a little information*.
- For large quantities of countable nouns, we use *many*: *Many houses were damaged by the storm. Are there many rooms in the hotel? I don't have many CDs.*
- For large quantities of uncountable nouns in negative sentences and questions, we use *much*: *There isn't much information. Do you have much homework?*
- We can use *a lot of*, or *lots of*, for large quantities of countable *and* uncountable nouns: *We had a lot of fun. I have lots of friends. Does she have lots of money?*
- If there is no noun after the quantifier, we use *a lot* without *of*: *I like him a lot*.
- We can use other words to refer to a quantity of an uncountable noun, e.g. *a bit of food, an amount of money, a drop of water*.

Prepositions of place

The prepositions *at*, *on* and *in* tell us where someone or something is.

- We use *at* for a point, e.g. *at the bus stop*, and in expressions like *at the top, at the back, at the station, at the seaside, at school* and *at a party*.
- We use *on* for surfaces, e.g. *on the table, on the wall*, and lines, e.g. *on the coast, on the border*.
- We use *in* when someone or something is in a space, e.g. *in a building, in a field, in the water, in South America*.

Countable nouns:	Uncountable nouns:
• use *a* or *an* in the singular, e.g. *a job, an animal* • can be made plural, e.g. *cars, books* • use *some* and *any* in the plural, e.g. *some friends, any answers*	• do not use *a* or *an* • cannot be made plural, e.g. *work, music* • use verbs in the singular, e.g. *the news is good, music helps me relax* • use *some* and *any* in the singular, e.g. *some food, any advice*

Some common uncountable nouns in English

accommodation	advice	countryside	damage	electricity	equipment
experience	food	furniture	homework	housework	information
knowledge	luggage	make-up	money	music	news
noise	paper	pollution	rain	research	scenery
shampoo	smoke	software	space	sugar	sunshine
time	transport	work			

Unit 2

Past simple and past continuous

Past simple

Be

I/he/she/it You/we/they	was (n't) were (n't)	at home yesterday (?)	
Was Were	I/he/she/it you/we/they		
	Yes	I/he/she/it you/we/they	was were
	No	I/he/she/it you/we/they	wasn't weren't

Most other verbs

I/you/he/she/it/ we/they		watched	
I/you/he/she/it/ we/they	didn't	watch	TV yesterday (?)
Did	I/you/he/she/ it/we/they	watch	
	Yes	I/you/he/she/it/ we/they	did
	No	I/you/he/she/it/ we/they	didn't

Past continuous

I/he/she/it You/we/they	was (n't) were (n't)	watching	TV yesterday at 6 pm (?)
Was Were	I/he/she/it you/we/they		
	Yes	I/he/she/it you/we/they	was were
	No	I/he/she/it you/we/they	wasn't weren't

Regular verbs in the past simple end in *-ed*: watch**ed**, arriv**ed**, play**ed**, etc.

 page 132 *Irregular verbs*

The past simple is used to describe:

- actions or events in the past: *I visited Egypt last year.*

- actions or events which happened one after another: *I saw the Pyramids, then I went to the Cairo Museum and later I went to a traditional restaurant.*

The past continuous is used to describe:

- activities that were already happening at a moment in the past: **We were doing a maths exam in class** *when my mobile rang.* (= We were in the middle of the exam when the phone rang.) *While* **I was walking to school**, *I met a friend.* (= On my way to school I met a friend.)

- activities when we are not interested in when the activity started and we do not know if this activity finished or not: *The sun was shining and I was feeling happy.* (= We know that the sun was shining at the same moment as I was feeling happy, but we don't know when these activities started or when they finished.)

We often use the past simple and the past continuous together to show that an action happened in the middle of an activity: *I was watching television when the telephone rang.* (= We started watching television and in the middle of this activity, the telephone rang.) (We don't know if I stopped watching TV after the telephone rang.)

I was watching television
→
↑
the telephone rang

Remember: state verbs are not normally used in the past continuous

page 117 *Present simple and present continuous*

When, while and as

- We can use *when*, *while* or *as* to introduce an activity in the past continuous:
  When/While/As *I was watching TV, the telephone rang.*

- We generally use *when* to introduce an action in the past simple:
  I was watching TV **when** *the telephone rang.*

Spelling of regular past simple and *-ing* forms

	infinitive	past simple	rule		*-ing* form	rule
most regular verbs	watch	watched	add -*ed*		watching	add -*ing*
verbs ending in:						
-*e*	arrive	arrived	add -*d*		arriving	usually remove -*e*, add -*ing*
consonant + *y*	study	studied	*y* changes to *i*, add -*ed*		studying	no change, add -*ing*
vowel + *y*	play	played	no change, add -*ed*		playing	no change, add -*ing*
one-syllable, consonant-vowel-consonant	plan	planned	double the last consonant, add -*ed*		planning	double the last consonant, add -*ing*
more than one syllable, as above, stress on final syllable	prefer	preferred	double the last consonant		preferring	double the last consonant, add -*ing*
more than one syllable, as above, stress **not** on final syllable	open	opened	no change, add -*ed*		opening	no change, add -*ing*
-*l**	travel*	travelled*	double final *l**		travelling*	double final *l**

* In British English (The final *l* is not doubled in US English.)

Used to

I/you/he/she/it/we/they		used to	
I/you/he/she/it/we/they	**didn't**	use to	play with dolls (?)
Did	I/you/he/she/it/we/they	use to	

Used to is used to describe things that happened regularly in the past but don't happen now: *I used to wear a school uniform but now I don't. We didn't use to get homework when we were younger but now we do.*

Note:

Used to is only used in the past. To talk about things that happen regularly in the present, use the present simple with an adverb like *usually, every day,* etc.: *I usually drink water with my lunch. He catches the same train every day.*

Unit 3

Verbs followed by *to* or *-ing*

Some verbs are followed by the *-ing* form of another verb: *Everyone enjoys listening to music. I've finished reading my book.* Other verbs like this include:

admit, avoid, dislike, fancy, feel like, imagine, mention, mind, miss, practise, put off, suggest.

Some verbs are followed by the *to* infinitive of another verb: *We expected to win the game. I can't afford to buy a bike.* Other verbs like this include: *agree, appear, attempt, begin, decide, demand, fail, hope, intend, learn, manage, offer, plan, pretend, promise, refuse, seem, want, would like.*

Some verbs are followed by the *-ing* form *or* the *to* infinitive of another verb with similar meanings: *I love playing tennis. I love to play tennis. It continued raining all day. It continued to rain all day.* Other verbs like this include: *begin, continue, hate, like, love, prefer, start.*

Some verbs are followed by the *-ing* form *or* the infinitive of another verb, but with a different meaning:

	verb + infinitive	verb + *-ing*
remember	*Did you remember to bring your running shoes?* (an action you have to do)	*I remember feeling very tired at the end of the race* (a memory of something in the past)
forget	*Don't forget to bring your tennis racket* (an action you have to do)	*I'll never forget winning my first tennis championship* (a memory of something in the past)
regret	*I regret to tell you the race has been cancelled (regret + to say / to tell / to inform means: I'm sorry to give you this information)*	*I regret not training harder before the race* (I'm sorry I didn't do this)
try	*I'm running every day because I'm trying to get fit* (my aim is to get fit)	*If you want to get fit, why don't you try swimming?* (swimming is a way to achieve what you want)
stop	*During the race, he stopped to drink some water* (in order to drink some water)	*When he realised he couldn't win, he stopped running* (he didn't continue)

Phrasal verbs

A phrasal verb consists of two or three parts. There are three main kinds of phrasal verb:

- verb + adverb, with object, e.g. *He picked up his coat.*
- verb + adverb, without object, e.g. *The plane took off.*
- verb + adverb + preposition, with object, e.g. *I got on with my work.*

Unit 4

Comparative and superlative adjectives

We use a comparative adjective to compare two people or things and to say one thing has more (or less) of a quality (size, height, etc.) than the other: *A blue whale is heavier than an elephant. Mount Everest is higher than K2.*

We use a superlative adjective to compare one person or thing with all those in the same group and to say this thing has the most (or least) of a quality: *There are many high mountains in the world but Mount Everest is the highest.*

Comparative adjectives	Superlative adjectives
• We add *-er* to one-syllable adjectives, e.g. *deep, high, tall. The Pacific Ocean is deeper than the Atlantic.*	• We add *-est* to one-syllable adjectives: *The giraffe is the tallest animal in the world.*
• We add *-er* to two-syllable adjectives ending in *-y* or *-ly*, e.g. *noisy, friendly. My brother is friendlier than me.*	• We add *-est* to two-syllable adjectives ending in *-y* or *-ly*. *The blue whale is the heaviest animal in the world.*
• We use *more* to form the comparative of most other two-syllable adjectives. *Gold is more expensive than silver.*	• We use *most* to form the superlative of two-syllable adjectives: *The mosquito is the most dangerous creature.*
• After the adjective we usually put *than*.	• Before the adjective we usually put *the*.
• The adjectives *good, bad* and *far* form irregular comparisons.	• The adjectives *good, bad* and *far* form irregular superlatives.
• We can sometimes use *less* instead of *more*: *A mobile phone is normally less expensive than a laptop.*	• We can sometimes use *least* instead of *most*: *This mobile phone is the least expensive.*

Spelling of comparative and superlative adjectives

Regular			
adjective	comparative	superlative	rule
deep	deeper	deepest	Most adjectives add -er or -est
			Adjectives ending in:
safe	safer	safest	-e add -r or -st
noisy	noisier	noisiest	-y change to -i, add -er or -est
big	bigger	biggest	one vowel + one consonant double the last consonant, add -er or -est
Irregular			
good bad far	better worse farther/ further	best worst farthest/ furthest	irregular

A bit, a little, much, far, a lot

We can't use *very* with comparatives but we can use *much*, *far* or *a lot*: Cheetahs are **much/far/a lot** faster than elephants. (**Not** ~~Cheetahs are very faster than elephants.~~)

We can use *a bit* or *a little* to describe a small difference: Canada is **a bit / a little** bigger than the USA.

(Not) as … as …

We use *as* + adjective + *as* to say two things are the same in some way: Tara is as tall as Hannah. (= Tara is the same height as Hannah.)

We use *not as* + adjective + *as* to say that one thing is less than another: Hannah is not as tall as her brother. (= Hannah is shorter than her brother.)

We can use *so* in negative sentences to replace the first *as*: Hannah is not so tall as her brother.

Remember: the form of the adjective does not change: ~~(not) as taller as~~   (not) as tall as.

Big and enormous (gradable and non-gradable adjectives)

- *Big* (*good, happy, surprised*, etc.) are *gradable* adjectives. We can say someone or something is *quite, very* or *really* big (*good, happy, surprised*, etc.) to talk about **how** big (*good, happy, surprised*, etc.) they are. We can also say something is *extremely big* which means it's much bigger than usual.

- *Enormous* (*fantastic, delighted, astonished*, etc.) are *non-gradable* adjectives, meaning *very big* (*good, happy, surprised*, etc.). We can say *really* or *absolutely enormous* but **not** normally *quite*, very* or *extremely enormous*.

*quite here means *a little* ⊙ page 126 quite *with non-gradable adjectives to mean* completely

Unit 5

Can, could, might, may (ability and possibility)

To say someone has (or hasn't) an ability, we use *can*, *can't*, *could* and *couldn't*:
Francesca can speak five languages, but she can't speak Russian. As a child, she could play the piano but she couldn't play the violin.

- The question forms are *can you* and *could you*: Can you swim? Could you run 20 kilometres when you were very young?

- We use *can* and *could* with *see, hear, smell, feel* and *taste*: From the top of the mountain you could see for more than 50 km. I can hear a strange noise coming from upstairs.

To express possibility about the present or future, we use *may, might* or *could*: I may come and visit you next summer. We might go to the cinema this evening if we finish all our work in time. We should go out for a walk now because it could rain later.

We use *may not* and *might not* for the negative (not *can't* or *couldn't*, which express certainty): Frankie is looking very pale: he may not be very well. Don't cook any dinner for me because I might not be back in time.

Should, shouldn't, ought to, must, mustn't, have to, don't have to (obligation and prohibition)

To give somebody advice we use *should* or, less often, *ought to*: You should get a new pair of shoes. You ought to have a rest now.

- Particularly in the negative, *shouldn't* is more common than *oughtn't*: You shouldn't work so hard. The question form is *should I/she*, etc: Should we go now?

- We often use *should* (and occasionally *ought to*) to talk about the right thing to do, but which is different from what really happens: I should do the housework instead of watching television in the middle of the afternoon. He should write his own answers instead of copying them from the Internet.

To express obligation, we use **must** and **have to**: *You must be quiet. I have to go now.*

- We use *must* when the obligation is something we agree with. Teacher to students: *You must hand in your homework on Monday.*

- We use *have to* when the obligation comes from someone else: *My teacher has given me a lot of homework which I have to do for Monday.*

- We use *must* for strong advice: *You must be careful if you stay out late at night.*

- The question forms are *must I/you*, etc. and *do I/you*, etc. *have to*: *Must we stop writing now? Do they have to wear uniforms at that school?*

To express prohibition, we use **mustn't**: *You mustn't go in there – it says 'No entry!'. You mustn't speak during the exam – it's forbidden.*

- Do not use *don't have to* to express prohibition: *You mustn't use your mobile phone in class* (it's not allowed). Compare this with: *You don't have to use your mobile phone to speak to Fayed. Look! He's over there* (i.e. it's not necessary).

- Never use *mustn't* about the past. For prohibition in the past, we can use *not allowed to*, e.g. *We weren't allowed to speak.* For something that wasn't necessary, we often use *didn't have to*: *Jo gave me a ticket for the concert, so I didn't have to pay.*

To say that there is no obligation, or it's not necessary, we use *don't have to*, *don't need to* or *needn't*: *This is a really good exercise on phrasal verbs for anyone who's interested, but it's not for homework, so you don't have to do it if you don't want to. You needn't learn all the vocabulary on this page – only the words you think are useful.*

Adjectives with -*ed* and -*ing*

There are many adjectives which can be formed with -*ed* or -*ing*.

- Adjectives with -*ed* express how the person feels about something: *She was terrified as Dracula approached her.*

- Adjectives with -*ing* are used to describe the person or thing which produces the feeling: *There's a surprising article in today's newspaper* (I felt surprised when I read it).

- Common adjectives like this include:

  amused/amusing annoyed/annoying disappointed/
  disappointing bored/boring relaxed/relaxing
  surprised/surprising tired/tiring depressed/
  depressing embarrassed/embarrassing interested/
  interesting amazed/amazing excited/exciting
  disgusted/disgusting satisfied/satisfying

Unit 6

Present perfect

I/you/we/they	have / 've		
he/she/it	has / 's	arrived	home (?)
I/you/we/they	have not / haven't		
he/she/it	has not / hasn't		
Have	I/you/we/they		
Has	he/she/it		

Regular verbs have the same form for the past simple and the past participle: *arrived, watched, played,* etc.

Some irregular verbs have the same form for the past simple and the past participle: *cut, felt, bought,* etc.

Other irregular verbs have a different form for the past simple and past participle: *done, given, written,* etc.

 page 132 *Irregular verbs*

We use the present perfect to connect the past with the present. It is used to describe something which started in the past and:

- has a connection with the present: *I've finished all my exams* (so I'm very happy now).

- continues into the present: *I've lived here for five years* (and I still live here now).

Just, already and *yet*

We often use the adverbs *just, already* or *yet* with the present perfect to talk about things that have happened before now but have a connection with the present.

- We use *just* to talk about things that happened a short time ago: *I've just eaten* (= I ate a short time ago and I'm not hungry now). *Magda's just gone out* (= She left a short time ago so you can't speak to her now).

- We use *already* to say something has happened, often sooner than expected. *'Do page 23 for homework!' 'We've already done that page.'* (= That page is finished now so we don't need to do it again.)
  'When are you going to tidy your bedroom?' 'I've already tidied it.' (= The room is tidy now so I don't need to do it again.)

Note: these two adverbs normally go in the middle of the sentence, between *have* and the past participle: *I've just bought some new trainers. She's already read that book.*

- We often use *yet* in questions and negative sentences when we expect something to happen. It means *until now*: *'Have you seen the new Kate Winslet film yet?'* *'No, I haven't seen it yet.'* (= No, I haven't seen the film at a time before now but I expect I'll go.)

  Note: *Yet* normally goes at the end of the question or sentence: *'Have you finished yet?'* *'No, I haven't finished yet.'*

Since and *for*

We often use *since* and *for* with the present perfect to talk about a time that started in the past and continues into the present.

- We use *since* to talk about the beginning of a period of time:

Michael Keen has written three novels	**since**	2007 last year Wednesday
He's played tennis three times		

- We use *for* to talk about the whole period of time:

I've been on the basketball team	**for**	three years three weeks a long time

- We often use *How long* to ask questions about this period of time: *'How long have you had those trainers?'* *'Since last year.'*

Present perfect or past simple?

Present perfect	Past simple
We normally use the **present perfect** when: • we are thinking about the past **and** the present: *I've broken my arm so I can't do the maths exam. Molly has bought a ticket for the concert tonight.* (= Molly has a ticket and plans to go to the concert tonight.) • we are **not** interested in *when* this action happened, but we are interested in the result *now*: *I've lost my keys* (and now I can't open my front door). *I've finished all my homework* (so I don't have to do it now). We can also use the **present perfect** to: • talk about experiences over a time that started in the past and continues until now, but we don't say *when*: *JK Rowling has written seven* Harry Potter *books.* (= She may write more.) *I've never been to Japan* (until now, but I may go in the future). • to give news: *Rafa Nadal has won again. I've had my hair cut.* Remember if we ask questions about a time that started in the past and continues into the present, we use the **present perfect**: *'How long have you lived here?'* *'I've lived here for three years.'* (= I'm interested in a time period that started in the past and continues until now.) *'How many matches have you played this week?'* (= I'm interested in a time period that started in the past and continues until now.)	We normally use the **past simple** when: • we are thinking about the past **but not** the present: *I broke my arm when I was riding my bike. Seth bought two tickets for last week's concert and he went with his friend Jim.* (= Seth went to the concert with Jim last week.) • we are interested in *when* this action happened: *I lost my keys* **yesterday** (and I couldn't open the front door). *I did my homework last night.* We use the **past simple**: • when these experiences happened over a time in the past: *JRR Tolkien wrote the* Lord of the Rings. (= Tolkien's dead so he won't write more.) *When I was in Asia, I didn't go to Japan.* (= I'm not in Asia now). • to add more details to this news: *He beat Roger Federer.* (**not** ~~has beaten~~) *I went to that new hairdresser's.* We use the **past simple** to ask questions about a time in the past: *'When did you move here?'* *'May 2009.'* (= I'm interested in a particular date in the past.) *'What time did the match start?'*

Unit 7

Ways of expressing the future

Here are some ways of talking about the future.

tense	use	examples
future simple	1 with things which are not certain, especially with *I think, I hope, I expect, probably* and *maybe*	*She'll probably phone later. I think it'll be warmer next week.*
	2 predictions for the future	*Sea levels will rise by several centimetres. The climate will change.*
	3 *will* can also be used to: • make requests • make promises • make offers • express a decision made at the moment of speaking	*Will you help me with my homework?* *I won't forget to give you a present.* *I'll buy you a sandwich if you're hungry.* *That's the phone ringing – I'll get it!*
***going to* future**	1 predictions about the future based on present evidence	*Your work is so good that I reckon you're going to get a Grade A.* *Look at the clouds! I think it's going to snow.*
	2 future plans and intentions	*I'm going to study biology at university.* *He says he's going to phone you tomorrow.*
present continuous	things arranged between people for the future	*I'm seeing the dentist tomorrow – I phoned her assistant yesterday.*
present simple	events fixed on a timetable	*The flight to Paris takes off at six.* *Our train leaves at 5.15.*

In some cases, more than one verb form is possible:

- In practice, an agreed arrangement (present continuous) may be almost exactly the same as a plan (*going to*): *I'm seeing Joey tonight. / I'm going to see Joey tonight.*

- When it is not clear whether a prediction is based on fact (*going to*) or opinion (*will*), we can use either of these forms: *Amy is going to pass her exam.* (I'm the teacher and I've seen some of her exam marks.) / *Amy will pass her exam.* (I know Amy and I think she's very clever.)

Prepositions of movement

To say how we travel, we normally use *by*: *We went to Paris by train.*

- Expressions like this include *by car, by plane, by ship, by boat, by ferry.*

- We also say *by road, by sea, by air, by rail, by metro, by underground.*

- But we say *on foot*, **not** ~~*by foot*~~: *There were no buses so we went on foot.*

- We can't use *by* with *a, the, her*, etc. in expressions like *a taxi, the plane, her bike.* Instead, we say *in a taxi, on the plane, on her bike.*

To talk about cars and taxis, we use *in*: *They arrived at the cinema in Liam's car. I decided not to go in my car. There were five of us in the taxi.*

- With *get*, and sometimes with other verbs such as *jump* and *climb*, we use *in/into* and *out of*: *Get in the car! Two people got into the taxi. I got out of the car and closed the door behind me. Sofia jumped into her car and set off quickly.*

To talk about public transport, motorbikes, bicycles and horses, we use *on*: *She left on the 7.45 plane. I usually go to school on my bike, but today I'm going on the bus. The best way to cross the hills is on a horse.*

- We use *on/onto* or *off* with *get*: *You get on the bus at the station, and get off at the shopping centre. Marlon left the café and got on his motorbike.*

Too and enough

Too means more than is needed or wanted: *She's too old to join the police.*

Enough means as much as is necessary or needed: *Have we got enough eggs to make a cake?*

Extremely, fairly, quite, rather, really, very

We can use the adverbs *very*, *extremely* and *really* before adjectives to make the adjectives stronger: *It was a very long journey. We were extremely tired yesterday (very tired). I had a really good sleep last night (very good).*

To make an adjective weaker, we can use *rather* or *fairly*:

It's rather cold today (cold, but not freezing).

Their apartment is fairly big (big, but not huge).

We can use *quite* to make **gradable** (e.g. *good*, *tired*, etc.) adjectives weaker, but with **non-gradable** adjectives (e.g. *sure*, *true*, *different*, etc.), *quite* can mean *completely*:

The town I live in is quite small (small, but not tiny).

I'm quite sure it's the right answer (I'm 100% sure).

too	enough
too + adjective (+ for somebody) (+ infinitive): • *He's too young to drive.* • *That suitcase is too heavy for me to lift.* ***too*** + adverb (+ for somebody) (+ infinitive): • *You're working too slowly. Please hurry up.* • *It was snowing too heavily for me to see the road ahead.* ***too much/too many*** + noun (+ for somebody) (+ infinitive): • *They brought too much food for us to eat.* • *I've received too many emails to answer.*	adjective/adverb + ***enough*** (+ for somebody) (+ infinitive): • *This coffee is not warm enough! Please heat it up again.* • *Franz didn't answer the questions well enough to get the job.* • *That hotel is not smart enough for her.* ***enough*** + noun (+ for somebody) (+ infinitive): • *Have you got enough money to get to London?* • *There isn't enough cake for me to give some to everyone.*

Unit 8

Zero, first and second conditionals

We use conditional sentences to talk about a possible situation or action (*If* ...) and the possible results of this situation or action:

If it rains,	*I'll get wet.*
(possible situation)	(possible result)

We can also talk about the result before we describe the situation:

I'll get wet	*if it rains.*
(possible result)	(possible situation)

Note: If the situation comes first, a comma is used. If the result comes first, no comma is used.

Conditionals are often divided into types:

Type 0 or zero conditional

***If* + present tense, present tense:** *If our team wins a match, our coach is happy.* (= He's happy every time we win.)

The zero conditional is used to talk about things which are always or generally true.

Type 1 or first conditional

***If* + present tense, future:** *If our team wins this match, we'll win the competition.* (= I think the team could win.)

The first conditional is used to talk about a real possibility in the future.

Type 2 or second conditional

***If* + past tense, *would* + infinitive:** *If our team won all the matches, we'd be the champions!* (= I don't think the team will win all the matches.)

The second conditional is used when the speaker is imagining a situation that will probably not happen.

When deciding whether to use the first or second conditional, you need to think about whether each situation is a real possibility or not for you:

If it rains at the weekend, I'll go to the cinema. (I think it could rain.)

If it rained in the desert, plants would grow. (I'm sure it won't rain.)

When, if, unless + present, future

We can use *when*, *if* or *unless* to talk about the possibility of things happening in the future:

- We use *when* for things we are sure will happen: *When I get home, I'll watch TV.* (I'm sure I'll get home today.)

- We use *if* for things that may happen: *If I get home before 8 pm, I'll watch the film.* (I'm not sure if I'll get home before 8 pm but it is possible.)

- *Unless* can generally replace *if … not* and means *except if: I'll watch the film unless I get home too late.* (= I'll watch the film *if* I *don't* get home too late. / I plan to watch the film *except if* I get home too late.)

So do I and *nor/neither do I*

We can use *so do I* and *nor/neither do I* when we reply to someone but we don't want to repeat the same words. We use these expressions to say that the same is true for me or someone else:

Someone says:	You agree:
I'm bored.	So am I.
I've got lots of cousins.	So have I.
Maya plays the guitar.	So does Lou.
We don't like rock music.	Neither/Nor do they.
You can sing well.	So can you.
They bought that new CD.	So did I.
Josh hasn't done his homework.	Neither/Nor have I.

We use:

- *so* in positive sentences: *'I live in Japan.' 'So do I.'*
- *nor* or *neither* in negative sentences: *'James can't swim well.' 'Nor/Neither can Matt.'*
- the same auxiliary verb in the reply: *'I**'ve** studied for the exam.' 'So **have** I.' 'Callum **is**n't here.' 'Nor/Neither **is** Hamish.'*
- *do* or *did* if there is no auxiliary verb: *'He **goes** to King William's School.' 'So **does** Kate.' 'I **did**n't watch TV last night.' 'Nor/Neither **did** I.'*
- the same word order as questions: *'I saw a great film at the weekend.' 'So **did I**'.* (**Not** ~~So I did.~~)

Unit 9

Which, that, who, whose, when, where clauses (defining and non-defining)

A clause is part of a sentence. The relative clause in this sentence is underlined:

The man <u>who phoned you</u> is my doctor.

Relative clauses start with these relative pronouns: *which, that, who, whose, where, when* and *why.*

Defining relative clauses

- Relative clauses which tell you which person or thing the speaker is talking about are called **defining relative clauses**.
- Defining relative clauses give **essential** information: *The doctor <u>who gave me the medicine</u> is my cousin.* The relative clause (underlined) tells us which doctor we are talking about.

Non-defining relative clauses

- Relative clauses which give you **extra** information are called **non-defining relative clauses**.
- Non-defining relative clauses give information that is not essential: *My doctor, <u>who belongs to the same tennis club as you</u>, gave me the medicine yesterday.* We already know which doctor (it's *my* doctor); *who belongs to the same tennis club as you* does not tell us which doctor we are talking about; it just adds extra information.

There are differences in grammar between defining and non-defining relative clauses:

Defining relative clauses	Non-defining relative clauses
• Don't have commas.	• Use commas (or pauses in spoken English).
• Use the following relative pronouns: *who, which, whose, where, when, why.*	• Use the following relative pronouns: *who, which, whose, where, when, why.*
• *That* can be used instead of *who* or *which.*	• Don't use *that.*
• *Who, which* or *that* can be omitted when they are the object of the clause: *The medicine (which/that) the doctor gave me should be taken twice a day* (*the doctor* is the subject and *which/that* the object of the clause).	• The relative pronoun cannot be omitted.

Past perfect

I/you/he/she/it/we/they	**had / 'd**		
I/you/he/she/it/we/they	**had not / hadn't**	**arrived**	home (?)
Had	I/you/he/she/it/we/they		

The main uses of the past perfect are:

- to show that we are talking about something which happened before something that is described in the past simple: *When he got to the station, his train had already left.* Compare this with: *When he got to the station, his train left.* This shows that the train left at the same time he arrived.

- it is often used with time expressions like *when, as soon as, after, before*: *She started driving before he'd fastened his seatbelt. When the terrible storm had ended, people started to come out of their houses.*

- it is often used with the adverbs *already, just, never*: *The thieves had already escaped when the police arrived. He'd never eaten a really good pizza until he went to Italy.*

Unit 10

Commands*

Commands are also known as *imperatives*.

'Stand up!'	'Don't touch the walls, children.'
'Be quiet, everybody.'	'Don't worry so much.'
'Have a good weekend.'	'Don't forget to phone me.'

We use:

- the infinitive without *to*: *'Be good!', 'Don't talk!'* (**Not** *'Don't to talk!'*)

- the same form when we talk to one or more than one person: *'Enjoy your holiday, everybody!'*

- this structure to *command, tell* or *ask* someone to do something, to *give instructions* or *advice, make suggestions, encourage, warn*, etc.

Have something done

I/you/we/they	**have**	
he/she/it	**has**	
Do	I/you/we/they	**have**
Does	he/she/it	

(the car **repaired** (?))

I	**'m (not)**	
You/we/they	**'re (not) are (n't)**	
He/she/it	**'s (not) (isn't)**	**having** the computer **mended** (?)
Am	I	
Are	you/we/they	
Is	she/he/it	

I/you/he/she/it/we/they	**had (didn't have)**	
Did	I/you/he/she/it/we/they	**have**

(the house **painted** (?))

- We use *have something done* when we ask someone else to do something for us: *We're having the car repaired.* (= The mechanic is repairing the car for us.) *I had my hair cut last week.* (= A hairdresser cut my hair for me.)

- We can also use *get something done*: *She **gets** her hair cut* (but usually only in informal situations).

- We can use *have* (or *get*) *something done* in any form or tense: *I'm thinking of having my hair cut. My watch is broken – I must have it repaired.*

Unit 11

The passive: present and past simple

The passive is formed by the verb *be* + *done* / *eaten* / *cleaned*, etc.: *Lunch is served in the hotel restaurant from 1 pm.*

Active	Passive
They ate all the food very quickly.	*All the food was eaten very quickly.*
We've sold the car.	*The car has been sold.*
It's nice when people invite me to dinner.	*It's nice when I'm invited to dinner.*
On a clear day you can see Ibiza from the mainland.	*On a clear day Ibiza can be seen from the mainland.*

The passive is used when:

- the speaker doesn't know who or what does/did something: *My bike was stolen last night.*

- the speaker doesn't need to say who or what does/did something because it's obvious from the situation or context: *The murderer was arrested* (obviously by the police).

- what happens is more important than who does it: *The post is delivered at 8.30.*

- when writing in a formal style: *Your documents were signed yesterday and they can now be collected from our office.*

More about the passive:

- If it is important to say who or what did something, we add *by* + noun: *This picture was painted by my aunt.*

- We sometimes leave out a relative pronoun and the form of the verb *be*: *The film, (which was) made in the 1990s, is still very popular.*

Comparative and superlative adverbs

We use a comparative adverb to compare two ways things are done: *Computers run more quickly than in the past. Lucy always talks more loudly than Stacey.*

We use a superlative adverb to compare one thing or person with all those in the same group: *There were a lot of good dancers in the competition, but Sam and Ricky danced the most brilliantly.*

Comparative adverbs	Superlative adverbs
• We use *more* to form the comparative of two-syllable adverbs, including adverbs ending in *-ly*: *Maria read the text more quickly than Susanna. She visits me more often than she used to.* After the adverb we usually put *than*. • We add *-er* to one-syllable adverbs, e.g. *hard, fast, straight*: *My mum works harder than my dad.* (**Not** *more hardly*) • The adverbs *well* and *badly* form irregular comparisons: *well → better*; *badly → worse*: *Dolphins can swim better than people. Your team always plays worse than mine.* • We can sometimes use *less* instead of *more*: *After a while, the wind began to blow less strongly.*	• We use *most* to form the superlative of two-syllable adverbs, including adverbs ending in *-ly*: *This machine works most efficiently of all.* • We add *-est* to one-syllable adverbs: *Max won the race because he ran fastest at the end.* • The adverbs *well* and *badly* form irregular superlatives: *well → best*; *badly → worst*: *They are all excellent students, but Mel speaks French best. We tested three cars, and this one performs worst.* • The superlative sometimes takes *the*, especially in more formal situations: *In the current economic situation, sales of our luxury model are growing the most slowly.*

Unit 12

Reported speech

We often use *say* and *tell* to report what people say:

- we use *tell* if we mention who we are talking to: *He told me he was from Casablanca.* (**Not** ~~He told he was from Casablanca.~~)

- if not, we use *say*: *She said she would help me.* (**Not** ~~She said me she would help me.~~)

Remember: you can leave out *that*: '*He said **that** he was tired*' and '*He said he was tired*' have the same meaning.

Tense changes

What people say ⟶	Reporting what people said
present simple '*I live in Berlin.*'	past simple *She said she lived in Berlin.*
present continuous '*I'm watching TV.*'	past continuous *He said he was watching TV.*
present perfect '*I've seen the film already.*'	past perfect *She said she had seen the film already.*
past simple '*I missed the concert.*'	past perfect* *He told me he had missed the concert.*

* We can also use the past simple: *He told me he missed the concert*

will '*I'll phone you soon.*'	*would* *She said she would phone me soon.*
am/are/is going to '*I'm going to play tennis.*'	*was/were going to* *She said she was going to play tennis.*
can '*I can run but I can't run fast.*'	*could* *He said he could run but he couldn't run fast.*

Other changes

We usually make the following changes:

What people say ⟶	Reporting what people said
I/you '**I** spoke to **you** earlier.'	he/she/they He said **he** had spoken to **her** earlier.
we '**We**'ve finished!'	they They said **they** had finished.
my 'I can't find **my** keys.'	his/her She said she couldn't find **her** keys.
your 'I'll come to **your** house later.'	my/his/her/their He said that he would come to **her** house later.
our 'We've tidied **our** bedroom.'	their They said they had tidied **their** bedroom.
today / this week / month / year	that day / week / month / year
tomorrow / next month / year	the next day / the following month / year
yesterday / last week / month / year	the day before / the previous day / the previous week / month / year; the week / month / year before
'I'm playing tennis **tomorrow**.'	She said she was playing tennis **the next day**.
here 'I've lived **here** all my life.'	there He said he had lived **there** all his life.

Reported commands

What people say ⟶	Reporting what people said
'Stand up!'	The teacher told them to stand up.
'Be quiet!'	He told the child to be quiet.
'Don't touch anything.'	The mother told her son not to touch anything.
'Don't worry.'	Her friend told her not to worry.

We generally use *ask* and not *tell* to report more polite requests:

'Open the window.'	He told her to open the window.
'Can you open the window?'	He asked her to open the window.

Reported questions

We can, use *ask*, *wonder*, *want to know*, etc. to introduce reported questions:

What people say ⟶	Reporting what people said
'Where do you live?'	He asked me where I lived.
'What are you doing after class?'	She wondered what he was doing after class.
'Have you finished your homework?'	He wanted to know if she had finished her homework.

To report a question, we make the following changes:

- change the word order in the question to the same as a normal sentence:

direct question:	'Where **can I buy** a dictionary?'
reported question:	He asked me where **I could buy** a dictionary. (**not** ... ~~where could I buy~~ ...)

- make the same tense changes as for reported speech:

  ◗ page 129 *Reported speech*

direct question:	'Where **have** you **been**?'
reported question:	She asked me where I **had been**.

- do not use *do*, *does* or *did* as an auxiliary verb:

direct question:	'**Do you like** strawberries?'
reported question:	He asked me if **I liked** strawberries. (**not** ... ~~if I did like strawberries~~)

- use a full stop, not a question mark at the end of the sentence:

direct question:	*'What time do you start school?'*
reported question:	*They asked us what time we started school.*

In reported questions, we use the same question words (*what, when, where*, etc.) but if there is no question word, we use *if* or *whether*.

Direct question	Reported question
'Why are you laughing?'	*The teacher asked us **why** we were laughing.*
'Are you going on holiday?'	*He asked me **if** I was going on holiday.*

Indirect questions

When we ask for information, we sometimes use indirect questions to sound more polite. Expressions used to introduce indirect questions include: *I was wondering …, I'd like to know …, I can't remember …, Could you tell me …,* etc.

Direct question	Indirect question
'Where do you live?'	*I was wondering where you lived.*
'What are you doing later?'	*Could you tell me what you are doing later?*
'Have you finished your homework?'	*I'd like to know if you have finished your homework.*

As for reported questions (see above), when a direct question becomes part of a longer, indirect question, we make the following changes:

- change the word order in the indirect question to the same as a normal sentence:

direct question:	*'How long **have you lived** here?'*
indirect question:	*I'd like to know how long **you've lived** here.*
	(**not** … ~~how long have you lived here.~~)

- do not use *do, does* or *did* as an auxiliary verb:

direct question:	*'**Do you play** tennis every day?'*
indirect question:	*Could you tell me if **you play** tennis every day?*
	(**not** … ~~if you do play tennis~~ …)

Also, as for reported speech, we use the same question words (*what, when, where,* etc.) but if there is no question word, we use *if* or *whether*:

Direct question	Indirect question
*'**Where** did you go?'*	*I can't remember **where** you went.*
'Did you stay in a hotel?'	*I'd like to know **if** you stayed in a hotel.*

However, unlike in reported questions, in indirect questions:

- the tense stays the same:

direct question:	*'Will he leave soon?'*
indirect question:	*I was wondering if he'll leave soon.* (**not** … ~~if he would leave~~ …)

- we use a question mark when the introductory expression is a question: ***Could you tell me** where the bank is?*

- we use a full stop when the introductory expression is **not** a question: ***I'd like to know** where the bank is.*

Irregular verbs

verb	past simple	past participle	verb	past simple	past participle
be	was/were	been	lend	lent	lent
beat	beat	beaten	let	let	let
become	became	become	lie	lay	lain
begin	began	begun	light	lit	lit
bend	bent	bent	lose	lost	lost
bite	bit	bitten	make	made	made
bleed	bled	bled	mean	meant	meant
blow	blew	blown	meet	met	met
break	broke	broken	pay	paid	paid
bring	brought	brought	put	put	put
build	built	built	read	read	read
burn	burnt/burned	burnt/burned	ride	rode	ridden
buy	bought	bought	ring	rang	rung
catch	caught	caught	rise	rose	risen
choose	chose	chosen	run	ran	run
come	came	come	say	said	said
cost	cost	cost	see	saw	seen
cut	cut	cut	sell	sold	sold
deal	dealt	dealt	send	sent	sent
dig	dug	dug	set	set	set
do	did	done	sew	sewed	sewn
draw	drew	drawn	shake	shook	shaken
dream	dreamt/dreamed	dreamt/dreamed	shine	shone	shone
drink	drank	drunk	shoot	shot	shot
drive	drove	driven	show	showed	shown
eat	ate	eaten	shut	shut	shut
fall	fell	fallen	sing	sang	sung
feed	fed	fed	sink	sank	sunk
feel	felt	felt	sit	sat	sat
fight	fought	fought	sleep	slept	slept
find	found	found	smell	smelt/smelled	smelt/smelled
fly	flew	flown	speak	spoke	spoken
forbid	forbade	forbidden	spell	spelt/spelled	spelt/spelled
forget	forgot	forgotten	spend	spent	spent
forgive	forgave	forgiven	spill	spilt/spilled	spilt/spilled
freeze	froze	frozen	spoil	spoilt/spoiled	spoilt/spoiled
get	got	got	stand	stood	stood
give	gave	given	steal	stole	stolen
go	went	gone	stick	stuck	stuck
grow	grew	grown	strike	struck	struck
hang	hung	hung	sweep	swept	swept
have	had	had	swim	swam	swum
hear	heard	heard	swing	swung	swung
hide	hid	hidden	take	took	taken
hit	hit	hit	teach	taught	taught
hold	held	held	tear	tore	torn
hurt	hurt	hurt	tell	told	told
keep	kept	kept	think	thought	thought
kneel	knelt	knelt	throw	threw	thrown
know	knew	known	understand	understood	understood
lay	laid	laid	wake	woke	woken
lead	led	led	wear	wore	worn
learn	learnt/learned	learnt/learned	win	won	won
leave	left	left	write	wrote	written

Writing reference

What to expect in the exam

The Writing section follows the Reading section of Paper 1. Paper 1 (both Reading and Writing) lasts 1 hour and 30 minutes. You do three tasks.

- In Part 1, there is one task which you **must** do.
- In Part 2, there is one task which you **must** do.
- In Part 3, you choose **one** of two tasks.

Part 1

Sentence transformations

You have practised sentence transformation for Part 1 in Units 1, 3 and 7.

In Part 1:

- there are five questions (Questions 1–5) and an example
- each question has a complete sentence followed by a sentence with a gap in the middle
- all the sentences, including the example, are about the same topic
- you get 1 mark for each correct answer, giving a total of 5 marks.

Part 1 tests your ability to:

- understand grammatical structures at PET level
- rephrase information
- write grammatically correct PET-level sentences.

How to do Part 1

1 Make sure you are familiar with all the grammar areas you need to study for PET. See the Grammar Reference on pages 116–131, and the *PET Handbook* published by Cambridge ESOL.

2 Study the example. This will introduce the topic of the five questions, and remind you of the kinds of changes you will have to make.

3 For each question 1–5, look carefully at the first sentence and think about its meaning.

4 Study both sentences and decide what grammar point the question is testing, e.g. active to passive, *too* and *enough*, comparative adverbs, etc.

5 Think of different ways of saying the same thing as the first sentence.

6 Choose the correct words and fill them in on the question paper. Remember that short forms like *don't* count as two words.

7 Read through both sentences again, checking that they mean exactly the same.

8 Write the one, two or three words on your answer sheet. Check that you haven't made any spelling mistakes.

Exercise 1

Read the Writing Part 1 instructions and study the example below. Why would each of answers a, b, c and d be wrong?

    a the firrst time

    b the time after

    c the first time that

    d never before that

- Here are some sentences about flying in a helicopter for fun.
- For each question, complete the second sentence so that it means the same as the first, **using no more than three words.**
- **Write only the missing words on your answer sheet.**
- You may use this page for any rough work.

Example: I had never flown in a helicopter before.

          It was ..the..first..time. **I had flown in a helicopter.**

Exercise 2

Complete sentences 1–5 using these words.

us to	spent	the most	any flights	as cold as

1 We went on a Saturday because you can't fly on Sundays.

    There aren't .... **on Sundays so we went on a Saturday.**

2 It was warmer inside the helicopter than I had expected.

    Inside the helicopter it wasn't .... **I had expected.**

3 'Please switch off your mobile phones,' the pilot said.

    The pilot asked .... **switch off our mobile phones.**

4 We stayed up in the air for half an hour.

    We .... **half an hour flying.**

5 I've never had such an exciting experience before!

    It was .... **exciting experience I've ever had!**

Exercise 3

In the example on page 133, *never before* changes to the expression *it was the* (*first time*) + past perfect simple. For each question 1–5, look at the difference between the first and the second sentence. What does each question test?

Part 2

You have studied and practised writing Part 2 in Units 2, 6, 8 and 10.

In Part 2, you:

- are asked to write a short message of between 35 and 45 words in the form of an email, note, postcard, etc.
- are told who you are writing to and why
- must include three content points which may ask you to *thank, invite, suggest, explain, apologise*, etc.
- should open and close the letter in a suitable way (e.g. *Hi, best wishes*)
- can get a maximum of 5 marks for this part.

Do not spend too long on this part or you may not have enough time to answer the longer Part 3 writing task where you can get a maximum of 15 marks.

Part 2 tests your ability to:

- read and understand a task
- write a clear message within a word limit
- organise and connect your ideas well.

You **must**:

- include all three content points or you won't be given more than 3 marks, even if it is a very good answer
- make sure your message is clear
- be careful with your grammar, punctuation and spelling
- remember that short forms like *don't* count as two words
- write your answer in pencil on the answer sheet.

You **mustn't**:

- write a lot more than 45 words or your answer might not be as clear as a shorter answer
- write less than 35 words. A short answer is unlikely to include all three content points. If you write 25 words or less, you won't be given more than 2 marks.

How to do Part 2

1 Read the task very carefully. Underline the following:

   why you are writing

   what you are writing

   who you are writing to

   the three content points.

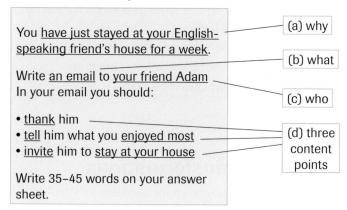

You <u>have just stayed at your English-speaking friend's house for a week</u>. — (a) why

Write <u>an email</u> to <u>your friend Adam</u> — (b) what
In your email you should: — (c) who

- <u>thank</u> him
- <u>tell</u> him what you <u>enjoyed most</u> — (d) three content points
- <u>invite</u> him to <u>stay at your house</u>

Write 35–45 words on your answer sheet.

2 Think of some ways to communicate each content point and note them down, e.g. *Thank you ever so much for … .*

3 Think about how you can connect your ideas with words like *but, and* or *because.*

4 Decide how you are going to open and close your message. Think about whether the message is formal or informal.

5 Write your complete text, including all three content points. Look back at the question, if necessary.

6 Don't waste time writing a rough copy. Remember you will need to leave enough time to do Writing Part 3.

7 Read the question and your answer again. Make sure you have:

- included all three content points
- written a clear message and connected your ideas with *and, but*, etc.
- checked you haven't made mistakes with grammar, spelling or punctuation
- opened and closed the message in an appropriate way
- written 35–45 words.

Messages

Exercise 1

Read the Part 2 writing task below and answer these questions.

1 Who are you writing to? Why?
2 Will your message need to be formal or informal?
3 What are you writing?
4 What are the three content points?

> You want to borrow your friend's camera.
>
> **Write an email to Eva. In your email, you should**
> * **explain why you want to borrow the camera**
> * **suggest when you can collect the camera**
> * **say when you will give it back.**

In the PET Writing Part 2 exam you may have to *thank someone, explain, invite, apologise, suggest, ask for something,* etc.

Ways of thanking someone

Thank you / Thanks (ever so much) for (giving me) such a nice present.

It was very kind of you to give me such a nice present. (FORMAL)

Ways of explaining

I can't come to your party because I have to study for my exams.

I have to study for my exams. That's why I can't come to your party.

Ways of inviting

I'm going to the new Turkish restaurant. Would you like to come?

I'm going to the new Turkish restaurant. I'd like you to come.

Ways of apologising

I'm so sorry for breaking your camera.

I'm so sorry that I broke your camera.

Ways of suggesting

Why don't we go to the cinema?

How/What about (going to) the cinema?

Shall we go to the cinema?

Ways of asking

Can I borrow your camera, please?

Could you lend me your camera, please?

Would it be possible to borrow your camera, please?

Exercise 2

Write what you would say in the following situations.

1 You can't meet your friend at the weekend. Apologise.

   I'm sorry that I can't meet you at the weekend.

2 You want to borrow your friend's camera. Explain why.
3 You spent two wonderful weeks at your English-speaking friend's house. Thank him/her.
4 Your English-speaking friend has never been to your country. Invite him/her.
5 You've arranged to meet an English-speaking friend. Suggest a place to meet.
6 You forgot your friend's birthday. Apologise.
7 You're going to Hugh's party. Ask him for directions to his house.

Exercise 3

Look at the following expressions we use to open and close messages and answer the two questions that follow.

Expressions used to open messages

Dear ...   Hello, ...   Hi ...

Expressions used to close messages

Best wishes   All the best   Yours   Love   Lots of love   See you soon

1 Which expressions can we use in both a formal and an informal message?
2 Which expressions can we only use in an informal message?

Exercise 4

👁 Read the three answers to the task in Exercise 1 written by PET candidates on the next page. Answer the questions by putting a tick (✓) or a cross (✗) in the correct column.

Has each candidate:	A	B	C
1 included all three content points?	✗		
2 written a clear message?	✓		
3 connected their ideas with *and, but,* etc.?			
4 opened and closed the message with an appropriate expression?			
5 written between 35 and 45 words?			

A

Dear Eva,

I'd like to borrow your camera next Friday. I'll need it for the weekend since I'm going to take part in a competition and my camera has just broken. I'll return it next Monday. Let's keep in touch.

Love,

B

Dear Eva,

How are you? I hope you're fine. I'm going to visit my friend this weekend but I have a big problem. Somebody stole my new camera. Could you lend me your camera? I can visit you on Friday. I'll return it next Monday. Write to me soon.

Love,

C

Dear Eva

You told me you can lend me your camera. I will give it back next Friday.

See you,

Exercise 5

Look at the PET Writing Part 2 marking scheme (adapted from the Cambridge ESOL website, with kind permission). What mark would you give each of the three answers in Exercise 4?

Writing Part 2 marking scheme

Mark	Reason
5	Candidate has included all 3 content points appropriately. The message is very clear.
4	Candidate has included all 3 content points. The message is generally clear.
3	Candidate has tried to include all 3 content points. The message is not clear in places. OR Candidate has only included 2 content points but these are clear.
2	Candidate hasn't included 2 content points or these 2 points are not clearly communicated. The message is not completely communicated. OR The answer is a little short (20–25 words)
1	Content points hardly included and/or message difficult to understand. OR The answer is short (10–19 words)
0	Content points not included OR message impossible to understand OR too short (under 10 words)

Exercise 6

Read the following Part 2 writing task and underline:

1 why you are writing
2 what you are writing
3 who you are writing to
4 the three content points.

> You are going to miss an English-speaking friend's birthday party tomorrow.
>
> **Write a note to your friend Ian. In your note, you should**
> - **apologise for missing his party**
> - **explain why you can't be there**
> - **suggest meeting another day.**
>
> **Write 35–45 words on your answer sheet.**

Exercise 7

Read three students' answers and decide which one was given the maximum 5 marks.

A

Hello, I am sorry but tommorrow I can't go to your party becouse I have my sister's wedding and she live in the USA. I must bring the train from Lyon and afterwards the plan from Paris. Shall we meet next weekend? Tanks,

Good idea to use your own words

There are 6 mistakes which make the message a little unclear

B

> Dear Ian, ¹I would like to apologise for missing your birthday party. ²I will have to go to the doctor with my younger brother because our parents won't be able to go with him. ³Why don't we meet on Saturday so I can give you a gift? Best wishes,

All 3 content points included

Clear message connected with *because* and *so*

C

> Hi Ian, I'm sorry for not going to your party yesterday. I had a bad cold and my sister had an accident. I went to the hospital and the doctor told her that she had a broken leg, so I couldn't be there. I will see you tomorrow. Yours,

2 content points are not correct. The party is tomorrow and the writer doesn't **suggest** another day

Exercise 8

Rewrite the other two answers so that they could also be given the maximum 5 marks.

Part 3

In Part 3, you must choose from **one** of two writing tasks.

- The tasks you choose from are an informal letter and a story.
- You are given some written information, but you must answer the task with your own ideas.
- You must write about 100 words.
- Your letter or story is marked out of a possible 15, so this is the most important part of the Writing section.

Part 3 tests your ability to:

- complete the task you have chosen
- organise your text well
- use a variety of grammatical structures and vocabulary
- link your sentences together
- write in a suitable style, e.g. friendly and informal in a letter to a friend
- use correct spelling and punctuation
- avoid making many mistakes
- avoid errors that make it difficult to understand your writing.

In this part you might need to show you can:

- describe a place, something you own, or a person you know
- give somebody practical information
- describe how something happened
- say how you feel about something, or about something that has happened
- express your opinions or say what makes you happy
- say what you hope for or what you regret.

How to do Part 3

1 Read the questions and choose the task you think you can do better. When you are deciding, think about what you are good at and what you are not so good at. Are you more confident writing letters to friends, or telling a story?

2 Read the task that you choose very carefully. Underline the following:

- **who** will read your text, e.g. an English-speaking friend, your English teacher
- the **key words** in the instructions, e.g. *story*, *begin*, *holidays*
- the main points you must write about, for example:

> There's a really big shopping centre quite near my apartment. I go there every Saturday.
> <u>What are the shops like near where you live?</u>
> <u>What do you like buying most?</u>

Main points that you must answer

3 Think about the topic and how you will write about it. Quickly note down as many ideas as you can.

4 Choose your best ideas and write a brief plan, putting these ideas under separate headings.

5 Think of some useful words and phrases for each paragraph and note them down, but don't write a full, rough copy. You won't have time to write it all twice.

6 Decide what style you need to write in: formal or informal.

7 Write your text, following your plan and keeping to the topic.

8 Try to make your handwriting as clear and easy to read as possible.

9 Use as many different kinds of grammatical structures and as much vocabulary as you can.

10 Form longer sentences by using linking expressions like *so* and *because*.

11 At the end, check you have written about the right number of words. If you have written fewer than 80 words, you will lose marks. If you write many more than 100, you might make more mistakes.

12 Make sure you leave enough time to check your completed text for mistakes and correct them. Making a lot of corrections doesn't matter if they are easy to read.

Informal letter

You have practised writing an informal letter for Part 3 in Units 4, 5 and 11.

When you write your letter, you **should**:

- imagine the short text you read is written to you
- organise your text properly, using short paragraphs
- put the opening, e.g. *Dear Amy*, the closing, e.g. *Love*, and your name on separate lines
- use friendly, informal language
- give reasons and examples, using linking words.

Expressions used at the beginning of an informal letter

Dear …   Hello …   Hi …

Thanks (very much) for your letter.   It was great to hear from you.

Sorry I've taken so long to write back, but …   Sorry I haven't written for so long, but …   I've got so much to tell you.   I'm writing to say …   This is just a quick note to say …

Expressions used at the end of an informal letter

Well, that's all for now.   I'd better finish now because …

Say 'hello' to your family from me.   Give my love to everyone.

Don't forget to write soon.   Looking forward to hearing from you.

Love,   Lots of love,   Best wishes,   All the best,   Bye for now,

Exercise 1

Read the Part 3 writing task on the right and answer these questions.

1 What are the key words in the instructions?

2 Who must you write to?

3 What does your English-speaking friend tell you?

4 What questions does your English-speaking friend ask?

- This is part of a letter you receive from an English-speaking friend.

> I've just had my fourteenth birthday! I had a great time with all my family. Please tell me about your birthdays. What happens? What do you do?

- Now write a letter, answering your friend's questions.

- Write your **letter** in about 100 words **on your answer sheet**.

Exercise 2

Study this model letter and the comments next to it. Answer these questions.

1 How does Stefan reply to Sam's questions?

2 Find as many informal words in the letter as you can.

3 What else shows that the style of the letter is informal?

4 Find an example and two reasons in the last two paragraphs. What linking words does he use?

Model letter

Dear Sam,

Thanks for your letter and congratulations on your fourteenth birthday! I hope you had lots of cool presents.

Mine isn't till July, but I'm already getting excited. I always get nice presents from my mum and dad, as well as loads of birthday cards – some of them are quite funny. There's a cake, too. This year it'll have 14 candles on it.

Later on, my mates take me out somewhere special, like a concert. That's always fun. But the best thing is that I can do what I like all day and no one can say anything because it's my birthday!

Anyway, that's all for now because I've got to go out. Write soon.

All the best,

Stefan

(Friendly beginning)

(Thank the other person for their letter and say something about what they wrote)

(Answer their questions)

(Say why your letter is quite short, and ask for a reply)

(Friendly ending)

Exercise 3

Read the Part 3 writing task below and answer these questions.

1 What are the key words in the instructions?

2 Who are you writing to?

3 What information does your friend give?

4 What does your friend want to know?

> This is part of a letter you receive from an English-speaking friend.
>
> > *I've just bought my tickets, so next month I'll see you!*
> > *Please tell me more about your country. Which are the best places to*
> > *visit? What can I do there?*
>
> • Now write a letter to this friend.
> • Write your **letter** in about 100 words **on your answer sheet**.

Exercise 4

⊙ Read the letter written by a PET candidate and answer questions 1–8.

1 Zoe has made one grammar mistake in each paragraph (1–4). Can you correct the mistakes?

2 Has she made any spelling mistakes?

3 Has she organised her letter well?

4 Is her letter about the right length?

5 Is her writing formal or informal? Give some examples.

6 Does she answer all Jamie's questions? In which paragraphs?

7 Which four common expressions does she use at the beginning and end of her letter?

8 Which linking words does she use to give reasons?

PET candidate's letter

Hi Jamie,

1 *Thanks for your letter – that's such <u>a good news!</u> I can't believe you are going to visit my country!*

2 *I think it's best to spend your time in a city because there are more things <u>for do</u> than in the countryside. Generally, in the cities you can watch films, go shopping and eat in good restaurants.*

3 *The nightlife in my country is wonderful! There are famous discos here and lively cafés. On Sundays there are cultural attractions for <u>people which</u> are visiting the cities.*

4 *I recommend <u>you to visit</u> the capital, as it's huge and there are lovely sandy beaches too. Also because I live here!*

Please write again soon.

Best wishes,

Zoe

Story

You have practised writing a story for Part 3 in Units 9 and 12.

When you write a story, you **should always**:

- check whether the words you are given in the instructions are the title or the first line
- write about the topic suggested by the title / use the first sentence you have been given
- get ideas by asking yourself *who?, what?, where?, when?* and *how?*
- decide before you start writing what will happen at the beginning, in the middle and at the end. Will the ending be happy, sad – or a mystery?
- make sure each part of your text develops the story
- use time expressions, e.g. *before, after, during, when, while, until, first, then, next, immediately, as soon as, suddenly, finally, in the end*
- use a variety of tenses, e.g. the past simple for events, the past continuous to describe the background, the past perfect for things that happened before something else when you are already talking about the past.

You **should try to**:

- set the scene at the beginning by using description
- include some interesting details
- use some unusual vocabulary to make the story more lively
- include some direct speech, e.g. '*What was that strange noise?*'

- say how you, or the main character, felt at different times in the story
- create interest during your story, possibly with a surprise at the end.

Exercise 1
Read this Part 3 task and answer the questions that follow.

> - Your English teacher has asked you to write a story.
> - Your story must have this title:
>
>   ***The lost wallet***
>
> - Write your **story** in about 100 words **on your answer sheet**.

1 What are the key words in the instructions?
2 Do the instructions give the title or the first line?
3 How many words should the answer be?

Exercise 2
Study this model story and the comments next to it. Answer these questions.

1 Is the text written in the first person (*I*), or the third person (*he/she/it*)?
2 What adjectives and adverbs are used to describe the scene and the people?
3 What kind of ending does it have?
4 Match each of comments a–f with words in the text.

Model story

a Good use of tenses to set the scene

b Describes how he felt

c Direct speech brings the story to life

d Creates interest

e Surprise at the end

f Partly explains what happened

The lost wallet

Rafa was standing on the crowded platform of a busy underground station when his wallet was stolen. Upset and angry, he realised that with it he had lost his identity card and all his cash.

He never expected to see it again, but months later there was a knock at the door. 'I believe this is yours,' said a nervous stranger, who handed him his wallet and then hurried off into the night. Rafa looked anxiously inside it.

He couldn't believe his luck, because his money was there and so was his ID card. Something, though, was wrong. That was his card, but with someone else's photo on it. Then he understood: they had wanted to steal his identity.

Exercise 3

Read the Part 3 writing task below and answer these questions.

1 What are the key words in the instructions?

2 Who will read your story?

3 Which words do you have to use? Where?

4 What are the key words in the sentence you are given?

5 Do you have to write in the first person (*I*), or the third person (*he/she/it*)?

- Your English teacher has asked you to write a story.
- Your story must begin with this sentence:

  When the phone rang, I knew immediately who was calling.

- Write your **story** in about 100 words **on your answer sheet**.

Exercise 4

Quickly read the story written by a strong PET candidate and answer this question.

- The story has three paragraphs 1–3. Which paragraph is mainly about the time:

a before the phone rang

b after the phone rang

c when the phone was ringing?

PET candidate's story

1 When the phone rang, I knew immediately who was calling. Before answering, I thought back to when I was taking part in the dance competition.

2 I had passed through the first, second, third and fourth rounds. After I had completed my dance in the fifth round, the judges said the winner would perform around the world.
I was informed that the results will be announced in two weeks, and now it was time.

3 Nervously, I took the call. 'You've won the National Dance Competition,' a voice said. I was amazed. I couldn't beleive it; it was a dream come true. After all, I was just 13 years old and at that age anyone would be the happiest person of the world.

▶ page 119 Grammar reference: *Past simple and past continuous*

▶ page 128 Grammar reference: *Past perfect*

Exercise 5

Read the story more carefully and answer questions 1–9.

1 Does the story keep to the topic of the first sentence?

2 Is it about the right length?

3 Find one incorrect verb form, a spelling mistake and a preposition error.

4 What verb tenses does she use? Give an example of each, e.g. past simple: *rang*.

5 Which time expressions, e.g. *when*, does she use?

6 Is her writing mainly formal or informal? Give some examples.

7 Where and how does she create interest?

8 Where does she use direct speech?

9 Which words and phrases describe how she felt?

Speaking reference

What to expect in the exam

The Speaking paper is Paper 3.

- It lasts 10–12 minutes.
- Sometimes it is on a different day from the written papers.
- You normally do Paper 3 in pairs.
- There are two examiners: one speaks to you and the other just listens.
- The Speaking paper has four parts.
- In Parts 1 and 3, you talk on your own. In Parts 2 and 4, you talk with your partner, not the examiner.
- You are not given time during the exam to make notes or think about your answer.
- Paper 3 is 25% of the marks for the whole PET exam.

Part 1

You have practised Part 1 in Units 1 and 8. It lasts 2–3 minutes.

In Part 1:

- the examiner asks you some simple questions about yourself
- you don't speak to the other candidate
- you will be asked to spell a word such as your name or country
- questions may be about your life at present, things you've done in the past or your plans for the future
- you may also be asked about your interests, your likes and dislikes, your opinions, etc.

Part 1 tests your ability to:

- hold a simple conversation about everyday subjects
- give basic personal information.

How to do Part 1

1 When you meet the examiners and the other candidate, be friendly and polite.

2 Listen carefully to the examiner when he or she asks you questions.

3 If you don't understand something, politely ask the examiner to repeat it.

4 Say more than just *yes* or *no* in your answers.

5 Speak clearly and loudly enough for the examiners and the other candidate to hear you.

6 Use a range of grammatical structures, including verb tenses.

7 Try to use as wide a range of vocabulary as you can.

8 Remember that one of the aims of Part 1 is to help you relax by getting you to talk about a familiar topic: yourself!

Exercise 1

Read suggestions a–g and this transcript from a candidate during Speaking Part 1. Match the candidate's (Emilio's) answers 1–7 with a–g.

a use future forms of verbs

b use past tense forms of verbs

c give one or more examples

d give more information by adding detail

e give one or more reasons

f add more answers to a question

g ask the examiner to say the question again

Examiner:	Now, what's your name?
Emilio:	My name's Emilio.
Examiner:	Thank you. And what's your surname?
Emilio:	Sánchez.
Examiner:	How do you spell it?
Emilio:	S-A-N-C-H-E-Z.
Examiner:	Thank you. Now, where do you live?
Emilio:	In Santiago. (1) ......*d*...... In a district called 'Independéncia', which is quite near ~~of~~ *to* the city centre.
Examiner:	And do you work or are you a student in Santiago?
Emilio:	I'm a student. I'm in my five year at secondary school.
Examiner:	And what subjects do you study?
Emilio:	Er … (2) .... could you repeat the question, please?
Examiner:	What subjects do you study?
Emilio:	Oh, um … maths, science, history, geography … things like that. (3) .... And English, of course. I do that at the school, and I have lessons at home, too, with a teacher that comes to my house.
Examiner:	Do you enjoy studying English, Emilio?

Emilio: Yes, I like learning it a lot (4) .... because so many of the Internet is in English, and also because most of the music I enjoy is too.

Examiner: Do you think that English will be useful for you in the future?

Emilio: Yes, definitely. (5) .... For instance, I'd really like to travel round Europe and North America, and for that (6) .... I'll need to know English. Except in countries as Spain and Mexico, of course, where I'll be able to speak in Spanish.

Examiner: OK, Emilio. What did you do last weekend?

Emilio: Last weekend … Oh yes, (7) .... I was at the sports centre on Saturday. We were playing basketball against one of the best teams in Santiago, and in the end we beat them. We never did that before!

Examiner: Thank you.

Exercise 2

Emilio makes six mistakes when he is speaking. Can you find and correct them?

Exercise 3

(26) Listen to the dialogue and decide whether these statements are true or false.

1 He sounds confident and relaxed.   *True*

2 He speaks loudly and clearly enough.

3 He sometimes speaks too much.

4 He is polite when he speaks to the examiner.

5 His mistakes sometimes make it difficult to understand him.

6 He probably got a good mark in Part 1 of the Speaking paper.

Exercise 4

Study the expressions below. Which would you use to:

● add more information?

● ask someone to repeat something?

● give examples?

> *for instance   as well as that   sorry, I didn't catch that*
> *could you say that again, please?   like   for example*
> *also   could you repeat that, please?   and sometimes*
> *such as*

Exercise 5

(27) Listen to this extract from Part 1 with another candidate, Isabel. Which of the expressions does she use?

Part 2

You have practised Part 2 in Units 3, 7 and 9. It lasts 2–3 minutes.

In Part 2:

● the examiner describes a situation and asks you and the other candidate to talk about it together

● there is a large page with pictures on it to help you with some ideas

● the examiner repeats the instructions

● you speak to the other candidate, not the examiner

● you give your own opinions about an imaginary situation – it isn't a role play

● you keep talking together until the examiner tells you to stop.

Part 2 tests your ability to:

● discuss a situation, taking turns with the other person

● do things such as *make suggestions, agree* or *disagree*, and *give reasons*.

How to do Part 2

1 Listen carefully to the instructions both times the examiner gives them. You can ask to hear them again if anything is not clear.

2 Look quickly at the pictures, and then say something like: *Shall I start, or will you?* or *Would you like to start, or shall I?*

3 Start talking about one of the pictures. You might want to give your opinion or make a suggestion, and then ask what your partner thinks, and why.

4 Talk briefly about each picture in turn, replying to what your partner says and giving reasons for your own suggestions, opinions and preferences. You can choose to agree or disagree (politely) with what he or she says.

5 Move the conversation along quite quickly, for example by saying: *What do you think of this one?* or *Shall we go on to the next one?*

6 Bring the discussion towards a conclusion by saying, for instance: *So which shall we choose, then?* or *Which do you think would be best?*

7 Try to reach a decision by suggesting one of the options, e.g. *Shall we go for that one?* or *I'm in favour of doing that.*

8 If you both decide on one of them, end by saying something like *OK, we agree; That's the one we'll choose* or *Right, let's go for that one, then.* But it doesn't matter if you don't: you can agree to disagree! *OK, we've both got our own ideas – let's leave it at that, then* or *Shall we agree to disagree, then?*

Exercise 1

Study the Part 2 instructions and pictures below, and answer these questions.

1 What do you have to imagine?

2 What two things do you have to do with your partner?

3 How many objects are in the picture? What is each one called?

> **Examiner:** I'm going to describe a situation to you. A school friend of yours is going to live in another country. Talk together about the different things the class could buy him or her as a leaving present and decide which one would be best. Here is a picture with some ideas to help you. All right? Talk together.

Exercise 2

🎧 28 Listen to Stella and Lee doing Speaking Part 2 and answer questions 1–6.

1 Do they ask the examiner to repeat anything?   *No*

2 Do they take turns properly?

3 Do they listen and reply to what each other says?

4 Do they discuss all the pictures?

5 Do they agree to choose one of the objects? If so, which?

6 Which candidate do you think got a better mark? Why?

Exercise 3

🎧 28 Listen again and look at the expressions below. Tick (✓) the ones that Stella and Lee use (they may not use exactly the same words).

Making suggestions

How about …?

What do you think of …?

Why don't we …?

Perhaps we should …?

So shall we … , then?

Agreeing with suggestions

Right.

Yes, that's true.

I think so, too.

Yes, I (completely) agree with you.

That's a (very) good idea.

Disagreeing politely with suggestions

I think it might be better to …

I think I'd rather …

I'm not so keen on …

I'm not really sure about that.

You may be right, but …

Giving reasons

… because …

For one thing …

For another …

The thing is …

I think the problem is that …

Part 3

You have practised Part 3 in Units 4, 5, 10 and 12. It lasts 3 minutes.

In Part 3:

- the examiner introduces the topic (e.g. *people at work*) and asks both candidates to talk in turn about a colour photograph for about one minute

- each candidate has a different photograph to talk about

- the photograph shows everyday situations, e.g. people at work, at home, on holiday, etc.

- the examiner stops candidates after a minute

- candidates are not asked to comment on their partner's photograph.

Part 3 tests your ability to:

- describe everyday situations using a range of vocabulary and structures
- organise your language in a long turn.

How to do Part 3

1   Listen carefully to the examiner's instructions as the examiner will tell you the topic of both photos, e.g. *people at work* or *teenagers at home*.

2   It is a good idea to imagine you are describing the photograph to someone who can't see it.

3   Talk about everything you can see in the photograph – the people, what they are doing, what they are wearing, their age, etc. Also talk about any other objects you can see, including their colour, size, etc.

4   Try to use a range of vocabulary and structures.

5   If you don't know the word for an object, use one of the *describing* expressions, e.g. *It's a thing for …*

6   Avoid pointing at objects – use *next to*, *behind*, etc. instead.

7   Speak for a minute – the examiner will say *Thank you* when it's time to stop.

8   When it's the other candidate's turn to talk about their photograph, listen but don't say anything.

Exercise 1

Read the example Speaking Part 3 task below and look at the photographs. Answer the question that follows.

Now, I'd like each of you to talk on your own about something. I'm going to give each of you a photograph of people **enjoying their free time**.

Photo A

Photo B

Please tell us what you can see in your photograph.

Look at the two photographs. Which of these things could you talk about for Photo A and Photo B? Put a tick (✓) in the *You* columns.

		You		Sofia	Tania
	Photo:	A	B	A	B
the place		✓	✓	✓	✓
the weather					
the time of day (morning, afternoon, etc.)					
the colours					
the food					
the transport					
the clothes					
the activities					

Exercise 2

🎧(29) Listen to Sofia and Tania doing the Speaking Part 3 task. Tick (✓) the things they talk about in the correct column in the table on page 145.

Exercise 3

🎧(29) Listen to Sofia and Tania again and decide if the following sentences are correct or incorrect for each one. Tick (✓) the box **if you think the sentence is correct**.

		Sofia	Tania
1	She describes things she can see in the photograph.	☐	☐
2	She uses a wide range of vocabulary and structures.	☐	☐
3	She uses expressions like *It's made of ...* .	☐	☐
4	She describes the location of objects.	☐	☐
5	She speaks for about a minute.	☐	☐
6	She probably got a good mark in this part.	☐	☐

Ways of talking about the photographs

In this photo I/we can see ...

It looks like + noun / It looks + adjective

I think it ... / I don't think it ...

It could/might be ...

There seems/appears to be ...

Ways of talking about an object you don't know the word for

It's a kind of ...

It's something like a ...

It's made of metal/plastic/wood, etc.

It's used for ...-ing

Ways of describing location

in   on the left (right)   between   opposite   on

inside   next to   behind   in front of   over

Part 4

You have practised Part 4 in Units 2, 5, 6 and 11. It lasts 3 minutes.

In Part 4:

- the examiner asks you to talk together with your partner about something connected to the photographs in Part 3
- the examiner will introduce the topic for discussion. You will usually need to consider two parts, e.g. *places you would like to visit* **and** *activities you would do there* or *activities you like to do* *on your own* **and** *activities you like to do* *with other people*
- you have a conversation with your partner, not the examiner
- you need to take turns to speak by asking and answering each other's questions
- you keep talking together until the examiner tells you to stop.

Part 4 tests your ability to:

- talk about your own experiences, opinions, likes and dislikes, etc. with another person on a topic
- take turns with the other person by asking them about their experiences, opinions, likes and dislikes, etc.

How to do Part 4

1 The examiner will ask you to have a general conversation with your partner about a topic which is connected to the photographs you both described in Part 3.

2 In this general conversation, you will need to talk about your own likes and dislikes, experiences and opinions and ask your partner about theirs.

3 Listen carefully to the examiner's instructions. You can ask the examiner to repeat them again if you do not understand, e.g. *Sorry, can you say that again, please?*

4 You will usually need to consider two parts in your discussion, e.g. *I'd like you to talk together about the types of television programmes you like to watch* **and** *when you like to watch them* or *the activities you like to do with your family* **and** *the activities you like to do with your friends*.

5 Turn your chair to face your partner.

6 Begin the conversation by talking about one part of the question but remember to invite your partner to join in, e.g. *What do you think?*

7 Listen carefully to what your partner says and reply in a suitable way, e.g. *I'm not so sure, I ...*

8 If you can't think of anything more to say, the examiner will ask you a further question.

9 After three minutes, the examiner will stop you by saying: *Thank you. That's the end of the test.*

Exercise 1

Read the Part 4 instructions below and underline the two parts you will need to consider in your discussion.

> **Examiner:** Your photos showed people enjoying their free time. Now I'd like you to talk together about the things you enjoy doing in your free time and the things you would like to try in the future.

Exercise 2

Make a list of some of the things you could talk about in the *You* row below.

Free-time activities

	now	in the future
You	Sports like basketball/ hockey	I'd like to try volleyball/skiing because ...
Agnes		
Marcos		

Exercise 3

(30) Listen to Agnes and Marcos doing Part 4. Make some notes on what they talk about in the table above.

Exercise 4

(30) Listen again and decide if the following sentences are correct or incorrect. Tick (✓) the box **if you think the sentence is correct**.

1 They talked about their experiences, opinions, likes and dislikes, etc. ☐

2 They asked each other questions and gave each other plenty of time to speak. ☐

3 They showed they were interested in what their partner said. ☐

4 They talked about both parts of the task. ☐

5 They didn't change the topic completely. ☐

6 They got a good mark in this part of the test ☐

Questions for taking turns	Showing you are listening and interested
What about ...?	*I'm not so sure.*
What do you think?	*Maybe.*
Don't you think so?	*Yes and no.*
Do you think ...?	*Really!*
Do you like ...?	*Good point!*
Have you got ...?	*I agree/disagree.*

PAPER 1: READING Part 1

Reading

Part 1

Questions 1-5

Look at the text in each question.
What does it say?
Mark the correct letter **A**, **B** or **C** on your answer sheet.

Example:

0

NO BICYCLES AGAINST GLASS PLEASE

A Do not leave your bicycle touching the window.

B Broken glass may damage your bicycle tyres.

C Your bicycle may not be safe here.

Answer: | 0 | A — | B ▭ | C ▭ |

1

FOR FREE PARKING
CUSTOMERS SHOULD
PICK UP AN EXIT
TICKET FROM INSIDE
THE SUPERMARKET

A Supermarket customers are not charged for parking but need to collect a special ticket.

B Supermarket customers should show their receipt at the exit to the car park.

C Supermarket customers have to pay for the car park inside the supermarket.

2

Graham,

Ring Otleys Books – the dictionary you ordered is no longer published. They recommended another one (£5 extra) – they could get a copy for tomorrow.

Marina

A Graham has to wait an extra day for the dictionary he ordered from Otleys.

B If Graham wants a dictionary from Otleys, it'll cost more than he expected.

C The dictionary Graham needs is unavailable at Otleys, so they recommend trying another shop.

3

From:	Li
To:	Chung

Thanks for lending me that surfing DVD – I'm glad you got it back OK. You can borrow my baseball one and return it on Sunday if you want.

A Li is offering to lend Chung a DVD.

B Li wants to return one of Chung's DVDs to him.

C Li is asking Chung to give back a DVD he has borrowed.

4

REDBRIDGE COLLEGE GENERAL OFFICE

Parcels cannot be collected here without a college identity card

A The college office will give you a card when you collect your parcels.

B When posting a parcel, take your college card with you to the office.

C The office will only give you your parcel if you prove who you are.

5

SPORTS CENTRE

Please report lost property immediately to any member of staff

A Ask a member of staff to show you the lost property list.

B Tell the staff what you have lost without delay.

C The staff will fill in a lost property report immediately.

Part 2

Questions 6-10

The people below all want to buy a book for the young person shown in each picture.
On the opposite page there are descriptions of eight books.
Decide which book would be the most suitable for the following people to buy.
For questions 6-10, mark the correct letter (A-H) on your answer sheet.

---

6  Gina wants a book for her nephew who is interested in nature. He's always asking questions about the world around him and Gina thinks he's ready to start learning a few simple facts.

7  Bruno is looking for a book his daughter will enjoy reading and which will also help with a project she is doing at school. She has to describe an important event from the past.

8  Edita's son loves animals and she would like to buy him a book with beautiful pictures and a strong message about the need to respect the environment.

9  Tony wants to buy a novel for his teenage sister. She likes stories that are true to life and that show people in difficult situations.

10  Lydia is looking for a book about animals for her granddaughter, who cannot read yet. She wants a book with several stories in it, and some attractive pictures.

BOOKS FOR CHILDREN

A I Wonder Why

The wonders of science come alive for children in this delightful book. As well as enjoying the lovely pictures, they will also learn about how plants grow, see how different birds care for their young and discover some interesting information about insects.

B Basic Technology

A love of knowledge begins early with this colourful reference book. Find out interesting facts and learn about important inventions in the last century. If you know a child who asks questions like 'What makes a car go?', then this is the book for you.

C Painting History

This is a beautiful book showing famous paintings through history. Each painting is described in detail, including simple facts about the people shown in them and their lives. Children are invited to look more closely at the pictures and to try some of the techniques themselves.

D The Hunter

In this exciting story, wonderfully illustrated by a famous wildlife artist, Jamina finds a baby elephant whose mother was killed by hunters. Looking for help, she travels back through the African bush and is able to enjoy the nature all around her. Her journey teaches her the importance of doing all we can to save and protect our world.

E Forest Tales

This book is a collection of seven well-known animal stories from different cultures around the world. They are particularly suitable for reading aloud and would make good bedtime stories. Each story is about six pages long with bright and colourful pictures on every page.

F Journey to the Past

Lying ill in bed, Lucien knows he is not like other boys. In this imaginative story he finds out just how different he is. He discovers that he has the power to transport his mind through space and time. This amazing novel will appeal to those who read to escape from the real world.

G Time Travellers

This very interesting set of stories shows what life was really like for people at certain points in history – the building of the Eiffel Tower, the sinking of the *Titanic*, the first moon landing. Written as diaries, these stories are historically accurate.

H Joanna's Search

Joanna was brought up by her aunt and uncle and has never known her parents. At 14, she decides to try and find the answers to the questions that she has always asked herself – 'Who am I?', 'Where do I come from?' The novel tells the moving yet funny story of Joanna's search for her identity.

PAPER 1: READING Part 3

Part 3

Questions 11-20

Look at the sentences below about two people who have visited Antarctica.
Read the text on the opposite page to decide if each sentence is correct or incorrect.
If it is correct, mark **A** on your answer sheet.
If it is not correct, mark **B** on your answer sheet.

---

11   Sara Wheeler went to Antarctica to do some scientific research.

12   Sara Wheeler was surprised by how few artists have travelled to Antarctica.

13   Philip Hughes was one of many artists to have paintings on display at the 'Antarctica' exhibition.

14   By 1975, Hughes realised that he needed to find other locations for his work.

15   Sara Wheeler particularly liked the fact that Antarctica is so different from other places on earth.

16   One of Hughes's paintings brought back happy memories of Antarctica for Sara Wheeler.

17   Hughes had to wear gloves whenever he drew a picture outdoors in Antarctica.

18   Hughes completed the painting *Christmas Day at Rothera* outdoors.

19   Hughes found it challenging to paint mainly in white.

20   Hughes missed having his mobile phone in Antarctica.

Antarctica

Journalist Sara Wheeler writes about her meeting with the artist Philip Hughes and the discussion they had about their experiences in Antarctica.

Antarctica has had a powerful effect on both explorers and scientists. In 1994 I discovered why, when I spent seven months there collecting material for a travel book. I have often thought the amazing emptiness of this region would attract the interest of many landscape painters and yet, throughout history, only a small number have actually been there.

In 2003, one of them, the 67-year-old painter Philip Hughes, opened a one-man show in London called simply 'Antarctica'. Until 1975, Hughes's paintings were mostly of the South Downs in England, but at this point, Hughes decided he wanted to paint more distant lands. First, he travelled to South America. Then in 2001, he spent five weeks in Antarctica, dividing his time between Rothera, a British research centre on Adelaide Island, and a science camp up on the West Antarctic ice sheet.

Antarctica simply isn't like anywhere else on this planet and for me this was the best thing about my visit. It is one-and-a-half times bigger than the United States but it is very peaceful. It also never gets dark. When I went to Hughes's show, we looked at his paintings together. He explained, 'I was just amazed by the beauty of Antarctica. It didn't matter that our nearest neighbours were 800 kilometres away.'

The temperatures can be extreme. At my camp they reached –115°C and at times I felt terrible. But back in England, looking at Hughes's painting *Leonie Island at Midnight*, I remembered what Antarctica was like when a storm ended. It was as if the world was new. Then I wondered why I came back. Hughes was there in summer, and the temperatures were around zero. He could draw in these conditions but if it got colder, he needed to wear gloves. The picture *Christmas Day at Rothera* was drawn on paper while Hughes sat on the ice. He didn't put paint on it until later when he went inside, a common technique with Hughes. Although there are colours in Antarctica, most of the continent is white. 'The technical difficulty involved in painting there,' explained Hughes, 'was working in white. When I used even a little blue and green, I had to work very carefully.'

I asked Hughes why he went to Antarctica. 'Today, people are controlled by things like mobile phones and email. I had to get away from this. You only become aware of the absence, say, of planes overhead, when there aren't any. When it's only you and the natural world, you completely understand its power.'

PAPER 1: READING Part 4

Part 4

Questions 21-25

Read the text and questions below.
For each question, mark the correct letter **A**, **B**, **C** or **D** on your answer sheet.

Indian films
Actor Amitabh Bachchan talks about his experiences

I have spent over 30 years in the Indian film industry and have worked with almost three generations of directors and actors. There was a time when life in the movies was very different. It was slower and everything seemed simpler. Now, there are so many things to be dealt with: the light needs to be right, the equipment needs to be returned, the actors have to be somewhere else. There also used to be a sense of magic about the movie industry and the stars were special. Now they are just one of a crowd.

However, in my experience, the new generation of film-makers take their work seriously and they are all very confident. Sometimes, when a young director is talking to me about a scene, I can see technical difficulties. For example, in the film *Aks* we needed wild dogs for a particular scene and I asked Rakesh Mehra how we would do that. He said it was not a problem. He found an address on the internet and we shot the scene in Romania. More often, Rakesh is anxious about getting the actors' dates right or sorting out the financial side.

Most of today's young directors have trained in the United States. They have learnt how to plan their productions in great detail and they are extremely well prepared. Before filming starts, they have already made decisions about the costumes, make-up, camera angles and so on. For an actor it means there's someone taking care of everything. It makes the filming go smoothly. I have little doubt that the future of our film industry is in very good hands.

21   What is Amitabh Bachchan trying to do in this text?

    A   suggest how Indian actors could improve their technique

    B   compare Indian films with those made in the USA

    C   encourage people to watch more Indian films

    D   describe changes in the Indian film industry

22   What does Amitabh Bachchan say about the Indian film industry today?

    A   Every stage of filming takes a long time.

    B   The film stars are famous around the world.

    C   The people involved in filming have a lot to do.

    D   It is difficult for young actors to start their careers.

23   What happened when Amitabh Bachchan and Rakesh Mehra worked together on *Aks*?

    A   They disliked working with one another.

    B   They argued about the best actor to use.

    C   They disagreed about acceptable levels of cost.

    D   They worried about different things in making the film.

24   What is Amitabh Bachchan's opinion of young directors?

    A   They have a professional attitude towards their work.

    B   They are careful not to annoy any of the actors.

    C   They like to discuss their decisions with others.

    D   They make sure that everyone is well trained.

25   How would Amitabh Bachchan describe the Indian film industry?

    A

> The films we made when I was younger were so much better – more money is available today but the acting is worse.

    B

> Indian film-makers know what they are doing – the industry is growing in strength and I think it will continue to do so.

    C

> Our new generation of film-makers depends too much on technology – they don't realise what makes a really good film.

    D

> There are some great young actors today – they have to film scenes unprepared and this makes them very special.

PAPER 1: READING Part 5

Part 5

Questions 26-35

Read the text below and choose the correct word for each space.
For each question, mark the correct letter **A**, **B**, **C** or **D** on your answer sheet.

Example:

0	**A** can	**B** should	**C** need	**D** would

Answer:

0	**A**	**B**	**C**	**D**
	—	=	=	=

Inventions

Great inventions are ideas that **(0)** .... sometimes change the world. The invention of

the radio has brought **(26)** .... places closer together, and the car has made it possible

to **(27)** .... a long way. An invention might also be a better way of doing something

– **(28)** .... example, a tool to make a job easier or a new farming method. Many

inventions, like musical instruments or sports equipment, have made life more comfortable or

enjoyable. The range of inventions is enormous.

Not **(29)** .... good idea leads to immediate **(30)** .... , however.

(31) .... the 15th century, Leonardo da Vinci wrote down his idea for chains

(32) .... were able to drive machines – but the technology to **(33)** ....

these chains did not **(34)** .... then. This shows that a great invention may be

unworkable **(35)** .... a future development makes it possible.

26	**A** far	**B** absent	**C** other	**D** distant
27	**A** reach	**B** travel	**C** transport	**D** arrive
28	**A** to	**B** with	**C** for	**D** of
29	**A** every	**B** any	**C** all	**D** each
30	**A** prize	**B** success	**C** win	**D** victory
31	**A** Between	**B** At	**C** During	**D** Since
32	**A** what	**B** who	**C** which	**D** where
33	**A** produce	**B** set	**C** record	**D** put
34	**A** last	**B** exist	**C** happen	**D** continue
35	**A** if	**B** while	**C** until	**D** when

PAPER 1: WRITING Part 1

Writing

Part 1

Questions 1–5

Here are some sentences about a football match.
For each question, complete the second sentence so that it means the same as the first.
Use no more than three words.
Write only the missing words on your answer sheet.
You may use this page for any rough work.

Example:

0   A lot of people went to the football match.

There were a lot of people .... **football match.**

Answer: | **0** | *at the* |

---

1   It was the most exciting football match I had ever been to.

I'd never been to .... **exciting football match before.**

2   I had to sit at the back, but I didn't mind that.

I didn't mind .... **sit at the back.**

3   Three players were given yellow cards by the referee.

The referee .... **yellow cards to three players.**

4   The home team didn't play as well as the visitors.

The visitors played .... **the home team.**

5   Their captain scored the winning goal just before the match ended.

Their captain scored the winning goal just before the .... **the match.**

Part 2

Question 6

You have moved to a new home and are writing to tell your friend about it.

Write a card to your English friend. In your card, you should

- explain why you have moved

- say what you like about your new home

- invite your English friend to visit you.

Write **35–45 words** on your answer sheet.

Part 3

Write an answer to **one** of the questions (**7** or **8**) in this part.
Write your answer in about **100 words** on your answer sheet.
Mark the question number in the box at the top of your answer sheet.

Question 7

- This is part of a letter you receive from an English friend.

> Yesterday I visited an exhibition about the future of my town. What do you think your town will be like in 20 years' time? Do you think you'll always live there?

- Now write a letter, answering your friend's questions.

- Write your **letter** on your answer sheet.

Question 8

- Your English teacher has asked you to write a story.

- This is the title for your story:

The best decision I've ever made

- Write your **story** on your answer sheet.

PAPER 2: LISTENING Part 1

 Part 1

Questions 1–7

There are seven questions in this part.
For each question there are three pictures and a short recording.
Choose the correct picture and put a tick (✓) in the box below it.

Example: Where is the girl's hat?

A ✓   B ☐   C ☐

---

1 Which band will the girl watch?

A ☐   B ☐   C ☐

2 Where does the boy feel pain now?

A ☐   B ☐   C ☐

3   Where is the computer now?

A ☐   B ☐   C ☐

4   How does the woman recommend travelling around the island?

A ☐   B ☐   C ☐

5   What do both girls decide to wear to the disco?

A ☐   B ☐   C ☐

6 Who gave the man the CD for his birthday?

A ☐ B ☐ C ☐

7 What is the man going to order?

A ☐ B ☐ C ☐

(32)   **Part 2**

Questions 8-13

You will hear the pilot Kate Gingford talking about the last few days of her flight around the world in a small aeroplane.

For each question, put a tick (✓) in the correct box.

---

8   In Norway, Kate's friends helped her

    A plan the route on the map. ☐

    B cook a meal before her flight. ☐

    C put on the clothes she would fly in. ☐

9   During the flight to Denmark, Kate

    A felt very tired. ☐

    B spoke to her son. ☐

    C enjoyed views of the sea. ☐

10   On Monday, Kate was worried because

    A she had to land unexpectedly. ☐

    B the plane was difficult to fly. ☐

    C a wheel was not working properly. ☐

11   While staying at her friends' farm, Kate

    A enjoyed hearing the birds sing. ☐

    B got annoyed about losing flying time. ☐

    C made sure she got some extra sleep. ☐

12   Kate had to arrive at the flying club in England

    A during the afternoon. ☐

    B while the weather was good. ☐

    C before it got dark. ☐

13   How did Kate feel when she arrived in London?

    A pleased she had done the trip ☐

    B keen to make another long trip ☐

    C nervous about seeing her family again ☐

PAPER 2: LISTENING Part 3

 Part 3

Questions 14–19

You will hear a recorded message about a tourist attraction called The Grand Palace.
For each question, fill in the missing information in the numbered space.

The Grand Palace

The Palace is now open again.

Repairs to the (14) .... are finished.

There is a display of (15) .... in the entrance hall to explain

the work.

In the music room, you can see the Queen's (16) ....

Light snacks are available in the tea-room or the (17) ....

The Palace is open 10:00 – 18:00 from June to (18) ....

A family ticket costs (19) ....

(34) **Part 4**

Questions 20-25

Look at the six sentences for this part.
You will hear a conversation between a boy, Tom, and a girl, Jemma, who are studying in different parts of the country.
Decide if each sentence is correct or incorrect.
If it is correct, put a tick (✓) in the box under **A** for **YES**. If it is not correct, put a tick (✓) in the box under **B** for **NO**.

		A YES	B NO
20	Tom and Jemma had arranged to meet each other.	☐	☐
21	The films at Kingsford cinema are usually rather out of date.	☐	☐
22	Tom is surprised that Jemma spends so much on entertainment.	☐	☐
23	Jemma did a free course to get a qualification.	☐	☐
24	Tom thinks Jemma will find working at a swimming pool boring.	☐	☐
25	Tom is sure Jemma will get a job at the holiday camp.	☐	☐

PAPER 3: SPEAKING Part 1

Phase 1

Interlocutor

A/B Good morning / afternoon / evening.
Can I have your mark sheets, please?

(Hand over the mark sheets to the Assessor.)

A/B I'm .... and this is ....
He / She is just going to listen to us.

A Now, what's your name?
Thank you.

B And what's your name?
Thank you.

Back-up prompts

B Candidate B, what's your surname? How do you spell it? Thank you. **A** And, Candidate A, what's your surname? How do you spell it? Thank you.	How do you write your family / second name? How do you write your family / second name?
(Ask the following questions. Use candidates' names throughout. Ask Candidate A first.) Where do you live / come from? ***Adult students*** Do you work or are you a student in ...? What do you do / study? ***School-age students*** Do you study English at school? Do you like it? Thank you. *(Repeat for Candidate B.)*	Do you live in ...? Have you got a job? What job do you do? / What subject(s) do you study? Do you have English lessons?

Phase 2

Interlocutor

(Select one or more questions from the list to ask each candidate. Use candidates' names throughout. Ask Candidate B first.)

Back-up prompts

Do you enjoy studying English?

Do you like studying English?

Do you think that English will be useful for you in the future?

Will you use English in the future?

What did you do yesterday evening / last weekend?

Did you do anything yesterday evening / last weekend? What?

What do you enjoy doing in your free time?

What do you like to do in your free time?

Thank you.

(Introduction to Part 2)

In the next part, you are going to talk to each other.

PAPER 3: SPEAKING Part 2

Visiting new city	Part 2
	2–3 minutes

Interlocutor

Say to both candidates:

> I'm going to describe a situation to you.
>
> A city wants to give better **information** to **tourists** who want to come and visit. Talk together about the different ways the city can **give** information and say which would be **best** for tourists.
>
> Here is a picture with some ideas to help you.

*Place **Part 2 booklet**, open at **Task 1**, in front of candidates.*

Pause

> I'll say that again.
>
> A city wants to give better **information** to **tourists** who want to come and visit. Talk together about the different ways the city can **give** information and say which would be **best** for tourists.

> All right? Talk together.

Allow the candidates enough time to complete the task without intervention.

Prompt only if necessary.

> Thank you. (Can I have the booklet please?)

Retrieve Part 2 booklet.

⏱ *About 2–3 minutes (including time to assimilate the information)*

PAPER 3: SPEAKING Part 3

Special occasions

Interlocutor

Say to both candidates:

> Now, I'd like each of you to talk on your own about something. I'm going to give each of you a photograph of a **special occasion**.
>
> Candidate A, here is your photograph. *(Place **Part 3 booklet**, open at **Task 1A**, in front of Candidate A.)* Please show it to Candidate B, but I'd like you to talk about it. Candidate B, you just listen. I'll give you your photograph in a moment.
>
> Candidate A, please tell us what you can see in your photograph.

(Candidate A)

Approximately one minute

If there is a need to intervene, prompts rather than direct questions should be used.

> Thank you. (Can I have the booklet please?)

Retrieve Part 3 booklet from Candidate A.

Interlocutor

> Now, Candidate B, here is your photograph. It also shows a **special occasion**. *(Place **Part 3 booklet**, open at **Task 1B**, in front of Candidate B.)* Please show it to Candidate A and tell us what you can see in the photograph.

(Candidate B)

Approximately one minute

> Thank you. (Can I have the booklet please?)

Retrieve Part 3 booklet from Candidate B.

PAPER 3: SPEAKING Part 4

Interlocutor

Say to both candidates:

> Your photographs showed special occasions. Now, I'd like you to talk together about special occasions you have enjoyed and say what you did to celebrate them.

Allow the candidates enough time to complete the task without intervention. Prompt only if necessary.

> Thank you. That's the end of the test.

⏱ *Parts 3 & 4 should take about 6 minutes together.*

Back-up prompts

1. Talk about special occasions **you've** enjoyed.
2. Talk about what you **do** on special occasions.
3. Talk about a **wedding / birthday party** you've been to.
4. Talk about the **clothes you wear / food / music** on special occasions.

Extra material

Student A activities
Unit 6
Grammar

Exercise 3

Page 56

Student A

The Disc Jockey (DJ)

DJ Jupiter played the guitar in a local band while at secondary school. He was often asked to choose the music at his friends' parties because he had a large collection of music. He began studying computing at uni but he became more and more interested in using software to mix music. In 2001, he began to work in local night-clubs and he has been a successful disc jockey since then. Last year, *DJ Today* named him 'DJ of the year'.

Unit 8
Speaking Part 1

Exercise 5

Page 75

Student A

1 received
2 centre (US center)
3 and
4 beautiful
5 colour
6 comfortable
7 then

Unit 12
Vocabulary

Exercise 1

Page 112

1 Where are Todd's keys?

2 Where's the sports shop?

3 Where's Elen, Imogen's cousin?

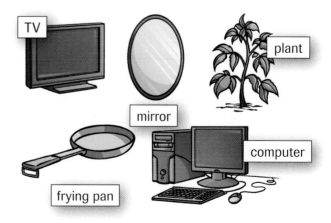

Unit 5
Starting off

Page 44

Key to quiz: How emotional are you?

1 a 2 b 0 c 1   2 a 1 b 0 c 2   3 a 1 b 2 c 0
4 a 2 b 1 c 0   5 a 0 b 1 c 2

8 or over: You have strong emotions and people always know how you're feeling. That can often be a good thing, but sometimes there's a danger of hurting others. A little more self-control might be good for you – and those around you!

4–7: You're not an extreme person. You're quite well-balanced: sometimes you show your feelings, but at other times you control them very well. It's important, though, to know when to show your emotions – and when not to!

3 or under: You're probably not a cold person, but perhaps you're controlling your emotions a little too much. Everybody needs to relax and express their feelings sometimes: it makes us feel better – and it may also do us good!

Unit 12
Vocabulary

Exercise 4

Page 112

Student A

Draw these objects on the plan on page 112.

TV
plant
mirror
computer
frying pan

Unit 8

Starting off

Page 70

Key to quiz: All in the family!

1 A Cinderella   2 A Maradona   3 C Rafa Nadal
4 A Brad Pitt & Angelina Jolie   5 B Bart Simpson's grandfather

Unit 9

Starting off

Page 80

Key to quiz: How fit and active are you?

1 A 1 B 2 C 0   2 A 1 B 0 C 2   3 A 0 B 1 C 2
4 A 2 B 1 C 0   5 A 2 B 0 C 1   6 A 1 B 2 C 0
7 A 0 B 2 C 1   8 A 0 B 1 C 2

0–5   You're not keen on exercise, are you? By not getting a minimum 30 minutes of activity a day you're missing the chance of having a better body and a great way to feel less stressed, sleep better and get more energy. As it's all new to you, start with a little at first. Remember you can do parts of your half hour at different times, so why not walk to work, clean the house, go for a swim – anything that stops you sitting on the sofa, really. You don't have to run 40 kilometres to improve your fitness.

6–11   You could be fitter. You're quite relaxed and, while taking it easy can be a good idea, it shouldn't take too much extra effort to do the recommended 30 minutes a day, five times a week. You enjoy spending time with your friends, so why not take up an activity together? It can be anything – from a street dance class to basketball. Or if you don't fancy organised classes, get together in the park for a game of football, or go out dancing instead of sitting around doing nothing.

12 or more   Well done! You're fit and active. Half an hour of activity a day is a minimum for you. While keeping active now means you look and feel great, you can also look forward to a healthy future. You shouldn't have to worry if you stay active. As you enjoy being fit, make sure you do all the activities you can: from hill walks and dancing to rock climbing and swimming. That way you'll never get bored with keeping active.

Student B activities

Unit 6

Grammar

Exercise 3

Page 56

Student B

The kickboxer

Both Lewis Young's parents were professional boxers. He began boxing when he was five. When he was eight he became interested in martial arts and when he was fourteen, he got his black belt. He began to fight professionally when he was eighteen. From the beginning he has been called a colourful fighter. He has won several important world competitions. He has just begun to write his first book on kickboxing.

Unit 8

Speaking Part 1

Exercise 5

Page 75

Student B

1 interesting   4 recommend   6 favourite
2 together   5 believe   7 thought
3 restaurant

Unit 12

Vocabulary

Exercise 4

Page 112

Student B

Draw these objects on the plan on page 112.

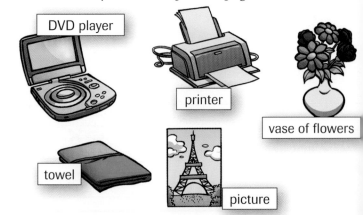

DVD player

printer

vase of flowers

towel

picture

Answer key

Note: You can use short forms to answer the questions, e.g. 'I am working' → 'I'm working', 'she has done' → 'she's done', etc.

1 Homes and habits

Starting off

❷ B

Recording script   CD1 Track 2

Julia: Hi. My name's Julia Davies and this is my room. I spend most of my evenings there and part of the weekend, though I'm out quite a lot then. It's not a particularly big room, but I've got all my favourite things there. There's my computer, which I use mainly for emailing, online chat and looking around on the Internet, and my mobile – I *love* texting people! I do my homework there too, as you can see from the pile of text books. They should really be on the bookshelf, but there just isn't any space there. I read a lot, actually – that's why there are so many books and magazines. Also I play the guitar a bit, and though I'm not very good yet my mum says I'm starting to get better! Then there's the DVD player. I don't often use that, but when I have someone round, we sometimes watch a film or two.

❸ 2 e 3 a 4 f 5 d 6 b

Listening Part 4

❷ *Suggested answers:*

1 doesn't shut late, lots of places stay open late
2 cost a lot of money, charge low prices
3 sometimes doesn't feel safe, is always very safe
4 get out of bed before, stay in bed longer
5 a sensible thing to do, not very clever

Recording script   CD1 Track 3

Lucas: When you're travelling abroad, Zoe, do you find that people do things at different times of the day?

Zoe: Well, I guess the first thing you notice is how early people have dinner here in the UK, maybe at 6 o'clock. And often in the USA and Canada, too. But in Spain or South America, for instance, they don't usually have their main meal until late in the evening, and they often go out after that. By then, in a town like this, everything's closing, isn't it?

Lucas: Well, I don't think that's *always* true. Some places stay open very late these days, particularly in the town centre.

Zoe: But how do you get home here? The buses and trains all stop running around eleven-thirty.

Lucas: There are usually taxis around after that. There always seem to be people getting into them, or waiting for them.

Zoe: Well, even if you can get one, they cost far too much, in my opinion anyway.

Lucas: You're right about that. That's why I never take them. But I suppose you could walk home.

Zoe: All the way from the town centre? You must be joking! And that's another thing. At night in places like Italy or Greece or the Middle East, there are always lots of people around. Families, I mean. So you don't worry about anything bad happening there, but when I'm here in your town there are times when I feel, well, not as safe. I know it seems silly, but it's true.

Lucas: You may be right that older people go to bed early most nights. But doesn't that make it more fun when you're out? Everyone you see is young!

Zoe: That's true!

Lucas: So do people in the south of Europe get up later the next morning?

Zoe: Well, school starts just as early as in the north of Europe so I don't think they stay in bed any later. And the school day is normally about the same as here.

Lucas: And when there's no school?

Zoe: They have lunch later, perhaps at two or three. A proper meal, that is – not just a sandwich. After that people sometimes have a quick sleep.

Lucas:	I think that's sensible, if it's just for a few minutes. I'd like to do that, every day.
Zoe:	It's certainly a good idea when it's hot. Maybe the different routines in different parts of the world are because of the weather there?
Lucas:	That's possible, yes.

3 1 No 2 Yes 3 Yes 4 No 5 Yes

Prepositions of time

4 2 in 3 on 4 at 5 in

5 AT half past two, bedtime;

IN the morning, summer, 2010, the holidays;

ON April 24, Saturdays

Grammar
Frequency adverbs; question forms

1 1 before 2 they go after it 3 at the end

2 *Suggested answers:*

2 I check my email every two hours.
3 I'm never late for school.
4 I sometimes write letters to friends.
5 I don't always have lunch at home.
6 I'm sleepy in the morning almost every day.
7 I hardly ever go out on Monday nights.
8 I stay in bed late most weekends.

Reading Part 5

2 Article; It's about a windmill built to be a home; C; On one side, near the top of the windmill (sails); around the lower part of the windmill (balcony).

Points in text: 1, 3, 4, 6, 7

3 2 ground 3 third 4 like 5 few 6 corners
7 as 8 in 9 job 10 electricity

4 News report; modern cave homes. Suggested points:
- As the climate becomes hotter, cave homes are becoming more popular.
- It's never very hot or cold in caves.
- Modern cave homes are pleasant places to live.

5 1 D 2 A 3 B 4 A 5 C 6 B 7 B 8 D

6 *Suggested answers:*

Reasons not to like it: the lack of natural light, the possibility of damp, claustrophobia.

Other places: tree houses, converted lighthouses, aeroplanes, boats, etc.

Grammar
Present simple and present continuous; state verbs

1 1 b 2 d 3 a 4 c

2 2 am/'m sitting 3 is 4 am/'m looking
5 love 6 stay 7 go 8 is getting /'s getting
9 leave 10 is blowing 11 am/'m having
12 don't think

3 All state verbs except: change, dream, fill, improve, paint, relax

5 2 Do you prefer to get up early or late? 3 Is anybody at your house watching TV at the moment? 4 What colour clothes are you wearing today? 5 Which things in your house belong to you? 6 What do you sometimes forget to do in the morning?

Suggested answers for replies: 2 I prefer to get up late.   3 No, nobody at my house is watching TV at the moment.   4 I'm wearing blue and black clothes today.   5 The small bed, the computer and the desk belong to me.   6 I sometimes forget to brush my teeth in the morning.

Vocabulary
House and home; countable and uncountable nouns

2 *Suggested answers:*

Living room: sofa, cushions, armchair

Bathroom: bath, cupboards, mirror, taps, toilet, towels, washbasin

Kitchen: cooker, cupboards, dishwasher, microwave, sink, taps, washing machine, fridge

Bedroom: blankets, cupboards, mirror, chest of drawers, pillow

Hall: bell

3 *furniture*

4 [U] tells you the noun is uncountable; [C] is the symbol for a countable noun.

Grammar

A few, a little, many, much, a lot of and *lots of* ;
prepositions of place

❶ **1** a few, a few   **2** a little, a little   **3** many, many,
many   **4** much, much, much   **5** a lot of/lots of, a
lot of/lots of, a lot, a lot

❷ **2** much / a lot of / lots of, a few   **3** a few / lots of /
a lot of, a lot of / lots of   **4** much / a lot of / lots of,
a lot of / lots of   **5** much / a lot of / lots of, a few, a
lot   **6** much / a lot of / lots of, many / a lot of / lots
of

❸ **2** in   **3** in   **4** on   **5** on   **6** on

Speaking Part 1

❶ **2** How do you spell it? d

3 Where do you live? a

4 What do you do? e

5 Do you enjoy studying English? c

❷ at (school etc.), in (a town, etc.), on (the coast, etc.)

❹ **2** in   **3** do you work   **4** are you   **5** at   **6** in
7 do you study   **8** 're studying   **9** do you
enjoy   **10** like   **11** at   **12** in   **13** go out   **14** in
15 at

❺

Recording script   CD1 Track 4

John: Maria, where do you come from?

Maria: I'm from Vari. It's a small town <u>in</u> Greece, near
          Athens.

John: And <u>do you work</u> or <u>are you</u> a student?

Maria: I'm a student, <u>at</u> a secondary school <u>in</u> the
          town.

John: What subjects <u>do you study</u>?

Maria: All the usual ones like maths and history, but
          this month <u>we're studying</u> modern music, too.
          It's really interesting.

John: Ah! What <u>do you enjoy</u> doing in your free time?

Maria: Well, I <u>like</u> listening to music <u>at</u> home, <u>in</u> my
          room. And I sometimes <u>go out</u> with friends <u>in</u>
          the evenings, or <u>at</u> weekends.

Writing Part 1

❶ **2** a little   **3** 'm waiting   **4** at   **5** often

❷ **b** 3   **c** 1   **d** 2   **e** 4

❸ **2** e   **3** b   **4** a   **5** d   **6** e

❹ **2** aren't / are not at   **3** is having / 's having
4 ever   **5** a little   **6** at the

2   Student days

Starting off

❶ **A** alarm clock rings   **B** set off for school   **C** catch
the school bus   **D** teacher takes register   **E** have
lunch in the school canteen

❷ **2** E   **3** D   **4** C   **5** B

Sounds that are heard: **2** knives and forks
3 teacher taking register and students answering
4 school bus arriving at bus stop   **5** student leaving
house for school

Recording script   CD1 Track 5

          One. [Alarm clock ringing]

          Two. [Sound of school canteen]

          Three. [Children coming into class]

Teacher: Kelly Ashby.

Kelly: Yes, Ms Truman.

Teacher: Max Atkinson.

Max: Yes, Ms Truman.

Teacher: Gemma Brown.

Gemma: Yes, Ms Truman.

          Four.

          [school bus]

          Five.

Boy: Bye mum!

Mother: Bye!

Reading Part 3

❶ *Suggested answer:*

The text is probably about the typical school day of
Wayne, a 16-year-old secondary school student in
Beijing, China.

❷ *Some possible guesses:*

Wayne sets off for school after breakfast; he catches the school bus near his house; when he gets to school, the teacher takes the register; he has lunch in the school canteen at 12.10.

❸ The general idea of the text is that Wayne's school day in China is long and hard.

❹ *Suggested words to underline:*

2 by car **3** punished, later than 07.20 **4** some sports facilities **5** midday, none, home, lunch **6** leaves, at 17.20 **7** homework until, dinner **8** never sleeps, more than six hours

❺ *Suggested words to underline:*
1 fry myself an egg for breakfast, My sister buys something from the market stalls
2 I sometimes go to school by bus. However, I normally go to school by bicycle
3 in school at least 20 minutes before lessons begin. It's a school rule. If you don't arrive on time, you can expect punishment (the clock in the next paragraph shows that lessons begin at 07.40).
4 didn't use to have a football pitch, basketball courts or a running track but now it does
5 All of us eat in the school canteen
6 We finish school but we can't go home; we have an exam after class
7 It takes me 30 minutes to eat and then I have to do my homework
8 I always wake up less than six hours later

2 B **3** A **4** A **5** A **6** B **7** B **8** A

Vocabulary
Take, sit, pass, fail, lose, miss, learn, teach and *study*

❷ **2** sitting **3** taking **4** missing **5** study **6** learn **7** teach

❸ *Suggested answers:*
1 How many marks do you need to pass exams at your school?
2 What happens if you fail an exam?
3 How often do you miss school?
4 Do you study every weekend?
5 Would you like to learn something new? What?

Grammar
Past simple

❷ **2** shopping centre **3** (large) cinema(s) (with choice of films) **4** Spanish **5** (being with) new family and friends

Recording script CD1 Track 6

Interviewer: Today we have Nadine with us to talk about the six months she spent in Chile. Hello, Nadine.

Nadine: Hi!

Interviewer: You're a normal 16-year-old school student. Where did you go last year?

Nadine: Last year I lived in Chile for six months as an exchange student. I lived with a Chilean family. I went to school every day and I had to wear a uniform. In Canada I don't have to wear a uniform. It's so uncool!

Interviewer: Where did you stay?

Nadine: I stayed in San Pedro de Atacama – high in the Atacama desert. Unlike Toronto, there's no disco, no shopping centre, no large cinemas with choice of films.

Interviewer: How did you feel when you first arrived?

Nadine: To tell you the truth, I was scared. San Pedro is so different from my home town.

Interviewer: Did you speak Spanish before you went?

Nadine: Yes, I did. I studied Spanish at school in Canada and I thought I was good at it. But when I got to Chile I couldn't say anything. It was awful!

Interviewer: What about school? What subjects did you study?

Nadine: I did maths, chemistry, biology, physics, history, Spanish and art.

Interviewer: Was it a good experience?

Nadine: Yes, it was. I'm really glad I went there. My Spanish improved and I even began to dream in Spanish. I also stopped missing expensive activities like going to the cinema or the disco and began to realise that fun in San Pedro was being with my new family and friends.

Interviewer: Thank you, Nadine … and if *you'd* like to know more about being an exchange student, contact our hotline number on 0800 444 …

❸ **2** Where did you stay? **3** How did you feel when you first arrived? **4** Did you speak Spanish before you went? **5** What subjects did you study? **6** Was it a good experience?

4 **b** stayed **c** was **d** studied **e** did **f** was … went

5 Regular: **a** lived **b** stayed **d** studied;
Irregular: **c** was **e** did **f** was, went

6 2 ~~plaied~~ → played (vowel before *y*)
3 ~~planed~~ → planned (consonant + vowel + consonant) 4 ~~traveled~~ → travelled (British English always doubles the l, although this answer would be correct in US English)
5 ~~openned~~ → opened (final syllable is **not** stressed) 6 ~~happend~~ → happened (add *-ed* to infinitive without *to*) 7 ~~studyed~~ → studied (consonant before *y*, the *y* changes to *i*)

7 2 ~~buyed~~ → bought 3 ~~choosed~~ → chose
4 ~~felt~~ → fell 5 ~~weared~~ → wore 6 ~~writed~~ → wrote

Past simple and past continuous

1 *Suggested answer:*

The sun was shining and Nadine was walking to school. Suddenly she saw a group of dogs. She was very frightened.

2

> **Recording script** CD1 Track 7
>
> Nadine: It was in my second week. The sun was shining and I was feeling good. I was walking to school when I saw a group of dogs. I was frightened but I didn't know what to do.

3

> **Recording script** CD1 Track 8
>
> Nadine: Suddenly a woman appeared from nowhere and she started screaming at the dogs. The dogs ran off. I said 'Gracias!' and went to school.

4 1 Underline: appeared, started, ran off

No, the actions happened one after the other. The dogs ran off last.

2 Circle: was shining, was feeling

We don't know when the sun started shining or if it stopped shining (but we do know that this activity was happening around the time of Nadine's journey).

3 Circle: was walking; underline: saw

No, Nadine began walking to school and in the middle of this activity, she saw the dogs.

5 2 past continuous 3 past simple 4 past continuous 5 past continuous 6 past simple

6 2 looked 3 was raining 4 had 5 got
6 drove 7 changed 8 was putting 9 started
10 were

7

> **Recording script** CD1 Track 9
>
> Tommy: This morning I woke up early to visit Ryukoku High School. I looked out of the window. It was raining. I had a quick breakfast and we got ready to go. We drove to school. At the school we changed our shoes for slippers. As I was putting on my slippers, my Japanese friend started looking at my feet. The slippers were too small!

Listening Part 1

1 *Suggested words to underline:*

2 do today, 11 am 3 What, buy 4 weather, tomorrow

2 *Suggested answers:*

1 **A** time: one fifty or ten to two **B** time: one forty-five or (a) quarter to two **C** time: two fifteen or (a) quarter past two

2 **A** a sports class **B** a (school) play/performance **C** a maths class

3 **A** table tennis balls **B** table tennis bats **C** trainers

4 **A** sunny weather **B** cloudy and rainy weather **C** cloudy weather

3 *Suggested answers:*

2 **A** 11 tomorrow **B** after break, finish 11.15 **C** 11.15
3 **A** cheap **B** lend brother's **C** got some
4 **A** too much sun **B** today **C** Internet dry but cloudy

> **Recording script** CD1 Track 10
>
> One. What time does John have to leave school today?
>
> Mrs Drew: Woodland High School. Mrs Drew speaking.
>
> Mother: Yes. This is John Fuller's mother. He's got another doctor's appointment today at a quarter past two. Last week I picked him up at ten to two but we got there late. Can I get him

five minutes earlier today – at a quarter to two?

Two. What are the students going to do today at 11 am?

Teacher: There'll be some changes to your timetable today. <u>After break</u> we're going to see <u>a play performed</u> by some Year 10 students. That should <u>finish by 11.15</u>. We'll do <u>maths then</u>. I know we <u>normally do sport at 11</u> but we'll have to <u>do that tomorrow</u> instead.

Three. What does Nathan have to buy?

Nathan: I've just joined the table tennis team but I'm not sure I've got enough money to buy the equipment.

Jacob: Don't worry! <u>The balls are really cheap</u> and <u>I can lend you my brother's bat</u>. He never uses it. You'll have to <u>get some good trainers</u> though.

Nathan: <u>I've already got some</u>.

Four. What will the weather be like tomorrow?

Father: Are you ready for your school trip tomorrow, Beth? You're going to those new outdoor swimming pools, aren't you? Lucky you didn't go <u>today</u>. <u>It hasn't stopped raining</u>.

Beth: That's what I'm worried about. Our teacher looked it up on the Internet and <u>it says it'll be dry, but cloudy</u>. Let's hope it's right.

Father: Yeah, that's <u>better than too much sun</u>, I think.

❹ 1 B   2 B   3 A   4 C

Grammar

Used to

❶ *used to*

❷ *Suggested answers:*

1 No (we can say *I/you/he,* etc. *used to* go)
2 There is no *d* at the end of *use* (*we didn't <u>use</u> to take exams*)
3 The infinitive without *to*

❹ *Suggested questions:*

1 Did you use to get a lot of homework?
2 Did you use to play in a team?
3 How often did you use to meet your friends?
4 Did you use to choose your own clothes?
5 What did you use to do in your free time?

Reading Part 1

❶ 1 B   2 C   3 C   4 B   5 A

Vocabulary

Earn, have, make, spend and *take*

❶ **2** make   **3** take   **4** spend   **5** earn

Speaking Part 4

❷ *Suggested answer:*

	Linh, Vietnam	*Marcelo, Colombia*
1	*No / Very few work* *Parents don't allow them* *They have to study hard*	*Yes* *Earn extra spending money*
2	*No*	*Yes, in father's office*
3	*No, but could be a good thing for some teenagers (learn about money and society)* *Studying is the most important thing*	*Yes, but with more rules / limit on number of hours worked* *Working can be good experience / can work more in school holidays*

Recording script   CD1 Track 11

Linh: <u>Do teenagers work in Colombia</u>?

Marcelo: <u>Yes, they do</u>. Teenagers in my country work to earn extra spending money. <u>What about in Vietnam</u>?

Linh: <u>Well, I don't work and actually very few teenagers in Vietnam work</u>. In my country, most parents don't allow their children to have a part-time job. We have to go to school and study hard. <u>In my opinion, it's not a good idea for teenagers to work and study at the same time</u>. What do you <u>think</u>?

Marcelo: I'm not so sure. I agree that teenagers need enough time to study and do their homework. If they work too many hours, their marks will go down. <u>However, working part-time can be a good experience … don't you think so</u>?

Linh: Maybe. For some teenagers, working could be a way to learn about money and society. However, we have to think about the future. <u>I think that studying is the most important thing</u>. Do you <u>agree</u>?

Marcelo: Yes and <u>no</u>. As I said before, <u>I think having a part-time job can be a good experience. However, we need more rules. For example, teens shouldn't work more than 15 hours a week and only two or three days a week, like at the weekend. I think they can work more hours during the school holidays.</u>

Linh: <u>Have you got a part-time job?</u>

Marcelo: <u>Yeah. I sometimes work in my father's office.</u> I have to deliver letters and documents around the building. I earn a little bit of extra money.

Linh: <u>Really?</u> That sounds interesting. What do your teachers <u>say</u>?

Marcelo: Teachers complain that students who work don't do their homework well and they often do badly in tests. I think that students can work to earn some pocket money if they are good students.

Linh: <u>Good point!</u> I haven't got a job. I'm going to concentrate on my studies and look for a job when I'm older.

❸ 1 think   2 so   3 agree   4 no   5 part-time job
6 Really   7 say   8 point

Writing Part 2

❶ *Suggested words to underline:*

can't, sports practice, note, coach, apologise, explain, suggest another time

❷ Answers for question 1: **1** email   **2** English-speaking friend, Isabel   **3/4** thank, tell, invite

Answers for question 2: **1** note   **2** coach, we don't know name   **3/4** apologise, explain, suggest

❸ **a** 1   **b** 2

❹ invite: would you like to come
suggest: why don't I train
explain: (I won't be able …) because (I …)
apologise: I'm sorry that …

❺ 1 an email   2 Jason   3 to tell him you can't meet him   4 apologise, explain, suggest

❻ *Model answer:*

Hi Jason,

I'm sorry that I can't meet you tomorrow. It's because I have exams next week and I have to study hard. I'll finish my exams on Friday. Why don't we meet then? We could go to the cinema.

Yours,

Vocabulary and grammar review   Unit 1

Grammar

❶ 2 in   3 on   4 in   5 in   6 at   7 In   8 at   9 in
10 at   11 at   12 in   13 on

❷ 2 a little   3 a lot   4 a little   5 time   6 much
7 a little   8 a few

❸ 2 ~~I call~~ I'm calling   3 ~~do you stand~~ are you standing   4 ~~Do you sleep ever~~ Do you ever sleep   5 ~~I'm never believing~~ I never believe   6 I make my own bed every day.   7 How often do you have a bath?   8 ~~I get normally home~~ I normally get home

Vocabulary

❹

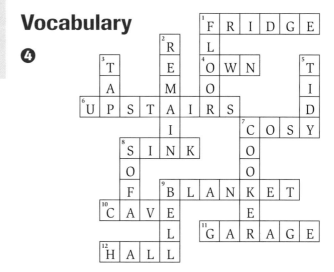

Vocabulary and grammar review   Unit 2

Vocabulary

❶ 2 study   3 had   4 made   5 take   6 missed
7 sitting   8 learn

Grammar

❷ 2 ~~planing~~ → planning   3 ~~payed~~ → paid   4 ~~founded~~ → found   5 ~~baught~~ → bought   6 ~~felt~~ → fell
7 ~~bringed~~ → brought   8 ~~studing~~ → studying
9 ~~teached~~ → taught   10 ~~puted~~ → put

❸ 2 was shining, were singing   3 was having, rang   4 chose, was   5 saw, was buying
6 escaped, was cleaning   7 thought, was
8 read, wrote   9 enjoyed   10 laughed, appeared

❹ *Suggested answers:*
2 used to go home for lunch
3 didn't use to live near our school
4 didn't use to be a good student
5 used to give us a lot
6 used to be very late for school

3   Fun time

Starting off

❶ b seeing   c going   d flying   e collecting
f playing   g surfing   h sending   i keeping
j diving   Pictures: 2 i   3 f   4 e   5 c   6 j

Listening Part 2

❶ a 2   b 1   c 4   d 3

❷ 1 B   2 A   3 C   4 B

Recording script   CD1 Track 12

Spencer: Hi, I'm Spencer Watson and I'm here to tell you about four unusual ways to have a great day out. First, how about going back in time with a steam train journey through the beautiful Scottish countryside? This is on the railway line made famous by the *Harry Potter* films. Starting at Fort William, near Britain's highest mountain, the train <u>departs each morning at twenty past ten</u>, getting into the lovely fishing village of Mallaig at 12.25. The return journey to Fort William starts at 14.10 and takes an hour and fifty minutes. The fares are good value for money and it's a great experience for steam train fans of any age. It's very popular in summer, so it's best to book ahead.

For a really exciting day out, *Go Wild* adventure courses offer hours of fun in seventeen different locations. For a fairly small admission fee, you can climb tall trees, go from tree-top to tree-top on a high wire, cross waterfalls far below, go through tunnels – and lots more. Before you start, though, they give you full safety advice. <u>To prevent accidents they put a belt round your waist and the tops of your legs</u>, and attach it to wires. And then you're

---

off – completely on your own! To take part you have to be fit, over nine years old and at least 1 metre 40 tall. Opening hours are usually 9.30 to 3.30.

If the adventure course isn't really your thing, but you like seeing really big wildlife, you can't do much better than dolphin and whale watching in Wales. *Voyages of Discovery* organises regular trips out to sea, passing small islands with their enormous sea-bird populations and then on to even deeper waters. And there, very occasionally, you will see whales, while <u>on almost all the trips dolphins will appear</u>. You may also see huge sharks, although they are quite rare these days. The voyage isn't cheap, but most people who've done it agree that it's well worth the money.

If instead you'd like to be up in the sky, try a balloon flight, from any of the hundreds of sites across the country. It usually begins early in the morning when you meet the pilot, crew and other passengers, and the huge balloon slowly fills with hot air. It rises gently, and then you go whichever way the wind is blowing. The actual flying time is about an hour, and although <u>I think it could last a bit longer</u>, it's certainly a wonderful experience. It's also possible to book a flight just for two, for any time of the year.

❸ 2 hours   3 fee   4 value   5 journey   6 advice
7 ahead

Vocabulary
Negative prefixes

❶ un- fit/fair/healthy, in- correct/dependent/active, im- possible/polite/probable

❷ 3 informal   4 unkind   5 untrue   6 impatient

❸ *Suggested answers:*

2 stay in all the time.   3 get up early to go somewhere.   4 fly in balloon number 13.
5 charge such high admission fees.   6 I sometimes have to run for the bus.

Reading Part 4

❷ *Suggested answer:*

tell the story of how a young person sailed alone across the Atlantic

❸ B

❹ **1** 'It feels fantastic … out of a can!' (second half of Paragraph 2)   **2** '… he too would like to break the record' (Paragraph 3)   **3** '… he hadn't felt afraid … never felt like giving up' (Paragraph 4)

❺ **1** C   **2** C   **3** B

❻ Yes, and they always are in Reading Part 4 questions on detail. (Exam question 5, however, usually requires understanding of different parts, or all, of the text, as does exam question 1, which normally concentrates on the author's purpose in writing the text.)

Grammar
Verbs followed by *to* or *-ing*

❶

Verb + *-ing*	Verb + infinitive
feel like, practise, admit, avoid, fancy, finish, mind, miss, suggest deny, dislike, can't help, imagine, mention, put off, can't stand	seem, afford, decide, expect, hope, learn, manage, promise, want, would like appear, attempt, intend, offer, pretend, refuse

❷ **2** ~~decided catch~~ decided to catch   **3** ~~enjoy to be~~ enjoy being   **4** ~~forget to visit~~ forget visiting   **5** correct   **6** ~~fancy to come~~ fancy coming   **7** correct   **8** ~~finished to eat~~ finished eating   **9** ~~forgot asking~~ forgot to ask   **10** correct

❸ *forget* and *remember* can be followed by both, with a change in meaning (see page 121 Grammar reference: Verbs followed by *to* or *-ing*

❹ **2** listening to   **3** to do   **4** going   **5** to bring   **6** to do

❺ *Suggested answers:*

2 I'm learning to speak a third language.
3 I decided to stop spending too much last week.
4 I'm planning to go shopping on Saturday.
5 I want to start learning to ride a motorbike.
6 I must remember to phone my best friend tomorrow.
7 I'll finish doing this exercise soon.

8 I shouldn't forget to watch that film on TV next weekend.
9 I always hate waiting for the bus.
10 I really love dancing to good music.

Vocabulary
Phrasal verbs

❶ **1** work out   **2** make up for   **3** look after

❷ **2** looking forward to   **3** turn (his dream) into   **4** set out on   **5** giving up   **6** go on   **7** deal with   **8** get on with

Three words: 2, 4, 8

Separated: 3 (*his dream*)

❸ **2** took up – c   **3** put (my name) down – b   **4** joined in – a   **5** go off (it) – f   **6** set off – d

❹ **2** went off   **3** take up   **4** put down   **5** gave up   **6** go on   **7** catch up with   **8** looking forward to

❺

> **Recording script**   CD1 Track 13
>
> **Chris:** Hi, Ava. Are you and Megan going away on holiday soon?
>
> **Ava:** Yes, on Saturday. We want to <u>set off</u> very early in the morning.
>
> **Chris:** Are you going to the coast?
>
> **Ava:** No, we <u>went off</u> beach holidays last summer. There were too many people. We've decided to <u>take up</u> skiing instead. We're off to the Alps.
>
> **Chris:** Do you know how to ski?
>
> **Ava:** Er, not really! That's why I'm going to <u>put</u> my name <u>down</u> for lessons.
>
> **Chris:** I tried it once but I found it really difficult. After three days I <u>gave up</u> and went home!
>
> **Ava:** Well, the lessons <u>go on</u> until late in the evening, every day, so I should improve quickly. Megan's a good skier and I've got a lot to learn, but I'm sure I can <u>catch up with</u> her. I'm really <u>looking forward to</u> trying, anyway!
>
> **Chris:** Yes, I'm sure you'll have a great time.

People's hobbies

6

hobby	person	equipment
chess	*player*	*board, pieces*
camping	camper	tent, backpack
collecting	collector	collection
cooking	cook	cooker, oven
cycling	cyclist	bike, helmet
music	musician	instrument
painting	painter	brush, paint
photography	photographer	camera

7 *Suggested answers:*

camping: sleeping bag, put up, fire, campsite

collecting: album, coins, stamps, objects, art, valuable

cooking: recipe, saucepans, frying pan, boil, roast, bake

cycling: wheels, seat, pedals, chain, lock, ride

music: practise, performance, solo, notes, keys, melody

painting: portrait, landscape, frame, picture, oils

photography: flash, focus, digital, zoom, close-up

Speaking Part 2

1 1 fishing   2 canoeing, water-skiing, rock-climbing, mountain-biking   3 mountain-biking

Recording script   CD1 Track 14

Olivia: There's never anything to do in this town, is there? Let's choose a hobby, an outdoor one, for the weekends and holidays.

Daniel: OK then, how about going fishing? We could go to the river in the valley over there, or even down to the lakes.

Olivia: Well, I think I'd prefer to do something a bit more exciting. And anyway I'd feel sorry for the poor fish! Perhaps we could try a water sport? Something like canoeing, or water-skiing, maybe.

Daniel: Yes, but we can't afford to hire a boat. I think we should do something cheaper. Or better still, free!

Olivia: All right, why don't we go rock-climbing? That's free, and it can be exciting, too.

Daniel: Hmm. I think it'd be better to do something less dangerous.

Olivia: OK, let me see … er, I know – what about mountain-biking? It's outdoor, quite safe, fairly cheap …

Daniel: … Yes, we could hire a couple of bikes and see if we like it. So shall we do that, then?

Olivia: I think it would be great. We could ride through the hills and into the forest. So, yes, let's go for that one.

2 2 prefer   3 could   4 should   5 why   6 better   7 shall   8 let's

3 The strongest stress is on:

1 fishing   3 water sport   5 rock-climbing   8 that
They give new information.

Recording script   CD1 Track 15

Daniel: OK then, how about going **fishing**?

Olivia: Perhaps we could try a **water sport**?

Olivia: All right, why don't we go **rock-climbing**?

Olivia: Yes, let's go for **that** one.

4

Recording script   CD1 Track 16

Olivia: Well, I think I'd prefer to do something a bit more exciting.

Daniel: I think we should do something cheaper.

Daniel: I think it'd be better to do something less dangerous.

Writing Part 1

1 1 have enough money for   2/3 *afford* is followed by the *to* infinitive, so it must be *afford to buy*

2 2 turned into / to: should be phrasal verb, is frozen now   3 setting out: should be -ing not infinitive after 'suggest', Let's leave the house   4 don't we: auxiliary and pronoun should be inverted in question form, It'd be a good idea to   5 forward to going: should be -ing not infinitive after 'looking forward to', can't wait to go

3 2 staying in bed   3 suggests going   4 start playing   5 have … lessons   6 too short

4 2 to get   3 about going   4 up   5 to learn to   6 on long

4 Our world

Starting off

➊ 2 go snowboarding 3 sunbathe 4 take photos
5 go trekking 6 go sightseeing 7 go snorkelling

➋ 1 snorkelling 2 snowboarding

Recording script CD1 Track 17

Toby:	Where did you go on holiday, Abi?
Abi:	Well, last year we went to Zanzibar. It's an island but it belongs to Tanzania, in East Africa.
Toby:	You always do exciting things, don't you? Which activities did you do in Zanzibar?
Abi:	Um, we stayed in Stone Town for a few days and <u>went</u> <u>sightseeing</u>.
Toby:	Ah! What did you see there?
Abi:	There were palaces and markets and <u>we visited the</u> <u>museums</u>.
Toby:	Do you like visiting museums?
Abi:	Um… it's OK, but I prefer going shopping.
Toby:	Did you buy anything?
Abi:	Oh yes! You know <u>I love</u> <u>buying souvenirs.</u> <u>I bought some</u> <u>clothes and jewellery.</u>
Toby:	Which activity <u>did you enjoy doing most</u>?
Abi:	Um… in the second week we stayed on the north coast and <u>I went snorkelling</u> for the first time. It was fantastic.
Toby:	Are there any activities you'd still like to try?
Abi:	Um… well <u>I've never been snowboarding. I'd</u> <u>love to try that.</u> All my friends say it's the most exciting winter sport. Have you tried it?

Reading Part 3

➊ *Suggested answers:*

trekking, snorkelling, sightseeing, buying souvenirs

➌ *Suggested words to underline:*

3 first part, sleep, city centre
4 water sports, South China Sea
5 airport, Sukau
6 animals, Sepilok, all sick or injured
7 impossible, get near, orang-utan
8 Orang-utans, only, meat
9 includes, free trip, Mount Kinabalu
10 buy gifts, after, sightseeing tour

➍/➎ *Answers and suggestions to underline (important words in* **bold***):*

1 B **Not** quite **as big as** its neighbour, the island of New Guinea

2 A Temperatures are generally **between 24° C and 30° C** all year round

3 A your comfortable **accommodation** in the **heart of this city**

4 A on the shores of the **South China Sea** where you can go **swimming or snorkelling** in its clear blue water

5 B **the only way to continue our journey** to Sukau … is **by bus**

6 B young orang-utans whose parents have died. **Some** of these animals arrive in **very bad condition**

7 B this extraordinary opportunity **to get close to** these creatures

8 B collect **the plants** that are part of **their diet**

9 B **For a small fee,** book our day trip to Mount Kinabalu

10 A And **when the tour is over,** it's a short ride to the modern shopping centres, local stores or markets **for** some last-minute **souvenirs**

Vocabulary

Travel, journey and *trip*

➋ 2 trip 3 travelled 4 trip 5 journey

Grammar

Comparative and superlative adjectives; (*not*) as … as …

➊ 1 False (New Guinea is bigger) 2 False (Kota Kinabalu is the most important city) 3 True 4 True

➋ 2 4 4 3

➌ 1 (the) noisiest 2 (the) biggest 3 (the) most beautiful 4 (the) best 5 (the) worst 6 (the) farthest or furthest 7 add -*r* or -*st* to adjectives that finish in *e* 8 double the final consonant if the adjective finishes in vowel–consonant 9 use *more* or *most* with adjectives with two or more syllables

4 2 more quiet → quieter   3 worse → worst   4 nearst → nearest   5 more better → better   6 hotest → hottest

5 *Suggested answers (other answers may be possible):*

3 the most dangerous   4 more intelligent
5 lighter   6 the noisiest   7 the slowest
8 the tallest   9 the biggest   10 the deepest
11 colder   12 larger

6

> **Recording script**   CD1 Track 18
>
> Fergus: And here are the answers to this week's general knowledge quiz. Did you know that <u>Asia is bigger than Africa</u>?
>
> Alyssa: Yes, and more people live in Asia than any other continent. Well, <u>Russia is the largest country in the world</u>.
>
> Fergus: And now for the animal facts. <u>The most dangerous animal on the planet is</u> not the lion or the shark but <u>the tiny mosquito</u> because it carries diseases. In the list of the top ten most intelligent animals <u>there are</u> dolphins, <u>orang-utans</u>, some types of elephant and whales – but <u>definitely no dogs</u>. The African elephant is the largest and heaviest land animal, but <u>the blue whale is the heaviest living creature</u>. On average, it can weigh around 150 tonnes – that's 150,000 kilos. I wouldn't like to share my home with <u>a howler monkey. They are the noisiest animals in the world</u>. <u>The slowest-moving fish is the sea horse</u>. It would take this fish about an hour to move 15 metres. <u>The tallest dog in the world is the Great Dane</u> and the smallest is the Chihuahua. You've got some answers about places, haven't you, Alyssa?
>
> Alyssa: Yes, I have. Did you know that <u>Nagoya train station in Japan is the biggest</u> in the world and <u>Shinjuku station in the same country is the busiest</u>? If you like diving, then you should go to Belgium. <u>Nemo 33 is the deepest pool</u> in the world.
>
> Fergus: And the last two answers. <u>Antarctica is the coldest</u>, driest and windiest continent. And while we're talking about large places, <u>the Amazon rainforest is larger than any other forest in the world</u>.

7 2 Mount Everest is a bit / a little higher than K2.
3 Arica is much / far / a lot drier (or dryer) than Death Valley.

4 Atlanta International Airport is much / far / a lot busier than Heathrow Airport.
5 The sperm whale's brain is much / far / a lot heavier than a human adult's brain.

8 1 True   2 True   3 False (the male is normally twice the size of the female)

9 1 *as* + adjective + *as*   2 not   3 no

10 2 large as   3 as straight as   4 as dangerous as / more dangerous than   5 as intelligent as

Vocabulary
Buildings and places

1 2 department store   3 youth club   4 market
5 port   6 fountain   7 bridge   8 town hall

3 2 wide   3 low   4 old (also ancient or old-fashioned)   5 clean   6 ugly   7 dull/calm
8 boring   9 dangerous   10 cheap   11 quiet
12 shallow   13 near   14 flat

Grammar
Big and *enormous* (gradable and non-gradable adjectives)

1 1, 2 and 3 (in any order) quite, very, really
4 and 5 (in any order) absolutely, really   6 and 7 (in any order) quite, very

2 *Suggested answers:*

2 small   3 hot   4 cold   5 bad   6 dirty
7 interesting   8 good

3 2 really   3 absolutely   4 quite   5 very

4 *Suggested answers:*

1 one hour from Stockholm, Sweden   2 not too crowded, interesting sights, safe   3 more nightlife (youth clubs / night-clubs)

> **Recording script**   CD1 Track 19
>
> Selma: Um … I come from Sweden. <u>I live in a town about an hour away from the capital, Stockholm</u>. There are only about 4,000 people – it's really tiny. <u>It's a very nice place to live in because it never gets too crowded</u>. <u>There are several interesting sights</u>, including a castle. Because it's a small town, <u>it's extremely safe</u>. Sometimes, I find living here quite boring. I'd like to live somewhere <u>with a more lively nightlife</u>. There are no youth clubs or night-clubs and we often have to spend the evening outdoors, even when it's absolutely freezing.

Listening Part 3

❶ *Suggested answers:*

  1 Oymyakon is a village in East Russia (Siberia).

  2 lowest temperature (−71.2° C); oldest man (109)

  3 Ewan McGregor visited Oymyakon in 2004 on his motorbike.

  4 Life for young people there is probably quiet.

❷ *Suggested answers:*

  1 date **2** number **3** noun **4** adjective **5** noun
  6 noun

❸/❹/❺ **1** 1926 **2** 9/nine **3** television **4** oldest
  5 mobile(s) (phone)(s) **6** motorbike

Speaking Part 3

❶ **2** Marrakech, Morocco **3** Machu Picchu, Peru
  4 The Great Wall, China **5** Hikkaduwa Beach, Sri Lanka

❷ *Suggested answers:*

  1 buy souvenirs, visit museums **2** buy souvenirs, go sightseeing **3** go trekking, go camping
  4 go trekking, take photos **5** sunbathe, go snorkelling

❸ She describes *all* eight things

❹ **2** looks like **3** looks **4** think, could be **5** seems to be **6** can see **7** appears to be **8** don't think

We use *look like* with a noun (it *looks like a traffic jam*) and *look* (without *like*) with an adjective (*the water looks really dirty*).

Writing Part 3

❶ **1** a letter
  2 about 100 words
  3 the name of a city in your country and more information about this city

❹ Yes (this is a model answer and would get full marks in the PET exam)

⑤ *Suggested expressions to underline:*

As you know, I've lived in … so why don't you write about …? It's one of the … cities in … In fact over … live there … is famous for … People say that … is on the east coast of … which are … they are … for (verb + -ing). There are absolutely … and … too. The weather is … because … I hope this is enough information

Vocabulary and grammar review   Unit 3

Vocabulary

❶ 2 unfit   3 unfair   4 unpopular   5 unhealthy
6 informal   7 impatient   8 unsafe
9 unnecessary   10 inactive

❷ 2 e   3 a   4 h   5 b   6 g   7 d   8 f

Grammar

❸ 2 to do   3 to get   4 going   5 to buy   6 to have
7 to look for   8 to see   9 spending   10 to buy
11 to do   12 being

❹ 2 a   3 c   4 a   5 c   6 b   7 b

Vocabulary and grammar review   Unit 4

Vocabulary

❶ *Suggested answers:*

2 fantastic/wonderful/great   3 coldest
4 freezing   5 lively/busy   6 enormous/huge
7 boring/dull   8 empty

❷ 2 than   3 very   4 far   5 travel   6 shopping
centres

Grammar

❸ 2 ~~more better~~ → better   3 ~~more safe~~ → safer
4 ~~that~~ → than   5 ~~as~~ → than   6 ~~then~~ → than

❹ 2 farther/further   3 most popular   4 better than
5 the hottest

5   Feelings

Starting off

❶ 2 happiness   3 sadness   4 anger   5 fear

❷ 2 anger   3 fear   4 happiness   5 jealousy

❸ *See the key to the quiz on page 173*

Listening   Part 4

❶ 1 I don't think, I'm a bit surprised, it seems to me, for me

2 *Suggested answers:* in my opinion, I think, I believe, I'm sure (that), I feel (that), as I see it, if you ask me, I'd say, I'm afraid, my view is that; the use of *might/could/may* for possibility.

❷/❸ 1 A   2 B   3 A   4 B   5 A   6 B

Recording script   CD1 Track 22

Erica:	So, Ben, how often do you and Liam actually get together these days?
Ben:	Whenever I can, Erica. Usually about once every two months.
Erica:	<u>I don't think that's enough, really, to keep a friendship going. Couldn't you visit him each month, or ask him to come here</u>?
Ben:	Well, it's a long way to go. More than 400 kilometres, I think.
Erica:	How long does it take?
Ben:	Over six hours, each way. So you spend half the weekend on the coach, going up and down the motorway. <u>It's so boring</u>!
Erica:	How about taking the train? Wouldn't that be quicker?
Ben:	<u>I don't think I could afford it. The fares are really high</u>.
Erica:	Why don't you get a student travel card? Your tickets would be a lot cheaper.
Ben:	Hmm. That's an idea.
Erica:	And Liam could get one, too. Then he could sometimes come here on Saturdays and Sundays to see you.
Ben:	<u>I don't think he's keen on doing that</u>. He likes his new town a lot. He wants to stay there at weekends, he says.
Erica:	I see. So you go and see him, but he never comes here.

❸ 2 e 3 f 4 a 5 b 6 d

Grammar

Can, could, might and *may* (ability and possibility)

❶ *Students should underline: can, could, might (not)*

might not is negative; 'not' goes after the modal verb (*might*); mightn't; *can't* and *couldn't*

❷ 2 ~~may seems~~ → may seem – the main verb following a modal is an infinitive without *to* so it does not add *s* in the 3rd person (*he/she/it*)

   3 ~~I'm not can~~ → I can't – forms of *be* are not used before modals; most modals form the negative by adding *not* or a short form of it at the end

   4 ~~we could~~ → could we – the question form of modals normally needs a change in word order of modal and subject and doesn't use the auxiliary verb *do*

   5 ~~can doing~~ → can do – modals are not followed by the *-ing* form of the verb

   6 ~~you will might see~~ → you might see – the future form of most modals is the same as the present form

   7 ~~It's could be~~ → It could be – forms of *be* are not used before modals

   8 ~~could met~~ → could meet – modals are followed by the infinitive without *to*, not a past form of the verb

❸ 1 can/could 2 may/might/could

❹ 2 might 3 couldn't 4 can't 5 can't 6 can
   7 Could 8 can't

❺ *Suggested answers:* I can't see my school friends, I can't stay out very late; I can go out with friends, I can stay in bed late, I can play computer games all morning, I might go to the cinema, play tennis, go dancing

Should, shouldn't, ought to, must, mustn't, have to and *don't have to* (obligation and prohibition)

❶ 1 B 2 A

❷ *Suggested answers:*

   A you ought to / should get a haircut, have a wash, mend your trousers, get some new shoes; you shouldn't go out like that, wear those clothes, have your hair like that.

   B You shouldn't go to school tomorrow, do any work, get too close to people; you ought to / should see the doctor, go to bed, lie down, have hot drinks, take an aspirin.

❸ 2 D 3 C 4 E

❹ b 3 c 2 d 1

❺ 2 must 3 mustn't 4 don't have to 5 have to
   6 must

❻ B

❼ 2 don't have to 3 have to 4 doesn't have to
   5 must 6 shouldn't 7 mustn't

Recording script   CD1 Track 23

Presenter: Internet sites like *MySpace, Bebo* and *Facebook* are a great way for young people to keep in touch with friends, but there are things you should do to stay safe. On some sites you don't have to use your real name if you don't want to, so invent a name for yourself. On most sites it's a rule that you have to give an email address, but this doesn't have to be your normal one – you can use any address. You can write lots of interesting things on your online page, but something you must never do is put your house address or phone number. In fact, you shouldn't give any information that could let strangers know your identity, because on the Internet you never know who is looking. Remember, too, that you mustn't put your friends' personal details on your page, or you could put them in danger. So the message is: have fun, but take care.

---

❽ *Suggested answers:* **2** I mustn't eat at my desk. **3** I don't have to go out early.   **4** I must work harder.   **5** I shouldn't eat cream cakes but I sometimes do!   **6** I ought to tidy my room but I probably won't.

Vocabulary

Adjectives and prepositions

❶ 1 with 2 of 3 about

❷ 1 of 2 with 3 about

❸ *Suggested answers:*

of: confident (also confident about), envious, frightened, etc.

with: pleased, cross, fed up, etc.

about: relaxed, excited, mad, etc.

❹ 2 with 3 of 4 with 5 of/about 6 of/about

Adjectives with *-ed* and *-ing*

❶ He wanted to contact her (and needed her details / phone number from them); They met again and got married.

❷ bor**ing**; it drops the final *-e* to add *-ing*

❸ bored

❹ 1 boring 2 bored

❺ 2 relaxed 3 surprising 4 tired 5 depressed
6 embarrassing 7 amused 8 annoyed
9 disappointed 10 interested 11 amazed
12 excited

❻ *Suggested answers:*

1 I'm always excited when I meet new people. It's always exciting to meet new people.

2 Dancing for a long time is tiring. I get tired when I dance for a long time.

3 I was disappointed that he didn't phone. It was disappointing that he didn't phone.

❼ 1 c 2 d 3 a 4 b

Recording script CD1 Track 24

Speaker 1: My brother took some CDs out of my room without asking. I wasn't happy about it because I wanted to play one of them.

Speaker 2: Usually my family all meet at our house on December 31st, but this year my cousins can't come. It's a shame.

Speaker 3: I don't want to go to that youth club again. There's never anything to do there and there's nobody to talk to.

Speaker 4: And then Jessica walked in. I couldn't believe it, because I thought I'd never see her again.

Reading Part 5

❸ *Suggested answers:*

1 when something bad happens to us 2 all the time / every day 3 our lives will get much better / we'll become much happier

❹ a 2, 5, 6 b 4, 8, 10 c 1, 7, 9 d 3

❺ 1 B 2 A 3 C 4 A 5 B 6 C 7 B 8 B 9 A
10 D

Vocabulary

Adjectives and their opposites

❶ 2 d 3 a 4 c 5 b

❷ 2 relaxed 3 positive 4 depressed 5 mean

❸ funny/serious, strange/ordinary

❹ 2 serious 3 awful 4 ordinary 5 strange
6 fantastic

Speaking Parts 3 and 4

❶ *Suggested answers:* **A**: I can see a girl. She looks like she's making a speech at her school or college. She seems nervous; **B**: I can see a boy. It looks like he's in a long queue for an event. He looks very bored.

❷ **A**: At the beginning, she felt nervous. After a few minutes she began to feel (more) relaxed. At the end, when everyone clapped, she was delighted; **B**: He was excited about going to the concert. After six hours in the queue he was very bored. In the end he was angry because some people bought tickets to make money.

❸ 1 did, feel 2 happened, end 3 did, have 4 was, reaction

Recording script CD1 Track 25

            Picture A.

Girl: Well, once I had to make a speech to nearly the whole school, in front of hundreds of other students.

Friend: How <u>did</u> you <u>feel</u>?

Girl: At first I was really <u>nervous</u> and I couldn't remember what I had to say. I needed to keep looking at my notes. But after a few minutes I started to feel a bit <u>more relaxed</u>, and then I just talked and talked.

Friend:	What <u>happened</u> in the <u>end</u>?
Girl:	Everyone clapped. I was <u>delighted</u> when I heard that!
	Picture B.
Boy:	I was really <u>excited</u> about that concert, I just had to see it, but thousands of other people wanted tickets too. That's why the queue was so enormous.
Friend:	How long <u>did</u> you <u>have</u> to wait?
Boy:	Six hours. I was so <u>bored</u>! But just before I got to the ticket office, it closed! They'd sold all the tickets.
Friend:	What <u>was</u> your <u>reaction</u> to that?
Boy:	I was <u>angry</u>. A lot of people had bought ten or twenty tickets each, so they could sell them later and make money.

Writing Part 3

❶ 1, 4, 5; you should also include reasons why you like to relax in that way.

❷ Points she includes: **1** (Where) her own room **4** (When) weekends, especially **5** (How) read an interesting book

Reasons (why): warm & cosy, she can listen to her favourite music, nobody comes in, no phone calls

❸ Lots of love (E), All the best (E), Don't forget to write soon (E), Dear George (B), Well, that's all for now (E), Thanks for your letter (B), This is just a quick letter to say (B), It was great to hear from you (B), Hi Lisa (B), Give my love to everyone (E), Sorry I've taken so long to write back (B)

❹ Hi Nathan, Thanks for your letter, it was great to hear from you, Write soon and let me know, All the best

❺ so (nobody comes in)

❻ **2** I never get tired of going to the cinema because there are so many good films. **3** Since I don't have much homework to do, I often go out in the evenings. **4** I enjoy water-skiing a lot because it's really exciting. **5** I've got some really good games so I'm on my PlayStation® every day.

❼ *Sample answer*

Dear Libby,

It's nice to hear from you. You ask about something exciting I do and the answer is easy: horse riding in the mountains!

It's great because on a horse you can get to beautiful places that are impossible to reach by car, or even by bike. Sometimes we're so high up that in winter and spring everything is covered in snow and the views are fantastic!

The paths along the mountain sides are very narrow, so it can be a bit frightening if you look down, but you're completely safe because the horses know the way – they've been there hundreds of times!

In your next letter tell me about the exciting things you do!

Bye for now,

Keira

6 Leisure and fashion

Starting off

❶ 2 documentary **3** quiz show **4** the news **5** comedy series **6** chat show

❷ They talk about: documentary, comedy series, chat show, the news.

Recording script	CD1 Track 26
Lucy:	Ben, you're watching TV again! What's on?
Ben:	It's <u>a programme about farmers in Kenya who are trying to save elephants</u>. Did you know that the elephant population has fallen by 80% there?
Lucy:	Yes, but how much TV do you watch a day?
Ben:	I'm not really sure. It depends on whether I have a lot of homework or not. I always watch *Alphabet Road*.
Lucy:	Oh? I haven't heard of *Alphabet Road*. What's it about?
Ben:	Oh, <u>it's the story of some neighbours on a crazy street</u>. It's on Thursdays and <u>it always makes me laugh</u>. What's your favourite programme?
Lucy:	I don't watch much TV but I love *The Luke Robinson Show*. <u>He interviews all kinds of people, including famous people</u>. Did you see his interview with Tom Cruise?
Ben:	You're joking! I can't stand those kinds of programmes. I prefer playing computer games to watching that.

Lucy:	Really? Look, it's 9 pm. Why don't we switch over <u>and watch the headlines? I like to know what's happening in the world.</u>
Ben:	Good idea! Here's the remote control.

Reading Part 2

❶ **2** Kids Rock **3** Found in Hong Kong **4** Best Friends **5** Prince of Mandavia **6** University Spotlight **7** Liala **8** Reggae Nights

❷ *Suggested answer:*

The important information has been underlined (what they want to do; what they don't want to do; extra information)

❸ G (Fight Planet) *suggested words to underline:* You haven't seen anything like this before (as they *would like to see something completely different*)

Reasons why they do not choose the other options:

University Spotlight – it says *book early*

Kids Rock, Prince of Mandavia, Liala, Found in Hong Kong and Reggae Nights all contain music and Silvie and Kat <u>don't want to hear more music</u>

Best Friends – there is *nothing different about this story*

❹ *Suggested words to underline:*

2 Teenagers visiting … with their parents, all love science fiction, Martha and Artie love live music, especially reggae, their parents want to see a musical

3 university students, want to have fun, can't afford … much money, like listening … music

4 Lily (19) … Ken (18) … 5-year-old cousin, Mai … mad about animals …, wants to drive … doesn't want to pay for parking

5 Lara … mum prefer something funny to serious drama, go to bed early, buy some presents before they leave

❺ **2** B **3** F **4** C **5** E

Suggested words to underline:
2 Set in the year 2306, live musicians play, this show
3 play their records … disco, Admission free
4 monkey, elephant and bear, Free parking for every two adult tickets
5 definitely good fun, Not to be taken seriously, Gift Shop open during interval

❻ *Suggested answer:*

Martha and Artie are teenagers and are going out with their parents. Their parents want to see a musical. *Reggae Nights* is a disco (not a musical) and is for over-18s only. It is likely that Martha and Artie are under 18. Also, there is no connection with science fiction, which they all like.

❼ *Suggested answers:*

1 Silvie and Kat are *best friends* (*Best Friends* is the title of H); they saw their *favourite band* last week (in C, 'Keith's Door' is everyone's *favourite band*)

3 Al and Ed are *university students* (A mentions students several times, e.g. *Special discounts for students*)

4 Mai is *mad about animals* (D mentions *no … animals here*; the musicians in E are dressed as *strange animals*)

5 Lara and her mum *prefer … funny to serious* (H mentions a *serious look*)

Vocabulary
Going out

❷ **2** admission **3** audience **4** live **5** review **6** subtitles **7** interval **8** venue

❸ Fight Planet

Recording script	CD1 Track 27
Liam:	Yes. It was brilliant! My uncle managed to get me a ticket for the <u>early performance</u>. When <u>Monkey</u> came on stage, the audience went wild. The only thing I didn't like was the venue. It was too crowded.

Grammar
Present perfect

❶ They decide to watch the film at home and have pizza there.

Recording script	CD1 Track 28
Tom:	Would you like to see a show tonight?
Evan:	Yeah! Why not? We haven't been out together for three months. What's on?
Tom:	Well, there's that musical *Kids Rock*. Have you <u>seen it yet?</u>

Evan:	'Fraid so. I saw it last week. I haven't <u>seen</u> the circus show *Liala* <u>yet</u>.
Tom:	I've <u>already seen</u> *Liala*. My cousin took me on Saturday.
Evan:	How about *Best Friends*?
Tom:	Fantastic idea. I've <u>just finished</u> reading the play.
Evan:	Oh no! It's not a play, is it? I don't fancy that!
Tom:	Let's stay in and watch a film on TV then.
Evan:	We can't do that. My dad's just taken the TV to be repaired. <u>We couldn't go to your house and watch the film, could we</u>?
Tom:	<u>Of course</u>! Why don't we <u>get a pizza</u> on the way to my house and <u>we can watch the film and have pizza</u>?
Evan:	What a great idea!

❷ 1 seen it yet 2 seen … yet 3 already seen 4 just finished

The present perfect is used in all four extracts.

❸ 2 already 3 yet 4/5 (in any order) already, just 6 yet

❹ 2 My dad hasn't found a new job yet.
   3 But he's/has started a course in computing.
   4 My mum's/has just won a prize in a photography competition.
   5 Have you seen the new *Kung Fu* film yet?
   6 I've/have already seen it three times. It's great!
   7 What about you? Have you finished your exams yet?

❺ *Suggested answers:*
   1 1998, etc.
   2 three years, etc.
   3 last year, my birthday, etc.
   4 (Name of teacher) / four months, etc.
   5 (Name of sport / *the* + instrument) / 2005, last year, etc.

❻ 2 How long have you been at your school?
   3 How long have you had your watch?
   4 How long has (name) been your English teacher?
   5 How long have you played (sport) / *the* (instrument)?

Present perfect or past simple?

❶ 2 Have … read 3 saw 4 haven't heard 5 won
   6 did … go 7 have … taken

❷ *Suggested answers:*
   1 Why did he decide to become a ………?
   2 When did he begin his career?
   3 Where did he first work?
   4 How did he feel when he first began working, do you think?
   5 How long has he been a ……… ?
   6 How many times has he won a competition?

Vocabulary

been/gone, meet, get to know, know and *find out*

❷ 1 been, been 2 meet 3 known 4 gone
   5 getting to know 6 find out

Listening Part 1

❶ *Make sure you can find these items:*

backpack, belt, blouse, boots, coat, dress, earring, glasses, glove, handbag, jeans, purse, pyjamas, sandals, shorts, skirt, socks, suit, sweater, sweatshirt, swimming costume, T-shirt, tie, tights, towel, tracksuit, trainers, trousers, umbrella, wallet

❷ 2 ~~beautifuls~~ → beautiful 3 a long ~~and~~ white → a long white 4 ~~fashion~~ → fashionable 5 ~~T-shirt~~ → a T-shirt 6 ~~a blue trouser~~ → blue trousers / a pair of blue trousers

❸ *Suggested answers:*

Words to underline: 1 Mark's sweater 2 Mary lost
3 John lost 4 coat

Differences between each: 1 There are three cotton sweaters – A is plain with a V-neck, B is patterned with a V-neck, C is plain with a round neck; 2 A is a towel, B a pair of earrings, C a purse; 3 A trainers, B socks, C sandals; 4 There are three long coats – A has 6 buttons and 2 pockets, B has 2 buttons and no pockets, C has 6 buttons and no pockets

❹ 1 C 2 B 3 A 4 C

Recording script CD1 Track 29

One. Which is Mark's sweater?

Mark: Excuse me. I've lost my sweater. I left it by the pool. It's <u>a plain one</u> – <u>there's no pattern or anything on it</u>. Has anyone handed it in?

Girl: Let me see … . We've only got three sweaters here, I think. Is it this one? It's got a V-neck.

Mark: Sorry, no! <u>Mine's got a round neck</u>. Oh! There it is! It's that one there! The cotton one! It was very expensive.

Girl: Well, be more careful with it next time! Here you are!

CD1 Track 30

Two. What has Mary lost?

Mary: Hi! I was emptying my backpack in the sports centre café because I needed to pay for something and I couldn't find my purse.

Girl: How much money was in it?

Mary: Oh … it's OK, I found that, but <u>I had a pair of earrings inside my bag too</u> … in a little kind of pocket … and <u>I think they fell out</u> when I pulled my towel out. <u>Has anyone brought them here</u>?

Girl: Sorry, no …

CD1 Track 31

Three. What has John lost?

Dad: We've come to pick up John and he's playing tennis in his sandals.

Girl: Really?

Dad: Yes! He's always losing things. We thought he'd lost his socks but we've found those. <u>Have you got his trainers</u>?

Girl: What do they look like?

CD1 Track 32

Four. Which coat is Barbara talking about?

Barbara: I was wearing my sister's coat and now I can't find it. She's going to be so angry with me.

Girl: We've got several coats. What does it look like?

Barbara: <u>It's quite long with five or six buttons down the front</u>.

Girl: Anything in the pockets?

Barbara: <u>It hasn't got any pockets</u>.

Speaking Part 4

❶ Things you like to do at home and things you like to do when you go out

❷ See answers below for Exercise 3

❸ (*Jon and Ivan do a model task, so these are also correct answers for them*):

2 ✓   3 ✗   4 ✓   5 ✓   6 ✗   7 ✗

Recording script CD1 Track 33

Examiner: Your photographs showed people going out. Now I'd like you to talk together about what you like to do at home and what you like to do when you go out.

Jon: So, Ivan, what do you like to do at home? Do you like watching TV?

Ivan: Yes, I love watching TV. We normally switch on the TV after dinner and watch a film, a football match or a documentary. What about you? Do you like watching films?

Jon: Yes, but I prefer watching sports to documentaries. I find documentaries a little bit boring. Did you see the basketball match last night?

Ivan: No, I didn't. When I'm at home I also enjoy playing cards or other games with my two brothers. On Sunday afternoons, we often stay in and play together. Do you ever play cards at home?

Jon: No, not really. When I go out with my friends we usually meet in the local shopping centre. It's not much fun. I love going to the cinema, but it's very expensive. Er, how often do you go to the cinema?

Ivan: I agree with you. The cinema is very expensive but I go with my parents once a month and they pay. Have you seen the new *Batman* film yet?

Jon: No, not yet. I like going to see shows with my family. I don't really like serious plays but I love musicals like *Cats*, *We Will Rock You!* and the *Lion King*. Do you like musicals?

Ivan: Er … I like some musicals but I think I prefer the cinema. My sister really loves the ballet. I've been once but I thought it was too long and slow. I think it was *Swan Lake*. Do you like classical music?

| Jon: | Oh no! My brother … er … plays the violin and we went to a classical music concert with him last year. It was awful! I wanted to wait outside but my mum said I had to sit there. It was two hours and there was no interval. |
| Ivan: | Two hours long? Poor you! |

4 1 True   2 False   3 False

5/**6** *(These are Jon and Ivan's answers but any full answer which doesn't change the topic completely is fine):*

2 No, I didn't. When I'm at home I also enjoy playing cards or other games with my two brothers. On Sunday afternoons, we often stay in and play together.

3 The cinema is very expensive but I go with my parents once a month and they pay.

4 No, not yet. I like going to see shows with my family. I don't really like serious plays but I love musicals like *Cats*, *We Will Rock You!* and the *Lion King*.

5 I like some musicals but I think I prefer the cinema. My sister really loves the ballet. I've been once but I thought it was too long and slow. I think it was *Swan Lake*.

7 The clothes you wear during the week and the clothes you wear at weekends

8 *Suggested answers:*

| When we have sport I wear a tracksuit. I often change my clothes when I get home from school. On Sundays, I often have to wear smart clothes. | What do you wear for sport? Do you change your clothes? Why (not)? What about you? |
| I like choosing my own clothes. I don't like wearing skirts very much. | Do you like wearing smart clothes? Can you choose which clothes you buy? If not, who chooses your clothes? What clothes do you <u>not</u> like wearing? |

Writing Part 2

1 *Suggested answer:*

The cat broke the vase. It knocked the vase off the furniture. Water spilled on the floor.

2 *Suggested words to underline:*

aunt's cat, She … sent … money, an email to … Aunt Kath, thank, what … buy, describe … cat did, 35–45 words

3/**4** Although 1 (Bettina's answer) is very well written (with no spelling mistakes and a very good use of grammar), well organised and the message is clear, she has not included the three content points (she does not describe what the cat did). She can only be given a maximum of 3 marks.

2 (Katia's answer) is less accurate but it is well organised and the message is clear. She has included all three content points and so her teacher could give her 5 marks.

5 *Sample answer:*

Dear Dorota,

Thanks so much for the money you sent me for my birthday. You know how much I love new clothes. I'm going to buy those tight black jeans I saw last week. Why don't you come with me next week to buy them?
Yours

Magda

Vocabulary and grammar review   Unit 5

Vocabulary

1 2 of   3 with   4 on   5 of   6 about   7 about   8 about   9 of   10 of

2 amazing, interesting, embarrassed, frightened, amused

3

Crossword answers:
Across: MEAN, AFRAID, EMOTION, AWFUL, OUGHT, LUCKY, LOVE
Down: SAD, HABBIT, JEALOUS, GRATEFUL, NEGATIVE, PROUD

Grammar

4 2 can't   3 should   4 Could   5 don't have to
6 might   7 have to

Vocabulary and grammar review   Unit 6

Vocabulary

1 2 Audiences   3 live   4 reviews   5 performances
6 admission   7 interval

2 2 C   3 A   4 A   5 B   6 B

Grammar

3 2 ~~since three years ago~~ → for three years / since
2007   3 ~~he's gone~~ → he went / he's gone to Dubai
(with no time adverb)   4 ~~gone~~ → been   5 ~~Already
I've~~ → I've already   6 ~~I looked~~ → I've looked
7 ~~never~~ → ever   8 ~~has given~~ → gave   9 ~~just came~~
→ has just come   10 ~~didn't decide~~ → haven't
decided   11 ~~has opened~~ → opened   12 ~~what
happened~~ → what has happened

4 2 've/have never lived / 've/have not lived /
haven't lived   3 since   4 've/have known   5 seen

7   Out and about

Starting off

2 2 temperature, hot, degrees, centigrade   3 showers,
get wet   4 gale, blowing   5 thunderstorm,
lightning   6 freezing, frost, snowfall

Listening Part 2

1 **a** Chloe   **b** an interviewer   **c** taking photos of
extreme weather conditions   **d** the weather in
her country, when she began taking photos of bad
weather, what she uses to photograph lightning,
where she takes photos during thunderstorms,
what she most likes photographing in winter, what
she photographs when it's windy   **e** the weather
in the speaker's country, bad weather, lightning,
thunderstorms, winter weather (ice/snow/frost),
windy weather.

2 1 B   2 B   3 C   4 C   5 A   6 B

Recording script   CD1 Track 34

Interviewer: Tell me, Chloe, have you always been
interested in the weather?

Chloe: Oh yes. It's really fascinating in this country
because it can be quite different in the north,
in the west and in the south, for instance, and
it doesn't usually stay the same for long. It can
be warm and sunny one moment; wet and cold
the next. In fact you can sometimes have all
four seasons in one day!

Interviewer: So when did you first photograph storms and
things like that? Was that while you were at
university? Or in your first job?

Chloe: No no, I was much younger than that. I was
just a kid, really. We were coming home from
holiday and we got caught in a thunderstorm.
I took some pictures and luckily they came out
really well. Since then I've done lots of other
kinds of photography, especially when I was a
student, but I still love photographing lightning.

Interviewer: That must be quite difficult. How do you get
good pictures?

Chloe: Well, the first thing is the right camera. It
doesn't have to be expensive, or particularly
modern – I've had mine for many years – and I
avoid using digital ones. But the main thing is
where you go to take your pictures.

Interviewer: Which are the best places?

Chloe: Well, some people take photos from their bedroom windows, but I live in a flat where there's no real view of the night sky and so I have to go out. Standing in fields and on hills during a thunderstorm is rather dangerous, <u>so I drive into the countryside, park, open the window and start taking pictures.</u> You're much safer with all that metal around you, like on a plane.

Interviewer: So what about photography during the day?

Chloe: I really enjoy taking winter photos, when it's really freezing.

Interviewer: Which are your favourite? Snowy scenes?

Chloe: I used to like doing those, just after snowstorms, and sometimes those beautiful shapes like flowers that you see on glass when it's frosty. But nowadays I prefer mountain scenes with lots of ice. Especially when you have <u>water flowing down valleys and over waterfalls, and it gets so cold that it freezes solid.</u>

Interviewer: Mm. And during the rest of the year?

Chloe: Um … storms, I think. You can get some great pictures when the wind is really blowing, particularly on the coast. <u>Whenever there's a gale, I go down to the beach and take loads of photos of the waves.</u> They can be amazing. Mm. And I'd like to take pictures of clouds, though it's often too dark to photograph them when it's stormy. Also forests, with everything bending in the wind. I've always wanted to try that, too.

❸ The extract answers question 3; the expressions 'photographing lightning' and 'How do you get good pictures?' show the information that you need to complete 'To photograph lightning, she uses …' will soon follow; A: <u>I avoid using digital ones</u>, B: <u>It doesn't have to be expensive</u>, C: <u>I've had mine for many years</u>; Yes, these are all close together; No, the order Chloe talks about them is not the same order as the options A, B and C.

Vocabulary

Extremely, fairly, quite, rather, really and very

❶ 1 really   2 rather   3 quite

Too and enough

❶ 2 before, *to* infinitive   3 uncountable, countable
4 as much as   5 before, after, *to* infinitive

❷ 2 ~~money for to buy~~ → money to buy   3 ~~too much~~ → very much   4 ~~for get~~ → to get   5 ~~too much expensive~~ → too expensive   6 correct
7 ~~for wearing~~ → to wear   8 ~~enough warm~~ → warm enough

Grammar

The future: *Will*, *going to*, present continuous and present simple

❶ 2 's going to rain   3 'm meeting   4 leaves   5 'll take

❷ b 'll take   c it'll stop   d 'm meeting   e 's going to rain

> **Recording script**   CD1 Track 35
>
> Mia: It's getting a bit late, Owen.
>
> Owen: Yes, but look at the rain! I'm hoping <u>it'll stop</u> soon, though I don't think there's much chance of that.
>
> Mia: No, the weather forecast said it's a big storm so <u>it's going to rain</u> for hours. What time do you have to be at the station?
>
> Owen: <u>I'm meeting</u> Jason and Mark there at 8.30, in the café near the main entrance. The train <u>leaves</u> at 8.45.
>
> Mia: It's quite a long walk to the station, isn't it? And it's 8.15 already. Look, <u>I'll take</u> you in the car.
>
> Owen: Thanks!

❸ *Suggested answers:*

2 When are you seeing your friends next week? I'm seeing them on Friday.   3 Where are you going to go this evening? I'm going to go to the cinema.
4 What date do your holidays begin this summer? They begin on July 5th.   5 When do you think you will get a job? I'll get a job in about eight years.
6 Do scientists say the Earth is going to get hotter? Yes, they say it's going to get a lot hotter.   7 When will you next send a text message? I'll send one right now!

❹ *Suggested answers:*

2 'm going on Monday / 'm going to go on Monday.
3 'll carry/take it for you.   4 leaves   5 'll have a glass of orange juice.   6 'm meeting friends.
7 's going to rain.

⑤ *Suggested answers:*

2 I'll help you / fix it (if you like). 3 It leaves / takes off at 9.30 in the evening. 4 There's going to be a storm. / The waves are going to get a lot bigger.
5 I'll call an ambulance. 6 I'm going to study medicine. / I don't know what I'm going to study.

Reading Part 1

❶ 2 email 3 notice 4 announcement/information
5 road sign

❷ b 3 ('strong winds', 'take care') c 5 ('wait' imperative) d 1 ('no parking') e 4 ('closes 30 minutes before …')

❸ 1 1 notice (near lift door, probably at an airport because of the reference to Passport Control)
2 Its purpose is to inform and advise (shown by the common phrase 'out of order' and 'Please use')

2 message; to inform and suggest something
3 Internet item description; to advertise something for sale 4 label; to give a warning 5 notice; to say what is (and is not) allowed 6 email; to inform and to suggest something

❹ 2 B 3 B 4 C 5 A 6 C

Vocabulary
Compound words

❶ crossroads, guesthouse, guidebook, hitchhike, overnight, railroad, sightseeing, signpost, suitcase

1 guidebook 2 suitcase 3 crossroads
4 hitchhike 5 railroad 6 backpack
7 signpost 8 overnight 9 guesthouse
10 sightseeing

❷ 2 guidebook 3 sightseeing 4 railroad
5 guesthouse 6 hitchhike 7 backpack
8 suitcase 9 crossroads 10 signpost

Prepositions of movement

❶ 2 on 3 on 4 off 5 on 6 in 7 out 8 of

❷ 1 on, off 2 in, out of 3 get, jump 4 by, by, on
5 on

❸ 2 ~~into~~ → on/onto 3 ~~at~~ → on 4 ~~on~~ → in/into
5 ~~on~~ → by 6 ✓ 7 ~~by~~ → on 8 ~~into~~ → on/onto

Speaking Part 2

❶ 1 Students should tick: bus, boat, metro, bike, tram 2 They decide to use bike and boat.

❷ 2 because 3 rather 4 not 5 one 6 another
7 about 8 like

❸ 2 b 3 d 4 a 5 b 6 b 7 c 8 d

❹ The underlined words are all weak forms.

	Three.
Mikel:	it's going to be really hot
	Four.
Mikel:	sail down the river
	Five.
Ingrid:	we can ride to the harbour
	Six.
Ingrid:	half an hour

Writing Part 1

❶ 2 too awful   3 quite close/near to   4 so much
5 are going   6 going everywhere on foot   7 I'd
rather

Recording script   CD1 Track 39

Pat:	Do you think people in 2020 will still <u>go everywhere by car</u>?
Kelly:	No, I don't. For one thing, the traffic will be <u>too awful</u> for us to go anywhere.
Pat:	Actually, we're <u>quite close to</u> that situation already.
Kelly:	Yes, I agree. And cars cause <u>so much</u> pollution, especially in cities.
	I think a lot of countries <u>are going</u> to reduce the number of vehicles.
Pat:	So do you think most of us will end up <u>going everywhere on foot</u>?
Kelly:	Yes I think we probably will, and I wouldn't mind that at all. In fact, I'd <u>rather</u> do that.

❷ 2 rise a lot   3 sunny   4 so … that   5 be … wetter
6 the coldest

❸ 1 cool enough   2 much higher   3 will/'ll shine
4 too warm   5 will/'ll rain   6 colder

❹ *Suggested answers:*

1 The areas around the coast will be badly affected, because sea levels will rise and a lot of the land will be covered in water.

2 The dry part of the country in the south-east will have even less rain, which will turn the area almost into a desert.

3 In the parts of the country where there are high mountains, there will be less snow, even in winter, so it won't be possible to ski there any more.

4 In the green areas in the north and west of our country it will rain much less, so there will be fewer plants and trees, with a bigger danger of fires because everything will be much drier.

8   This is me!

Starting off

❷ 1 A Cinderella   2 A Maradona   3 C Rafa Nadal
4 A Brad Pitt & Angelina Jolie   5 B Bart Simpson's
grandfather

Reading Part 3

❷ Toni Nadal

❸/❹ A life coach helps people to think about what they want and how they are going to get it.

❺ *Suggested words to underline:*

3 used to work … radio   4 Jem … do a degree … before … Africa   5 Jem's parents … like … his degree … another country   6 singing … study … nearly perfect … science   7 Irina … happy … any university   8 Irina … always … keen on keeping fit   9 Mo … worked … children younger than six   10 Some … Regina's friends … new school play basketball

❻ 2 B   3 C   4 C   5 C   6 D   7 D   8 D   9 E   10 E

❼ 1 Correct – I get on very well with Irina
2 Incorrect – Until now, life coaches have helped adults … Now it's the turn of our young people
3 Correct – a former radio producer
4 Incorrect – he has decided to take part in a volunteer project in central Africa first
5 Incorrect – This experience abroad will help him grow up before he goes to university here
6 Correct – Once she made up songs to learn by, she achieved 99 per cent in her tests
7 Incorrect – Now she hopes to get into a top university
8 Incorrect – She has even taken up exercise for the first time in years
9 Correct – Mo Ahmed has coached children as young as five years old
10 Correct – By joining the school basketball team Regina has made several new friends

❽ *Suggested answers:*

3 *used to → former*

4 *do a degree → got a place at university* (*before* and *first* have opposite meanings)

5 *do his degree → study medicine / goes to university*; *in another country → abroad* (*here* has the opposite meaning)

6 *used singing → made up songs*; *nearly perfect marks → 99 per cent*

7 *would be happy → hopes* (*top* has the opposite meaning of *any*)

8 *keeping fit → exercise* (*for the first time in years* has the opposite meaning of *always*)

9 *younger than six → as young as five*

10 *some → several*

Vocabulary
Phrasal verbs

❶ bringing up, set up, sort out, grow up, found out, made up, has ... taken up

Suggested answers for meanings:

bring up (a child) – to look after a child and teach them until they are old enough to look after themselves

find out (something) – to get information about something, or to learn a fact for the first time

get on with – if two or more people get on, they like each other and are friendly to each other

grow up – to become older or an adult

make up – to invent

set up (something) – to start a company or organisation

sort out (something) – to successfully deal with something, such as a problem or difficult situation

take up (something) – to start doing a particular job or activity

❷ **2** brought me up   **3** sort out   **4** set up   **5** take up
6 get on (well) with   **7** make up   **8** found out

Grammar
Zero, first and second conditionals

❷ **1** Kristian's dad says that Kristian isn't sure about his future.   **2** get training by going to acting classes after school; get experience by being a film extra

Recording script   CD1 Track 40

Mo:	Hi Kristian. How are you?
Kristian:	Er ... OK.
Mo:	Your dad's got in contact with me because he says you're not very sure about your future. Let's have a little chat about it. What are your favourite subjects?
Kristian:	No, that's not the problem ... I'm very sure about my future. I'd really like to go to drama school. You see, everyone says I'm quite good at acting.
Mo:	How old are you, Kristian?
Kristian:	That's the problem. I'm only fifteen. I'll need my parents' permission if I want to go to drama school. They say I have to stay at school until I'm eighteen. But if I stay at school until I'm eighteen, it'll be too late.
Mo:	Too late for what?
Kristian:	If you want to be an actor, you have to start your training at an early age.
Mo:	Maybe we should look at other ways of getting training. Have you thought about going to acting classes after school?
Kristian:	Yes, but I'd have to give up football if I went to classes after school. That's why I think drama school would be a good solution. If I studied at drama school, I'd have enough time for everything.
Mo:	Have your parents seen you performing on stage?
Kristian:	No, not for a long time. I wasn't in this year's English play because none of my friends were in it.
Mo:	I see. Let's think about ways you can get some more acting experience. Have you thought about being a film extra?
Kristian:	What's that?

❸ **1** want   **2** stay, 'll be   **3** want, have   **4** 'd have, went   **5** studied, 'd have

❹ **1** No. Josh doesn't want Kristian to join the drama club because the football team will lose its best player.

2 No

3 (6) is a real possibility but (7) is not

❺ b Type 1: 2, 6 **c** Type 2: 4, 5, 7

❻ *Students should underline:*

b snows, 'll make; **c** snowed, would go

Forms of the verb: Type 0: *if* + present, present; Type 1: *if* + present, future; Type 2: *if* + past simple, *would* + infinitive without *to*

❼ We use a comma if the conditional sentence begins with the *if* clause. We don't use a comma if the sentence begins with the result.

❽ 1 The first conditional has been used because the weather forecast says it will rain, so this is a real possibility.

2 We would use the second conditional when rain is not likely (e.g. in the middle of a very dry summer – *If it rained, the plants would get some water.*).

❾ *Suggested answers:*
2 If I saw a friend cheating in an exam, I wouldn't tell the teacher. / If I see a friend cheating in an exam, I'll tell the teacher.
3 If I get good marks at school, I'll be very happy.
4 If I found a lot of money in a rubbish bin, I'd take it to the police station.
5 If I got lost in a foreign country, I'd ask someone for directions. / If I get lost in a foreign country, I'll ask someone for directions.
6 If I get a lot of homework, I won't go out tonight with my friends.

❿ *Suggested questions:*
1 What would you do if you lost your mobile phone? / If you lost your mobile phone, what would you do?
2 What would you do if you saw a friend cheating in an exam? / If you saw your friend cheating in an exam, what would you do?
3 What will you do if you get good marks at school? / If you get good marks at school, what will you do?
4 What would you do if you found a lot of money in a rubbish bin? / If you found a lot of money in a rubbish bin, what would you do?
5 What would you do if you got lost in a foreign country? / What will you do if you get lost in a foreign country? / If you got lost in a foreign country, what would you do?
6 What will you do if you get a lot of homework from your teacher? / If you get a lot of homework from your teacher, what will you do?

When, if, unless + present, future

❶ A: this teenager will definitely call her parents (**when** she gets there); **B:** this teenager may not call his parents (if he gets there too late);
C: this teenager may not call her parents (only if she needs something)

❷ 1 when **2** if **3** unless

❸ 2 if **3** unless **4** unless **5** unless **6** unless

Listening Part 3

❶ They are in the crowd scenes/background.

❷ 1 noun **2** noun **3** number **4** noun **5** day **6** name

❸ 1 (a) market(s) **2** website **3** 18/eighteen (years old) **4** face(s) **5** Sunday(s) **6** Kavanagh

Recording script CD1 Track 41

Vanessa: What's an extra? An extra's an ordinary person – just like you or me – who's interested in TV or movies and would like to be on TV or in a movie. Extras aren't movie stars but they are people who appear in the background as members of a crowd, or <u>shoppers in a market</u> or fans in a sports stadium. Imagine the satisfaction of pointing to the screen and saying 'That's me!'.

Many people believe that films are only made in major cities like Los Angeles or New York. But that's where most people are wrong. Yes, movies *are* filmed in Los Angeles and New York City, but movie companies very often travel round the world to find suitable locations. <u>Check our website</u> regularly to see if something's being filmed near you soon.

Finding movie extra jobs is easy because it doesn't matter what you look like or how old you are, although your parents will need to give their written permission if you <u>aren't yet eighteen years old</u>. Directors are looking for all kinds of people. At the moment our directors are looking for young people who look about sixteen years old, who are no more than 1.7 metres tall and of course who have <u>interesting faces</u>.

Working as a movie extra isn't always exciting. Be ready to get up at 6 am or earlier and work very long days – anything up to sixteen hours

– but very rarely seven days a week. Filming may begin on Monday, often <u>with a break on Sunday</u>. This will depend on the director. Remember to wear comfortable clothes and shoes as you may have to stand for long hours.

All movies need movie extras. All you have to do is let these directors know you are willing and available to work. Give our agency a ring and ask for <u>Vanessa Kavanagh, that's K-A-V-A-N-A-G-H</u> or visit our website: www. extrasextras.com.

Vocabulary
Describing people

❶ B

Marti: Harry, is that you?

Harry: Marti! How's things?

Marti: Great! Great! Look, Darrilus is looking for a teenager to play Dean Darrick's son in his latest movie. Have you got anyone?

Harry: Dean Darrick, eh? What should this teenager look like?

Marti: He should be medium height, look around sixteen with long, straight hair – although we could change that if we had to. He should probably be rather good-looking, too.

Harry: Um … we've got this new young actor, but he's got rather <u>a large scar on his chin</u>. Any good?

Marti: Mm. <u>Not really.</u> He needs to look <u>young and fresh</u>, preferably with <u>no beard or moustache</u>.

Harry: I've got this one here. He's got <u>pale eyes</u>; he's <u>very attractive</u> and everyone says he's honest and reliable.

Marti: Let's get in touch with him then.

❷ *Suggested answers:*

hair: curly, straight, wavy, long, short, bald, grey, blond(e), red, dark, fair
build: slim, broad shoulders, medium height
skin: pale, dark
other: scar, beard, attractive, good-looking, moustache, beautiful, plain

❸ *Suggested answers:*

2 stupid **3** quiet **4** generous **5** polite/pleasant
6 nervous **7** shy, nervous **8** cold

❹ *im*patient *un*pleasant *dis*honest *un*reliable

❺ wonder*ful* beaut*iful* hope*ful*/hope*less* cheer*ful* (also possible: cheer*less*)

No – *hopeful* = feeling positive about a future event or situation (e.g. *I'm hopeful about my future*) but *hopeless* = very bad (e.g. *I'm hopeless at sport*)

❻ Finn*ish* Turk*ish* Brit*ish* Swe*dish* Scott*ish* self*ish* child*ish* fool*ish* baby*ish*

❼ **b** ~~hair and eyes black~~ → black hair and eyes **c** ~~young handsome~~ → handsome young **d** ~~white beautiful~~ → beautiful white **e** ~~black short~~ → short black **f** ~~green big~~ → big green

Speaking Part 1

❶/**❷**

eɪ	iː	e	aɪ	əʊ	uː	ɑː
A, H, J, K	B, C, D, E, G, P, T, V	F, L, M, N, S, X, Z	I, Y	O	Q, U, W	R

Man: /eɪ/ – A, H, J, K

Woman: /iː/ – B, C, D, E, G, P, T, V

Man: /e/ – F, L, M, N, S, X, Z

Woman: /aɪ/ – I, Y

Man: /əʊ/ – O

Woman: /uː/ – Q, U, W

Man: /ɑː/ – R

❸/**❹**

1 because **2** there **3** which **4** two **5** where
6 to **7** wear **8** their **9** too **10** different

         Write down the correct spelling of the words you hear. One.

Woman: *because* – I'm going to bed <u>because</u> I'm tired. Two.

Man: *there* – <u>There</u> isn't any milk in the fridge. Three.

Woman: *which* – I did a maths test yesterday <u>which</u> was really easy. Four.

Man: *two* – I've lived here for <u>two</u> years. Five.

Woman:	*where* – She can't open the door. She doesn't know <u>where</u> her keys are.
	Six.
Man:	*to* – Could you give this <u>to</u> your grandma, please?
	Seven.
Woman:	*wear* – Older people often <u>wear</u> hats at weddings in my country.
	Eight.
Man:	*their* – Rob and Simon didn't do <u>their</u> homework.
	Nine.
Woman:	*too* – I didn't get a part in the film. They said I was <u>too</u> young.
	Ten.
Man:	*different* – Do you think working in TV is <u>different</u> from working in radio?

Recording script   CD1 Track 45

	One.
Woman:	because – B-E-C-A-U-S-E
	Two.
Man:	there – T-H-E-R-E
	Three.
Woman:	which – W-H-I-C-H
	Four.
Man:	two – T-W-O
	Five.
Woman:	where – W-H-E-R-E
	Six.
Man:	to – T-O
	Seven.
Woman:	wear – W-E-A-R
	Eight.
Man:	their – T-H-E-I-R
	Nine.
Woman:	too – T-O-O
	Ten.
Man:	different – D-I-F-F-E-R-E-N-T

5 Student A's words: **1** received   **2** centre (US center)   **3** and   **4** beautiful   **5** colour   **6** comfortable   **7** then

Student B's words: **1** interesting   **2** together   **3** restaurant   **4** recommend   **5** believe   **6** favourite   **7** thought

6 **1** Brunner   **2** Murakami   **3** Switzerland   **4** Japan   **5** French   **6** beautiful   **7** future   **8** yesterday evening   **9** free time

Recording script   CD1 Track 46

	One.
Examiner:	What's your name?
Angela:	My name's Angela.
Examiner:	Thank you. What's your surname?
Angela:	It's 'Tedesco'.
Examiner:	How do you spell it?
Angela:	T-E-D-E-S-C-O
Examiner:	Thank you. Where do you live?
Angela:	I live in Italy.
Examiner:	Do you study English?
Angela:	Yes, I do. I study it at school.
Examiner:	Do you like it?
Angela:	Yes, I love English because I like travelling and meeting people from other countries.
Examiner:	Thank you. Angela, do you think English will be useful for you in the future?
Angela:	I'm not sure, but when I'm older I'd like to be an architect and I think I'll need to read a lot of books in English.
	Two.
Examiner:	Now, what's your name?
Eduard:	My name's Eduard.
Examiner:	Thank you. What's your surname?
Eduard:	My surname's '<u>Brunner</u>'.
Examiner:	How do you spell it?
Eduard:	<u>B-R-U-N-N-E-R</u>
Examiner:	Thank you. Where do you come from?
Eduard:	I come from <u>Switzerland</u>.
Examiner:	Do you study English?
Eduard:	Yes, I go to an English school twice a week.
Examiner:	Do you like it?
Eduard:	Yes, I like English, but I prefer <u>French</u> because it's easy for me.
Examiner:	Ah. Thank you. Eduard, what did you do yesterday evening?
Eduard:	Sorry, can you say that again?
Examiner:	Yes. Did you do anything yesterday evening?
Eduard:	Oh yes. I went to the cinema with my brother and cousins and we saw a film. It was very nice.

	Three.
Examiner:	What's your name?
Yuji:	Yuji.
Examiner:	Thank you. What's your surname?
Yuji:	Murakami.
Examiner:	How do you spell it?
Yuji:	M-U-R-A-K-A-M-I
Examiner:	Thank you. Where do you come from?
Yuji:	I'm from Japan.
Examiner:	Do you study English?
Yuji:	Yes, I have English lessons at school and I also do extra English at H & P English School.
Examiner:	Do you like it?
Yuji:	Yes.
Examiner:	Why?
Yuji:	I think English is useful for me and it's a beautiful language.
Examiner:	Thank you, Yuji. What do you enjoy doing in your free time?
Yuji:	Um … I really enjoy playing sports. Er, after school, I play ping pong with a team and I also like baseball. I also like reading books and watching TV.

7 *Suggested answers:*

1 Yes, they answer well because they use full answers with examples (Yuji: *After school I play …*), reasons (Angela: *I'll need to read … in English*) and opinions (Eduard: *we saw a film. It was very nice*).

2 Sorry, can you say that again?

3 No, he answers with a (slightly) different question: Did you do anything …?

Grammar
So do I and *nor/neither do I*

1

Recording script   CD1 Track 47

Ken:	My name's Ken.
	I'm 15 years old.
	I've got two brothers.
	I live in Taipei.
	I don't like football.
	I went to the cinema yesterday.
	I haven't been to Paris.

2

Recording script   CD1 Track 48

Zosia:	My name's Zosia.
	I'm from Krakow. It's a very beautiful city in Poland.
	I've got one sister.
	I get on very well with my sister.
	I love going to the cinema with my friends.
	I went to the cinema yesterday with my best friend.
	I don't like staying at home.
	I haven't travelled very much …
	… but I've been to Warsaw, the capital city of Poland.

Writing Part 2

2 1 I am keen on **T**-shirts (also *t-shirt* or *tee shirts*), trousers and jackets**.**
2 **I**'ll send a present to **M**arina**. I** hope she likes it**.**
3 **S**ay 'Hi' to your sister**. S**ee you soon, Gari
4 **I** can't come to your **E**nglish lesson on **M**onday**.**
5 **M**y blanket is like a penguin's skin**. It**'s black and white**.**

3 *Suggested words to underline:*

meet your cousin Myra, station, never met … before, an email to Myra, describe yourself, ask Myra … describe herself, suggest … place to meet … station, 35–45 words

6 Three points: 1 Im tallish … cap 2 what do you look like? 3 Lets meet outside the resturant wich is in the station

Words to connect points (with correct spelling): because, with, and, which

Spelling mistakes: **1** becouse → bec**a**use   **2** an → an**d**   **3** fav~~orit~~ → fav**ourite** (UK) / fav**orite** (US)   **4** res~~tur~~ant → res**taur**ant   **5** ~~wich~~ → **whi**ch

Punctuation mistakes: **1** ~~Im~~ → I'm   **2** ~~i~~ → I   **3** ~~what~~ → What   **4** ~~Lets~~ → Let's   **5** ~~station~~ → station.

Corrected letter:

Hi Myra,

I am very happy because you are coming. I'm tallish with short hair, blue eyes and I always wear my favourite (or favorite) blue cap. What do you look like? Let's meet outside the restaurant which is in the station.

Pablo

Vocabulary and grammar review   Unit 7

Grammar

❶ 2 big enough   **3** warm enough   **4** thick enough   **5** too sleepy   **6** old enough   **7** too cold   **8** too expensive

❷ 2 'm meeting   **3** 'll go   **4** leaves   **5** 'll   **6** are going

Vocabulary

❸ 2 f   **3** a   **4** b   **5** c   **6** e

❹

```
 1                          2
 T                          B
 R        3        W        O         4
 A        E        5 C    6 S  A  I  L
 7 M  E  T  R  O           R         O
                  O        D         U
 8                9              10       D
 F                B  L  O  W        Y
 L                I         11 D  R  Y
 I                K         I
 13 G  A  L  E           14 15 M  I  L  D
 H                       C         E
 T              16 F  E  R  R  Y
```

Vocabulary and grammar review   Unit 8

Vocabulary

❶ 2 B   **3** A   **4** C   **5** D   **6** B   **7** A   **8** C   **9** D   **10** C

❷ 2 ~~becouse~~ → because   **3** ~~did'nt~~ → didn't   **4** ~~sisters~~ → sister's   **5** ~~italian~~ → Italian   **6** ~~wich~~ → which   **7** ~~were~~ → wear   **8** ~~belive~~ → believe

Grammar

❸ *Suggested answers:*

2 … someone broke my new skateboard.
3 … I can't wake up in the morning.
4 … I'd keep it.
5 … I say something stupid.
6 … I'll have my party in the garden.
7 … I pass all my exams.
8 … my parents get angry.

❹ 2 has / has got / 's got   **3** so   **4** unless   **5** 'd/would travel

9   Fit and healthy

Listening   Part 4

❶ 1 I agree with you   **2** I'm not sure about that

Recording script CD1 Track 49	
Kelly:	They keep saying on TV things like 'today's teenagers are unfit and unhealthy', and I just don't believe it.
Jason:	<u>I agree with you</u>. There's all this stuff about us not getting enough exercise because we're watching TV or playing computer games all the time, when in fact, nowadays everyone is mad about sports.
Kelly:	Well, <u>I'm not sure about that</u>, but certainly a lot of young people are doing active things. Perhaps more than older generations did.

❷ *Suggested answers:*

<u>Agreeing</u>

I totally agree; I agree completely; (you're) right; absolutely; that's true; yes, I think so (too) because …; yes, I do too; so do I; neither do I

Disagreeing politely

I don't really agree; I don't think so because …; you may be right, but …; I don't know; actually, I think …; I know, but …; I'm not (so) sure (about that)

Disagreeing (showing strong disagreement)

I don't agree with you (at all); I (completely) disagree; that's not true; I don't think so because …; that's not the way I see it

❸ 1 NO 2 YES 3 YES 4 NO 5 NO 6 NO

Recording script   CD1 Track 50

Jason:	It's true, isn't it, Kelly, that people eat more these days, so they're getting bigger and heavier?
Kelly:	Er, yes, I think so, Jason. But lots of people are vegetarian now, aren't they? And I think that kind of food is really good for you. So people might eat more nowadays but <u>that doesn't mean that what they eat is worse for them</u>.
Jason:	No, it's just different. But there's more to being healthy than just exercise and eating, isn't there? I mean, there's so much stress in everyday life. And there are a lot of people that don't get enough sleep.
Kelly:	I don't know whether people are any more stressed, but <u>you're right that everyone seems to go to bed late</u>, even when they've got school or work the next day. I suppose it's all the late films on TV, or staying on the Internet until two in the morning.
Jason:	Or on the PlayStation®. There are so many fun things to do. So even if people manage to get up on time the next morning, they're too tired to do anything.
Kelly:	Hmm, I'm not so sure. These days, <u>when they go to school, a lot more students are going by bike</u>. Especially now that in some cities you can hire one cheaply and then just leave it anywhere you like. And that's quite healthy, isn't it?
Jason:	Hmm, it might be. But the air's really bad nowadays, especially in the cities. There's all that pollution from cars and lorries.
Kelly:	Actually, <u>I think the situation has improved a bit</u> since they started making everyone pay to drive into the city centre. There's not so much traffic now.

Jason:	You may be right, but it still makes me cough in the morning. Which reminds me: don't you think people get sick more often nowadays? <u>I'm always fine, and I'm sure you are too</u>, but we know a lot of people whose health is terrible, don't we?
Kelly:	Hmm, I don't know about that. I think it's mostly coughs and colds and sore throats; perhaps a headache or a stomach ache which lasts a day or two. Usually nothing more serious than that. And teenagers have always had those kinds of illnesses. In most cases, I don't think their basic health is any different.
Jason:	Well, <u>that's not the way I see it</u>, but I *hope* you're right!
Kelly:	Me too!

Vocabulary

Illnesses and accidents

❶ Phonetic script for underlined words: cough: /kɒf/; cold: /kəʊld/; sore: /sɔː/; throat: /θrəʊt/; headache: /hedeɪk/; stomach: /stʌmək/; ache: /eɪk/ Meanings: cough: make air come out of your throat with a short sound; cold: common illness which makes you sneeze and makes your nose produce liquid; sore throat: pain inside the throat; headache: pain inside your head; stomach ache: pain in your stomach

Recording script   CD1 Track 51

Kelly:	coughs and colds and sore throats; perhaps a headache or a stomach ache

❷

accidents	illnesses	treatments
injury	flu	medicine
cut	disease	plaster
bruise	high temperature	pill
wound	earache	tablet
sprain		bandage
fracture		aspirin
		X-ray
		operation
		injection
		plaster cast

❸ *Suggested answers:*

1 My brother fractured his leg.   **2** I think I've sprained my ankle.   **3** You've cut your finger. **4** She's bruised her leg.   **5** I've got a bad earache.   **6** The patient has a serious wound. **7** A nurse put a plaster cast on his broken arm. **8** You should have an X-ray.   **9** I don't like taking medicine.   **10** You need to have an injection now.

❹ *Suggested answers:* 'I had a bad cough, a sore throat and a terrible headache', 'I had an X-ray, they put on a bandage and I took some tablets for the pain'.

Grammar
Which, that, who, whose, when and *where* clauses (defining and non-defining)

❶ **2** who   **3** which   **4** whose   **5** that   **6** when **7** where   **8** that

❷

Recording script   CD1 Track 52

Presenter: Most people <u>that</u> do regular sport are healthier, and often feel happier, than those <u>who</u> do little or no exercise. Care must be taken, though, to avoid the injuries <u>which</u> sport can sometimes cause. People <u>whose</u> favourite sports are running or jumping, for instance, may injure their ankles or knees. Training <u>that</u> involves doing the same exercise again and again can do serious damage, particularly to athletes in their early teens, <u>when</u> their bodies are still developing. It is important not to do too much too soon. Everyone should 'warm up' before they begin – if possible in the place <u>where</u> they are going to exercise. It is essential, too, to follow any safety advice <u>that</u> they receive.

❸ **2** who   **3** that/which   **4** which/that   **5** when **6** where   **7** whose

The other relative pronouns which are the object and could be left out are: **7** where and **8** that

❹ **1** stress caused by busy living   **2** find something they enjoy doing every day

❺ (alternatives in brackets): **2** whose   **3** which (that)   **4** that (which)   **5** when   **6** which (that) **7** where

❻

Recording script   CD1 Track 53

Presenter: People <u>who</u> work very hard, and individuals <u>whose</u> lives are busy in other ways, may suffer from a kind of stress <u>which</u> can actually damage their health. One way <u>that</u> they can reduce stress levels is to find a time, every day, <u>when</u> they can relax. They should find something <u>that</u> they enjoy doing, such as reading, in a place <u>where</u> they feel comfortable and unlikely to be disturbed.

❼ We could leave out: **4** which   **5** when   **6** that **7** where

❽ **2** who/that swim   **3** where accidents   **4** not necessary / illness that   **5** whose tooth **6** not necessary / time when

❾ *Suggested answers:* **2** I do my homework / I listen to music   **3** I hate / I really like   **4** I stay in bed late / I go swimming   **5** always helps you / listens to you   **6** ticket wins a prize / health is really good

❿ **1** which   **2** which is very healthy   **3** separate it from the rest of the sentence   **4** yes   **5** no   **6** no

⓫ **2** a doctor, works in the hospital.   **3** I went for a swim, was very cold.   **4** sister is a nurse, is my best friend.   **5** was 12, the sports centre opened. **6** really enjoy, is popular in my country.

⓬ **2** I am visiting my mother, who is ill.
  3 He has a son, who is about my age.
  4 The last book (that) I read was 'The Lord of the Rings'.
  5 I've met a guy whose name is Daniel.
  6 I'm in Brazil, which is a beautiful country.
  7 That is all (that) I can tell you.
  8 There are many places that/which are very beautiful.
  9 I'll tell everyone (who) I know.
  10 I have to go to the airport, which is quite far from the city.

Vocabulary
Sports

❶ **1** B   **2** C   **3** A

❷ (do) gymnastics; (go) paragliding; (play) basketball

❸

do	go	play
gymnastics	paragliding	basketball
boxing	cycling	ice hockey
athletics	surfing	volleyball
	running	football
	swimming	squash
	climbing	tennis
	skiing	golf
	jogging	baseball

❹ *Suggested answer:*
Patterns: *go* is usually used with outdoor sports, which are often over long distances; *play* often goes with sports that end *-ball* and ball sports generally. We often use *do* with sports that do not take *go* or *play*. (Note: in informal speech, *do* can be used with most activities [e.g. 'she *does* cycling in her free time'].)

❺ 2 ~~make~~ → do   3 ~~make~~ → go   4 ~~done~~ → played   5 ~~made~~ → did   6 ~~played~~ → went

❻ *Suggested answers:*
court: tennis, squash, basketball, volleyball, etc.
gym: gymnastics, aerobics, martial arts, etc.
pitch: football, rugby, hockey, baseball, etc.
ring: boxing, wrestling, kickboxing, etc.
stadium: football, rugby, baseball, etc.
track: athletics, running, cycling, etc.

❼ clothes: boots (football, rugby, skiing, etc.); gloves (boxing, football goalkeeper, ice hockey, skiing, etc.); helmet (horse riding, motorcycling, baseball, etc.); trainers (running, jogging, tennis, etc.)

equipment: bat (baseball, cricket, table tennis, etc.); board (surfing, windsurfing, snowboarding, etc.); racket (table tennis, squash, badminton, etc.); net (tennis, table tennis, volleyball, etc.)

❽ 2 score   3 draw/lose/win

Reading Part 5

❶ 1 ice hockey: team, competitive;   2 squash: individual, competitive   3 aerobics: individual, non-competitive   4 scuba diving: individual, non-competitive

❹ 1 A   2 D   3 B   4 B   5 A   6 D   7 D   8 C   9 B   10 C

Speaking Part 2

❶ 2 sure   3 totally   4 so   5 way   6 all   7 true   8 too

❷ **a** agree: 3, 7, 8   **b** disagree strongly: 5, 6   **c** disagree politely: 1, 2, 4

❸ 2 really sure   3 totally agree   4 think   5 I   6 at all   7 true   8 I

❺ 2 then   3 agreed   4 what   5 both   6 So   7 thing   8 glad

❻

❼ Stressed words are: good idea, that, agreed, That's, both, that, best thing, glad

Writing Part 3

❶ 1 story   2 title   3 first person   4 story, title, frightening, experience, my (which answers 3)

❷ **b** 1   **c** 3   **d** 3   **e** 3   **f** 1

Past perfect

❸ 1 she had disappeared; had she gone; I'd gone; she'd heard; she'd found

2 *had* + subject + past participle (Had she gone …?) 3 *'d* + past participle (I'd gone / she'd heard / she'd found)

④ 2 I had/'d walked all the way home   **3** arrived at the stadium, the match had started   **4** had/'d left my trainers at home, I couldn't run in the race   **5** had/'d decided to get fit, I took up squash

⑤ 1 story   **2** the first line   **3** first person   **4** I (the answer to 3), nervous, game, began.

⑥ *Sample answer:*

I felt nervous when the game began. Fifty thousand people were watching me in the stadium, as well as a television audience of millions. I had always dreamt of playing for my favourite team, and at last I had my chance.

For the first hour everything went fine. We were playing well and I had started to feel less nervous. Then, suddenly, it all went horribly wrong: I made a terrible mistake and the other team scored. I felt awful.

Then I thought back to what the coach had said to me, about never giving up, and I knew that I simply had to win the match for my team. So, in the last few minutes, I scored the two most important goals of my life.

10 A question of taste

Starting off

❶ The types of food and drink have been organised according to colour. *Suggested answers:* white: yoghurt, onion, cream; red: meat, pepper, steak; yellow: mustard, corn, oil, lemon; orange: peach, pumpkin, marmalade

Reading Part 2

❶ *Suggested answers:*

The short texts probably describe unusual restaurants; match groups of people with suitable restaurants

❷ *Suggested answers to underline:*

1 teacher prefers ... fish; interesting views; isn't too expensive
2 summer wedding anniversary; next Tuesday; hate being with other groups; normally orders steak; Jack ... something different

3 try another character restaurant; this Thursday; aren't keen on fish; can't afford anywhere expensive
4 special views; on Sunday; Jon ... prefer ... meat rather than fish or vegetarian
5 on Sundays; love foreign food; eat alone; leaves Sweden

❸ *Suggested answers:*

1 cheap/inexpensive/reasonable/not expensive
2 They could hire the whole restaurant or book a private room.
3 Chef Mickey Mouse/Cowboy Café, etc.
4 No, restaurants in these places are unlikely to have windows with a view
5 Sweden (so they won't want to go to a Swedish restaurant)

❹ 1 B   **2** F   **3** A   **4** H   **5** C

Grammar
Commands

❶ 1 D   **2** A   **3** H

> **Recording script**   CD2 Track 2
>
> One.
>
> Waitress 1: Hi. How are you? Just before I take you to your table, <u>put on these gloves and snow boots</u>. Children, don't touch the walls please! OK, follow me. Here's your table. I'll bring you <u>some hot soup</u> while you look at the menu.
>
> Two.
>
> Waiter: Here's the bill. I hope you enjoyed your meal, sir. And remember – bring your friends with you next time – but, <u>don't tell your enemies where we are – it's a secret</u>!
>
> Three.
>
> Waitress 2: Go over to the butcher's table. Choose <u>a steak</u>. The butcher will weigh it for you. <u>Take your steak to the barbecue</u> and tell the chef how you'd like your meat. <u>Don't touch the grill</u> or you'll burn yourself!

❷ 2 don't touch   **3** bring   **4** don't tell   **5** Take   **6** Don't touch

Form of verb we use: **a** infinitive without *to*; **b** *don't* + infinitive without *to*

Form of the verb does NOT change when we talk to more than one person

③ *Suggested answers:*
1 Take off your coat and give it to me.
2 Mind your head.
3 Sit down here.
4 Here's your food. Don't touch the plate, it's hot.
5 Pick up your knife and fork.
6 Enjoy your meal.

Vocabulary

Course, dish, food, meal and *plate*

② 2 meals   3 plate   4 courses   5 dish

Listening Part 1

① 2 three   3 short   4 twice   5 try to tick (✓) the correct box

③ 2 loaf of bread   3 packet of biscuits   4 tin of pineapple

④ B

Recording script   CD2 Track 3
What did Jamie buy?
Jamie: I'm back, Mum! I got most of the shopping. <u>I got a tube of toothpaste and a loaf of bread</u>, but <u>I don't think they had any tins of pineapple left</u>. I couldn't see them anyway.

⑤ No, the correct answer is now A

Recording script   CD2 Track 4
Mum: Don't worry. <u>What about the biscuits</u>?
Jamie: I couldn't find them at first because they've changed the packet. <u>Is one packet enough</u>?
Mum: Plenty. Thanks, Jamie. Keep the change!

⑥ *Suggested answers:*

2 <u>What</u> will they <u>take</u> to the <u>party</u>?

You need to listen to find out if they take cake, ice-cream or soft drink and type (e.g. chocolate, cola, lemonade, etc.).

3 What <u>time</u> is the <u>boy's appointment</u>?

You need to listen for the times: 4.10 pm, 4.45 pm and 6.30 pm, and decide which one is the correct time for the boy's appointment.

4 <u>What</u> did the <u>girl buy online</u>?

We know that the girl buys one or two objects. You need to listen to find out if she buys a T-shirt and a pair of shoes, a T-shirt and a pair of pyjamas, or a pair of pyjamas only.

5 What is the <u>free gift</u> today?

You need to listen to find out if the free gift is a laptop, software or a mouse mat.

6 <u>What</u> is <u>nearest</u> to <u>Rick's Diner</u>?

You need to listen to find out which place: the bridge, station or roundabout, is the nearest to Rick's Diner.

7 Where has the <u>mother been</u>?

You need to listen to find out if she has been to the post office, fishmonger or hairdresser.

⑦ 2 B   3 A   4 C   5 C   6 A   7 B

Recording script   CD2 Track 5
Two. What will they take to the party?
Boy: Shall we take <u>a chocolate cake</u> to John's party?
Girl: Good idea, but <u>I'm not going to make one</u> and I'm sure <u>they're expensive to buy</u>. What about <u>some cans of soft drink</u>?
Boy: <u>You're right about the cake</u>. <u>John said he was going to buy some lemonade and some orange juice</u>. Have we <u>got enough to buy some ice-cream</u>?
Girl: Not really, but <u>my mum's got some in the freezer. Let's take that</u>.
Now listen again.
CD2 Track 6
Three. What time is the boy's appointment?
Man: I'd like to make an appointment for my son to get his hair cut one afternoon this week. Could you manage that on Thursday? I can bring him here after school.
Woman: Um, <u>Thursday's going to be busy</u>… um … but we could do that if you come at say … <u>half past six</u>? Would that be okay? If not, I've got <u>free appointments on Tuesday at ten past four</u> or <u>a quarter to five</u>.
Man: Er, thanks. <u>The earlier one that day would be best</u> for us.
Woman: Fine!
Now listen again.

CD2 Track 7

Four. What did the girl buy online?

Girl: Shopping online? Everyone says <u>shoes are cheaper if you buy them online</u> but you can't try them on, can you? <u>I ordered some pyjamas for my mum</u> and they were fine. You'd also think it would be safe to buy <u>a T-shirt</u> from the web <u>but my mum bought one</u> a month ago and it was just too tight.

CD2 Track 8

Five. What is the free gift today?

Announcer: Good afternoon, shoppers. To celebrate the fifth year of our very successful electronic department, we are offering <u>great discounts off all software bought today</u>. Computer expert, Gene Reedy, will also be in the store today to give you <u>free advice on how to improve your laptop's performance</u>. And for today only, you won't have to pay anything for one of our anniversary mouse mats – just pick one up from one of our shop assistants.

Now listen again.

CD2 Track 9

Six. What is nearest to Rick's Diner?

Message: This is Rick's Diner. We're open Monday to Saturday from 12.30 to late and you won't find better Moroccan food anywhere else outside Morocco! If you haven't visited us before, turn left at <u>Links Roundabout</u> into Trent Street and <u>we're 100 metres on the right, just before West Bridge</u>. And if you're coming by public transport, <u>it's a five-minute walk from the station</u>. See you soon!

Now listen again.

CD2 Track 10

Seven. Where has the mother been?

Boy: Hi, Mum, <u>did you collect my parcel</u>?

Mother: There was a terrible traffic jam and <u>you know the post office closes at six</u>. <u>I had to get fish for dinner</u>. Hope you don't mind. <u>I wanted to buy some sausages</u>, but by the time I managed to park the car, they were closed too! <u>I'm having my hair cut tomorrow</u> – I think I'll go by underground!

Boy: Could you get my parcel then?

Now listen again.

Vocabulary

Shops and services

❶ We use 's only with the place. (However, it is possible to describe the place with or without 's – *hairdresser/hairdresser's.*)

❷ **2** dentist   **3** dry cleaner   **4** library   **5** garage   **6** butcher   **7** post office   **8** travel agent

❸ **1** (hairdresser's),   **2** (dentist's) (possible but not usual),   **3** (dry cleaner's),   **6** (butcher's),   **8** (travel agent's) (possible but not usual)

❹ *Suggested answers:*

1 dentist('s), garage, hairdresser('s)   **2** butcher('s), post office   **3** library   **4** travel agent('s)   **5** dentist ('s), dry cleaner('s), garage   **6** butcher('s), dry cleaner('s), garage, hairdresser('s), travel agent('s)

❺ **1** hairdresser('s)   **2** garage   **3** dry cleaner('s)

Recording script   CD2 Track 11

One.

Madison: What have you <u>done to your hair</u>, Layla?

Layla: Oh don't! I normally <u>have my hair cut at Gabrielle's</u> but I wanted something different, so I went to that new place on the High Street.

Madison: Oh no! Was it very expensive?

Two.

Andrew: Are you coming to the party tonight, Lewis?

Lewis: I can't. I'm not allowed to go out.

Andrew: Why's that?

Lewis: I had a little accident <u>on my scooter</u>. My dad says it was my fault.

Andrew: What about your scooter? You only got it last week for your birthday.

Lewis: That's why my dad is so angry. <u>We're having the scooter repaired</u> and I'm going to have to look for a job to pay for it.

Three.

Vicki: Oh no! Callum! That's cola <u>you've spilt</u> down my dress.

Callum: Sorry, Vicki. It was an accident.

Vicki: My mum's going to go mad. <u>We had this dress cleaned last week</u> for this party and it wasn't cheap ...

6 *Suggested answers:*

1 Layla should complain and get her money back and then go to a better hairdresser.   **2** Lewis should find a part-time job by looking in the newspaper, asking friends or family or asking in shops and cafés. (He should also take better care of his scooter!)
3 Callum should offer to pay for the dry cleaning.

Grammar
Have something done

2 Vinnie is the slob.

3 **1** has his meals cooked for him   **2** 's having her nails done today   **3** had his flat cleaned last year

4 **2** I had my bike repaired two weeks ago.
3 John is having his bedroom painted now.
4 We have our photo taken once a year.
5 Our grandma has her hair coloured every three weeks.
6 I can't send an email because we are having our computer mended at the moment.

6 *Words and phrases to underline:*

he had his hair cut; have his head decorated; Jack has his head shaved; some of the teachers have their hair coloured regularly; footballers have their hair shaved

Speaking Part 3

(The objects illustrated are **A** hammer   **B** hairdryer **C** iron   **D** plug (electrical)   **E** fork   **F** frying pan **G** ladder   **H** tin-opener   **I** knife   **J** key)

1 They ask for: B, I and G.

3 **1** True   **2** True   **3** True   **4** False (you don't have to talk about things 'outside' the photograph, e.g. feelings, previous activities, etc.)   **5** False (you should use some of the expressions from the table in Exercise 2 in this section)

4 A

5 1, 3, 4, 5

Writing Part 2

1 **2** three   **3** Connect   **4** spelling   **5** between **6** open and close   **7** included

2 *Suggested words to underline:*

1 have pizza with your class; celebrate … end … year; forgotten to ask Ryan; email to Ryan; apologise; invite; explain where … eat; 35–45 words

2 shopping centre; nearby city; school holidays; email to … Paula; invite; explain why you want to go; suggest … place … meet; 35–45 words

3 stayed at your cousin's; left something behind; email to Alex; thank him; describe what you left; suggest how ... get ... object back; 35–45 words

❸ 2 because   **3** to come   **4** meet   **5** inviting

❹ *Suggested expressions to underline:*

thank someone: It was very kind of you to ...; Thank you very much for ...

explain: That's why ...; ... because ...

invite: How about ...; Would you like ...

apologise: I'm very sorry that ...; I'm so sorry for ...

suggest: Why don't we ...; Let's ...

❺ *Model answers:*

Hi Ryan,

I'm very sorry that I forgot to invite you before. We're going out on Friday night. Would you like to come too? We'll have a great time. We've decided to go to the new pizza restaurant. Let me know if you can come.

Yours,

....

Dear Paula,

I'm going to the shopping centre tomorrow. Why don't you come too? I want to go there because I want to have my hair cut at Dani Bridell's new hairdresser's. Why don't we meet outside the station?

See you soon,

....

Hi Alex,

Thank you very much for inviting me to stay for the weekend. I had a lot of fun.
I think I left my pencil case at your house. It's made of blue plastic. Can I come to your house tomorrow to get it?

Lots of love,

....

Vocabulary and grammar review   Unit 9

Grammar

❶ 2 d that   **3** f when   **4** a who   **5** b where
  6 e whose

❷ 2 In summer, when the weather is good, we play tennis.
3 Stevie, whose team won, was the best player of all.
4 In the city centre, where we live, there is a lot of pollution.
5 My brother, who had an accident, is feeling better now.
6 Volleyball, which is a team sport, is played on a court. / Volleyball, which is played on a court, is a team sport.

❸ 2 had practised   **3** felt   **4** had/'d brought
5 had/'d put   **6** was   **7** had/'d rained   **8** didn't seem   **9** was   **10** had left   **11** started   **12** realised
13 had/'d played   **14** was   **15** slipped   **16** fell
17 knew   **18** had/'d twisted   **19** went   **20** had not/hadn't broken   **21** wore

Vocabulary

❹ 2 sore   **3** beat   **4** nurse   **5** have   **6** bat
  7 athletics   **8** pill   **9** bruise   **10** ring

Vocabulary and grammar review   Unit 10

Vocabulary

❶ *Suggested answers:*

  2 complain   **3** book   **4** borrow   **5** repair

❷ *(Other answers are also possible)*

  2 ~~interesting~~ interested   **3** ~~resturants~~ restaurants
4 Chinese food ~~are~~ is   **5** ~~kind~~ nice   **6** all ~~kind~~ kinds   **7** chicken ~~food~~ dishes   **8** I think chicken ~~are~~ is   **9** ~~my~~ I think   **10** ~~enjoy with~~ enjoy your meal

Grammar

❸ 1 (*Also possible:* had <u>it</u> washed)   **2** is having/has her hair/it cut   **3** had it/one/a photo taken
4 have our windows/them cleaned   **5** had the car/it repaired   **6** had the walls/them painted

❹ 2 Put   **3** didn't   **4** had   **5** I would/'d

11 Conserving nature

Starting off

① B 3   C 7   D 8   E 1   F 4   G 6   H 2
2 T   3 T   4 F   5 T   6 F   7 F   8 T

② 1 tigers – Asia   2 polar bears – the Arctic
3 kangaroos – Australia   4 ostriches – Africa
5 lions – Africa/Asia   6 elephants – Asia/Africa
7 bats – all continents except Antarctica   8 bears –
South America/North America/Europe/Asia

Listening Part 2

① *Suggested answers:*

India: located in southern Asia – the world's biggest
democracy and country with the second-largest
population – independence in 1947 led by Gandhi
and Nehru – religions include Hinduism, Buddhism
and Sikhism – many languages are spoken but
Hindi is the official language and English quite
widely used – nowadays has a rapidly growing
economy and is an emerging superpower

Biggest cities: Mumbai; Delhi (both over 10 million
people)

Famous for: River Ganges; Taj Mahal; Bollywood
films

Wildlife: tigers; elephants; monkeys; snakes and
many other tropical rainforest plants and animals

② 2 one or two   3 twice   4 six   5 three   6 kind
7 key   8 similar   9 own   10 second

③ *Suggested answers:*

2 guide, knew, tiger   **A** he, seen   **B** another,
watching   **C** animals, noticed

3 got on, elephant   **A** ladder   **B** tree   **C** car

4 saw, tiger   **A** resting, meal   **B** sleeping
C looking, food

5 safe, believed   **A** never attack, humans   **B** not
attack, elephant   **C** too old

6 allowed   **A** get out   **B** feed   **C** photograph

④ 1 B   2 C   3 C   4 A   5 B   6 C

There were no rules against taking pictures of tigers, so I took lots with my new camera; but then, sadly, we had to leave. We passed some monkeys in the trees soon after and Mel wanted to throw them some food but Ajay stopped her, saying it wasn't good for them. Soon we reached the car and on our way back we drove around a lake. It was just wonderful there and I asked the guide if we could stop and go for a short walk. But he said we had to stay in the vehicle at all times. Except to climb onto an elephant, of course!

Vocabulary

Suffixes: -ion, -ation, -ment

❶ **1** advertise, prepare, direct **2** (suffixes are underlined) advertise*ment*, prepar*ations*, direc*tion*; *preparations* is the plural noun **3** *preparations* drops the final 'e' from the verb form *prepare*; (because) the suffix begins with a vowel

❷

-ment	-ation	-ion
announcement	*admiration*	attraction
development	confirmation	celebration
disappointment	examination	collection
enjoyment	information	completion
entertainment	invitation	connection
excitement	relaxation	creation
improvement	reservation	discussion
movement		education
replacement		invention
		pollution
		prevention
		protection
		translation

❸ attraction, celebration, collection, completion, confirmation, connection, creation, development, disappointment, discussion, education, enjoyment, entertainment, examination, excitement, improvement, information, invention, invitation, movement, pollution, prevention, protection, relaxation, replacement, reservation, translation

Patterns: the stressed syllable is normally before the suffix, or the *a* in the case of *-ation* suffixes. (Although there are exceptions, e.g. ad*ver*tisement, *ar*gument.)

❹/❺ **2** invention **3** direction **4** movement **5** connection **6** translation **7** invitation **8** disappointment **9** attraction **10** celebration

❻ (underlinings show word stress) **1** infor*ma*tion **2** in*ven*tion **3** di*rec*tion **4** *move*ment **5** con*nec*tion **6** trans*la*tion **7** invi*ta*tion **8** disap*point*ment **9** at*trac*tion **10** cele*bra*tion

Presenter: Seven.

Man: Invit**a**tion

Presenter: Eight.

Woman: Disapp**oi**ntment

Presenter: Nine.

Man: Att**ra**ction

Presenter: Ten.

Woman: Celebr**a**tion

Grammar

The passive: present and past simple

❶ 1 A and C are active; B and D are passive   2 C and D describe an event in the past   3 B and D
4 A: subject – tigers; object – people. B: subject – people; agent – tigers (using *by*)   5 C: subject – guides; object – tourists. D: subject – tourists; no object
6 information not in sentence D: *who* allowed the tourists to take photos (the guides)

❷ 2 A   3 P   4 A   5 P

❸ 3 are seen   4 was chased   5 are the crocodiles fed
6 was not noticed

❹

Recording script CD2 Track 17	
	One.
Man:	These are known as the 'Spring Gardens'.
	Two.
Woman:	The flowers were planted in March.
	Three.
Man:	The grass was cut in April and May.

❺ 2 Two giraffes were seen near the trees.   3 A poem was written about this waterfall.   4 Rice is grown in the east of the country.   5 The moon was hidden by one small cloud.   6 Cars aren't/are not allowed in the National Park.   7 The forest was partly destroyed by fire.   8 We weren't/were not told about the crocodiles in the river.

❻

Recording script CD2 Track 18	
	One.
Woman:	A lot of fish are caught here.
	Two.

Man:	Two giraffes were seen near the trees.
	Three.
Woman:	A poem was written about this waterfall.
	Four.
Man:	Rice is grown in the east of the country.
	Five.
Woman:	The moon was hidden by one small cloud.
	Six.
Man:	Cars aren't allowed in the National Park.
	Seven.
Woman:	The forest was partly destroyed by fire.
	Eight.
Man:	We weren't told about the crocodiles in the river.

Reading Part 4

❶ b 4   c 7   d 3   e 1   f 6   g 8   h 5

❷ 1 C

❸ 1 D (correct answer)   2 C (the word *import* tells us that the oil and gas come from abroad, not from under the sea)   3 A (the text says the opposite: there is still *no pollution*)   4 B (text says they are *in danger* – not that they have already disappeared)

❹/❺ 3 A 'the only way to prevent the situation getting even worse' (it is not certain it will get worse – there is one way to prevent it)

B 'the air pollution that leads to global warming' ('leads to' means 'cause')

C (correct answer) 'Chinese student Ding Yinghan'; 'it is unfair to say that just one country – his own – is causing climate change'; 'the air pollution that leads to global warming comes from many parts of the world'

D 'the air pollution that leads to global warming comes from many parts of the world, including poorer countries' (poor countries also cause it)

4 A 'her articles have been published in her local newspaper' (passive – somebody else publishes them)

B (correct answer) 'changes in the way teenagers behave are an important way of influencing choices that are made by parents'

C 'For her, changes in the way teenagers behave are an important way' (she wants young people to do things differently rather than follow their parents' example)

D 'She's against young people's general lack of interest in politics' (she thinks they should become interested in politics)

5 B *Suggested answers:*

A: 'I'm the only one from our country' (Every country has three champions: 'Each country involved selects three teenagers'.)

C: 'already three of us from every country in the world' (Not 'every country in the world', only 13: 'At present, 13 countries are involved'; 'more countries are expected to join soon'.)

D: 'Some of us are teenagers' (All of them are teenagers: 'young people of school age'; 'three teenagers'.)

Exam round-up

1 yes   **2** opinion and attitude   **3** general meaning   **4** the text   **5** yes   **6** usually in one paragraph

Grammar
Comparative and superlative adverbs

❶ 1 Students should underline – comparative adverbs: more quickly, more efficiently, worse; superlative adverb: most brightly   **2** by adding *more* in front of the adverb   **3** worse   **4** than   **5** by adding *most* in front of the adverb

❷

adverb	comparative	superlative
quietly	more quietly	(the) most quietly
carefully	more carefully	(the) most carefully
slowly	more slowly	(the) most slowly
easily	more easily	(the) most easily
fast	faster	(the) fastest
badly	worse	(the) worst
hard	harder	(the) hardest
well	better	(the) best

❸ 2 hardest   **3** more cheaply   **4** worst   **5** more cleanly   **6** more heavily

Speaking Part 4

❶ *Suggested answers:*
They are wasting water by watering the lawn with a sprinkler instead of leaving the grass to go yellow / waiting for it to rain. They are watering the pots with a hose pipe / with an irrigation system instead of using a watering-can or using collected rainwater from the garden. They are consuming unnecessary water by having a water fountain and a swimming pool. They are using a lot of water to wash the car with a hose pipe and instead could wash the car by hand.

They are wasting water by using a washing machine and dishwasher instead of washing dishes and clothes by hand. They have left the tap running, instead of putting a glass of water in the fridge to cool down.

❷ 1 water plants later in the day   **2** use a bucket and a sponge to wash the car   **3** wash small quantities of plates or clothes by hand

❸ 2 say   **3** for example   **4** like   **5** such as

Recording script   CD2 Track 19

Jake:	Well, there's lots you can do to save water at home. In the garden, <u>for instance, it's best to water the plants later in the day</u>. Because if you water them at two o'clock, <u>say</u>, when it's hot, the sun just dries everything out again.
Lily:	Right. And if you really *must* wash the car, <u>there are better ways of doing it than that. With a bucket of water and a sponge, for example</u>. You'd waste much less water, and get a bit of exercise, too.
Jake:	It's the same in the kitchen, isn't it? All those things <u>like</u> dishwashers and washing machines that do everything for you. They use a huge amount of water.
Lily:	I suppose they save people a lot of hard work when they're full. But if you don't have much to wash, <u>such as</u> a few plates or some socks, <u>you can do them much more quickly by hand. And avoid wasting all that water</u>.

❹ *Suggested answers:* 'If you want a cold drink, it's better to keep a jug of water in the fridge than run a tap until it gets cold'; 'Don't run the tap while you're brushing your teeth – use a glass of water'; 'Don't wash fruit, vegetables or salad under the tap – use a bowl'; 'Water used for cooking can be re-used, when it's cool, to water plants'.

Answer key (217)

2 connected with   **3** keep to this topic   **4** a range of tenses   **5** take turns   **6** listening to   **7** asking for more details and their opinions   **8** give reasons and examples

Writing Part 3

❶ 1 paragraph A: the wildlife in your country; paragraph B: favourite animal; paragraph C: Are there many of them?

2 ~~seen~~ are seen (present simple passive), ~~better~~ best (superlative adverb), ~~easyly~~ easily (spelling of comparative adverb)

❷ 2 G, I really enjoy being here.   **3** G, ... a new film about animals which is called 'The life of animals' ...   **4** Sp, ... a film with plenty of excitement ...
5 WO, I don't know what the name of the mountain is.   **6** V, I hope I haven't made a lot of mistakes.

❸ 2 True   **3** False   **4** True   **5** False   **6** True   **7** False
8 True

❹ *Sample answer:*

Hi Justin,

It was great to hear from you. We love pets here and almost everyone has a dog, cat, bird, rabbit or other animal.

People keep pets for different reasons. Many people, particularly those who live on their own, like to have a pet for company. Others need an animal at home, for instance a huge dog to protect the house, or a cat to catch mice!

Hamsters are my favourite pet. They're friendly, cute and – because they're so tiny – they don't take up much space! Sometimes our hamster Frankie is allowed out of his cage so that he can run round more freely. He really enjoys that!

Well, that's all for now. I hope you can write again soon.

Best wishes,

Ana

12   What did you say?

Reading Part 3

❶ 1 geek   **2** dude   **3** dork

❸ *Suggested answer:*

The text is about Martian. This language has been created by Chinese teenagers to talk with their friends online.

❹ *Suggested words to underline:*
   2 Young people ... first ... Martian ... Taiwan
   3 film *Shaolin Soccer*, Zhao Wei comes ... Mars
   4 Teenagers ... use the Internet ... called Martians
   5 Software companies ... selling programs ... help ... write ... Martian
   6 Ms Li ... never ... read messages ... Mei's computer
   7 When Mei starts writing ... Martian ... uses other people's work
   8 Wang Haiyong allows ... students ... homework in Martian
   9 Bei Bei Song considers herself ... up to date
   10 Bei Bei ... approves of Martian

❺ Sentence 2; No, you don't need to understand *spread* to know if the sentence is correct or incorrect.

❻ 1 Correct – 80% of teenagers aged between 15 and 19 in China use this language when they send messages or chat with each other online
   2 Correct – It became popular in Taiwan in 2004 and three years later, it spread to mainland China
   3 Incorrect – She isn't really a visitor from Mars
   4 Incorrect – anyone who acts strangely there is known as a Martian ... the language which teenagers in China enjoy creating is also known as Martian
   5 Correct – people are buying special software to translate between Chinese and Martian
   6 Incorrect – she could not understand the emails from Mei's friends
   7 Correct – At first, I just copy words from texts which my friends have already written in Martian
   8 Incorrect – I refuse to mark my students' work when they use this language
   9 Correct – but she doesn't think she's old-fashioned
   10 Incorrect – she thinks that this language is really silly

❼ *Suggested answers:*

1 incorrect / false   2 words / information / details   3 text   4 word / phrase / sentence

Vocabulary

Speak, talk, say, tell and *ask for*

❷ 2 told   3 speak   4 say   5 told   6 ask for

❸ 1 talk   2 speak   3 say   4 tell   5 ask   6 ask for

Suggested answers:
1 (together) about a topic, online
2 to someone (about)
3 something to somebody, *cheese* (when you take someone's photo)
4 the time, the difference (between)
5 someone to do something, someone about something
6 more food, someone's opinion

❹ *Suggested questions:*
1 How many languages can you speak well?
2 Do you always say 'hello' to everyone when you walk into the classroom?
3 Are you good at telling jokes?
4 If you don't understand, do you ask questions?
5 Do you talk to your friends about your future plans?

Grammar

Reported speech and reported commands

❷ Scott: disco; William: football match; Gina: non-uniform day (students pay to wear the clothes they want to school)

Recording script   CD2 Track 20

Ruby: Shh! Be quiet! Close the door, Paul!

Paul: OK!

Ruby: Thanks. Er, Tania, can you take notes today?

Tania: Oh, is it my turn to be secretary? OK.

Ruby: Right. As you know, we have to decide what event we're going to organise for the *Schools for All* project. Er, any ideas? Yes, Scott?

Scott: OK. Last year <u>we organised a disco to collect money. We can organise a similar event again.</u>

Ruby: Hmm. I think Year 10 are going to organise a party this year. Has anyone else got any other ideas? William?

William: Yeah, <u>we've thought about organising a football match</u>.

Ruby: Another football match? There are matches here every Saturday.

William: <u>In my sister's school, the students are going to play against the teachers</u>.

Ruby: But the teachers here wouldn't want to play football.

William: <u>It doesn't have to be just teachers.</u> Ellie's dad could play. He used to play football for United.

Ruby: But how are we going to raise money?

William: <u>The adults will have to pay to play</u>.

Ruby: Sounds good. Hmm. Er, anyone else? Gina?

Gina: Yes. <u>Today we're all wearing school uniform</u> and we all look the same. Who hates wearing school uniform?

All: Well … I really don't like …

Gina: So <u>our idea is to have a day when we don't wear school uniform</u>. We can wear what we want to school.

Ruby: And the money?

Gina: <u>We'll pay to wear what we want</u>.

Ruby: Oh! Thanks. Right. Think about the suggestions. And don't forget the meeting tomorrow. We'll take a vote then.

---

❸/❹ 1 had organised a disco to collect money
2 could organise a similar event again
3 'd/had thought about organising a football match
4 were going to play against the teachers
5 (that) it didn't have to be just teachers
6 were all wearing school uniform
7 would pay to wear

Recording script   CD2 Track 21

Nina: Hi Tania. Sorry I didn't get to the meeting yesterday. What did you decide?

Tania: Oh, hi Nina. There's going to be another meeting today at 1 pm to take a vote. We have to think about the three suggestions.

Nina: What three suggestions? Did anyone take notes?

Tania: Yeah! I was the secretary. I've got them written here. Let me see. Oh yes, Scott said that <u>they had organised a disco to collect money the year before</u> and they <u>could organise a similar event again</u>.

Nina: But isn't Year 10 going to organise a party?

Tania:	Er, yes, that's what Ruby said. Then William said <u>they had thought about organising a football match</u>.
Nina:	Not another football match.
Tania:	Well, not exactly … he said in his sister's school, <u>the students were going to play against the teachers. He also said that it didn't have to be just teachers.</u> It could be any adult – like Ellie's dad who used to be a football player. <u>William said the adults would have to pay to play</u>.
Nina:	You said there were three suggestions, didn't you?
Tania:	Yes, the third came from Gina. <u>She reminded us that we were all wearing school uniform that day</u> and that she hated wearing school uniform. She suggested a day when we wouldn't have to wear school uniform. She said <u>we would pay to wear</u> what we wanted.
Nina:	Oh… Good idea!

❺ 2 past continuous **3** past perfect **4** past perfect / past simple **5** *would* + infinitive **6** *was/were going to* **7** *could*

❻ 2 the year before **3** his/her **4** they/we

❼ 2 (that) someone had left/left their/his/her MP3 player in the kitchen after the party
3 (that) he was having a great time there
4 (that) he wanted to sell his bike so he could buy a new one

❾ 2 to close the door **3** to think about the suggestions **4** to forget the meeting

❿ 2 not to worry **3** not to touch anything **4** not to forget to phone

Listening Part 3

❶ 1 True **2** False (there is extra information which you don't need to understand to complete the notes) **3** True **4** True **5** False (you should use the second listening to check your answers)
6 False (you should make a guess – you will not lose marks for a wrong answer)

❷ *Suggested questions:*
1 How old do I have to be to enter the competition?
2 Can I enter with a friend?
3 Can I choose the topic of my website?
4 What language should I write the website in?
5 When do I have to send you my website?

❹ 1 coach **2** 19 **3** (school) subject **4** (online) library **5** Australia **6** November

Recording script   CD2 Track 22

Head:	Quiet!! I'd like to introduce Gerry Tremain from *Web Challenge*. He's going to tell you about an exciting website competition.
Gerry:	Thank you. Hi everyone! I'm going to talk about the *Web Challenge* which is an exciting competition for young people all over the world who are interested in designing websites. Although the website should be written in English, we do encourage you to provide links to translations into several other languages, including your own. Firstly, you'll need to get your team together. <u>All teams need a coach</u>. The coach should be a teacher, librarian or assistant working in a school. In each team, there should be three to six members who are school students, in addition to the coach.

The competition is open to students who are in full-time education who are no younger than nine and <u>no older than nineteen</u>. There are three age groups: <u>19 and Under</u>, 15 and Under and 12 and Under.

Once you've got your team together, you'll have to choose a topic that interests you. <u>Think about a favourite school subject</u>, or things you like to do in your free time. You're now ready to build your website. Don't forget that your website will need to be uploaded to our server.

Prizes for competition winners include laptop computers, digital cameras and money for your school to spend on new technology. <u>Every team that enters will have their site published on our online library</u>. First-prize winners in each age group <u>will win a seven-day trip to Australia</u> where you'll take part in workshops, events and excursions.

And finally a word about dates. All interested teams need to register for the competition <u>by the end of November</u>. Your final website should be on our server by April 14th. Now winners will be announced on July 1st. You can get further information by contacting our hotline on 098764444 or by looking at our website: www.webchallenge.com.

Grammar

Reported questions

❶ *Suggested questions:*

What software can we use to design the website?

Does the topic have to be very original?

How big should the website be?

❷/❸ 2 Jade   3 Julian   4 Hamad   5 Haley

Recording script   CD2 Track 23

Head:	Thank you, Gerry. I'm sure some of you have got questions. Yes, Nadia?
Nadia:	<u>Can I enter the competition on my own</u>?
Gerry:	Interesting question. No … the aim of the competition is to encourage young people to share ideas and work together.
Head:	Who's next? Yes, Jade?
Jade:	<u>Does our coach have to work in our school</u>?
Gerry:	No, not in *your* school, but this person does need to be working in *a* school, for example it could be the French assistant in Woods High School.
Head:	Yes, Julian?
Julian:	Sounds brilliant. <u>How do we register for the competition</u>?
Gerry:	It's easy. Log on to our website and fill in the application form online.
Head:	I think you're next, Hamad?
Hamad:	<u>What do we do if we have technical problems</u>?
Gerry:	Very good question. If you read the rules on our website, you'll see that if you are unable to upload your website because of problems with our server, we'll do everything we can to help you.
Head:	Anyone else? Yes, Haley?
Haley:	If we win, <u>what will we see in Australia</u>?
Gerry:	Once again, full details of the prizes are on our website but I can tell you that it will be a trip you'll never forget!

❹ 2 Does our coach have to work in our school?
   3 How do we register for the competition?
   4 What do we do if we have technical problems?
   5 What will we see in Australia?

❺ **b** usually changes like in reported speech
   c never   **d** isn't   **e** don't use

❻ 2 she was   3 Do you want   4 they were going
   5 if they had

Indirect questions

❶ *Suggested answer:*

Nadia says they took a boat trip around Sydney harbour and that their hotel had views over the harbour.

Recording script   CD2 Track 24

Journalist:	Hello, Nadia. Congratulations on winning the prize! <u>I was wondering if I could ask you some questions about your trip</u>. It must have been amazing!
Nadia:	Thanks. Yes, it *was* an amazing trip. We saw so many things.
Journalist:	I'm sure. So, your flight landed in Sydney, didn't it? <u>Firstly I'd like to know what you thought of Sydney</u>.
Nadia:	Well, before we won the prize, I thought Sydney was the capital of Australia, but it isn't. Canberra is the capital. Anyway, Sydney is enormous but the thing I noticed first was all the water. On the first day <u>we took a boat trip around Sydney harbour</u>.
Journalist:	<u>I can't remember where you stayed in Sydney. Could you tell me where your hotel was</u>?
Nadia:	Yes, we stayed in <u>a hotel with views over the harbour</u>.
Journalist:	<u>Tell me what you visited in Australia, apart from Sydney</u>.
Nadia:	Well, we went to …

❷ 2 thought   3 you stayed   4 your hotel was   5 you visited

❸ 2 you think of Sydney   3 you stay in Sydney
   4 your hotel   5 you visit in Australia apart from Sydney

❹ 2 stays the same   3 never   4 isn't   5 sometimes

❺ In *reported* questions the *tense changes* and we *never* use a question mark. In *indirect* questions the *tense doesn't change* and we *sometimes* use a question mark.

Vocabulary
Prepositions of place

❶

Recording script CD2 Track 25

One. Where are Todd's keys?

Adam:	Hi Todd.
Todd:	Hi Adam. I was wondering if you could do me a favour?
Adam:	Depends. What?
Todd:	Look, I've left my keys at home. Can you bring them to school?
Adam:	Sure. Where are they?
Todd:	Right. Go into my bedroom. On my desk, next to the lamp is a box. The keys should be inside the box.
Adam:	OK. In a box on your desk. I'll ring you back if I can't find them.
	Two. Where's the sports shop?
Karyn:	Dayton Sports. Karyn speaking.
Kylie:	Hi. I'd like to know if you've got any football gloves, size 8.
Karyn:	I'll just have a look for you … hmm … yes, we do.
Kylie:	Great. Could you tell me where your shop is?
Karyn:	Yes. Do you know where the central library is?
Kylie:	Er, yes.
Karyn:	Go past the library, over the bridge. We're between a bookshop and a hairdresser's, opposite the pet shop.
Kylie:	Ah! I think I know where you are.
	Three. Where's Elen, Imogen's cousin?
Nick:	I've never met your cousin Elen. What does she look like?
Imogen:	I think I've got a photo of her. Yes, here it is.
Nick:	Wow! Is that your family?
Imogen:	Yes. Can you see my aunt holding a baby? In front of her are my five little cousins.
Nick:	Ah! They look lovely. Has your aunt really got six children?
Imogen:	No! Three of them are my dad's brother's children.
Nick:	Oh! So where's Elen?
Imogen:	Well, on the right is my uncle. He's wearing sunglasses.

Nick:	Oh yes. Why didn't he take them off for the photo?
Imogen:	I don't know. My cousin Elen is standing behind my uncle. She's starting at our high school in September.
Nick:	She looks fun. I can't wait to meet her.

❸ *Suggested answers:*

Picture 1: Label the box *on the desk*, the lamp *next to the box*, the keys *in / inside the box*

Picture 2: Write *over* above the bridge, label the sports shop *between bookshop and hairdresser*, also label sports shop *opposite pet shop*

Picture 3: Label five little cousins *in front of aunt*, uncle with sunglasses *on the right*, Elen *behind uncle*

Speaking Part 3

❷ 1 on your own / one minute
2 describe what you can see
3 use one of the expressions from Unit 10
4 use a suitable preposition

Writing Part 3

❷ 1 A story
2 Your English teacher
3 About 100 words
4 In the first question, you are given the *first sentence* of the story and in the second question, you are given the *title*.
5 No, you can choose between a story and a letter

❸ 1 1   2 The ringing phone belonged to the teacher

❹ All the sentences are correct so the story is a good answer.

❺ Types of mistake: past tenses and plural forms

1 believed → believe   2 forgot → forgotten
3 student → students   4 left → leave   5 stoped → stopped

❻ *Model answers:*

1 I realised that I hadn't locked the door.

I was at the bus stop. I telephoned my sister to ask her if she could go home but she didn't answer her phone. Then I decided to telephone my mum to tell her the truth. My mum told me to go home. As I got to my street I saw a fire engine outside my house. 'Oh no!' I thought. I saw a neighbour and asked him what had happened. He said that a cat was in a tree and couldn't get down. I was so happy. Finally I got to my house and locked the door.

2 The message began, 'Congratulations! You've won first prize!'

I couldn't believe it! I was the winner. Two months before, I had entered a drawing competition in a shop. I telephoned my best friend who told me to phone the shop. She also asked me what the prize was but I said I didn't know. I decided to walk to the shop. I was so excited. I went into the shop and found a shop assistant. I told her my name and said that I had received a message. She said, 'Oh, you're the winner. Congratulations! You've won a weekend in Paris.' I was delighted.

3 I was in class when my mobile phone rang. *Model answer with five mistakes on page 113 (corrections listed above)*

4 As I got on the train, I saw an empty seat next to my favourite actor.

Davey Shaw was on the train. I couldn't believe it! I asked him if I could sit next to him. I told him that he was my favourite actor and I'd seen all his films. Davey asked me where I was going. I told him I was going to meet my friends to go to the cinema. The journey went really quickly and we were soon in the city centre. When I found my friends, I told them that I had sat next to Davey Shaw on the train but they thought I was telling lies again.

Vocabulary and grammar review Unit 11

Grammar

❶ 2 was built **3** seems **4** rises **5** is washed **6** reaches **7** was completely flooded **8** disappeared **9** is done **10** know **11** were saved **12** was put up

❷ 2 more quickly **3** (the) best **4** more frequently **5** harder **6** (the) worst **7** more strongly **8** more carefully

Vocabulary

❸ (More than one answer is sometimes possible)

2 great / much excitement **3** a reservation **4** a quick examination **5** celebrations often **6** no information

❹

			¹G	I	R	A	F	F	²E			
³R									N			
U	⁴P			⁵S	N	A	K	E			
B	E			O				R			
⁶B	A	T		L		⁷D		G			
I	R			A		U		Y			
S	⁸O	S	⁹T	R	I	C	H		¹⁰W		
H	L		I			K			A		
	G		G						S		
¹¹S	A	V	E						T		
	¹²R	E	C	Y	C	L	E				

Vocabulary and grammar review   Unit 12

Vocabulary

❶ 2 ~~infront of~~ → in front of **3** ~~At the right~~ → On the right **4** ~~next~~ → next to **5** ~~in~~ → on **6** ~~behind of~~ → behind **7** ~~inside of~~ → inside **8** ~~on~~ → over

❸ 2 told **3** said **4** ask for **5** asked **6** to tell/telling **7** tell

Grammar

❹ 2 ~~what was the team called~~ → what the team was called
3 ~~why didn't I go~~ → why I didn't go / why I hadn't gone
4 ~~why was I crying~~ → why I was crying
5 ~~what was I going to do~~ → what I was going to do
6 ~~where should she go~~ → where she should go
7 ~~when am I going~~ → when I am going

❺ 2 she was not/wasn't very keen **3** she loved comedies **4** she hadn't gone/didn't go **5** they had just finished **6** she would go to the cinema that day if she could

6 *Suggested questions:*
2 'Are you keen on thrillers?'
3 'Do you love comedies?'
4 'Did you go to the cinema last week?'
5 'Have you (just) finished your exams?'
6 'When will you go to the cinema?'

7 *Suggested answers:*
2 I asked you if you were keen on thrillers.
3 I asked you if you loved comedies.
4 I asked you if you went to the cinema last week.
5 I asked you if you had finished your exams.
6 I asked you when you would go to the cinema.

Writing reference

Part 1

Sentence transformations

Exercise 1

a spelling mistake (*first*)
b does not mean the same as the first sentence
c too many words
d grammatically wrong

Exercise 2

1 any flights 2 as cold as 3 us to 4 spent
5 the most

Exercise 3

1 *any* + change of verb *fly* to noun *flights*
2 comparative *-er* + *than* changes to negative *not as ... as*
3 direct to reported speech *asked us to*
4 *stayed ... for* changes to *spent* (no preposition)
5 *never ... such an* changes to superlative *the most ... ever*

Part 2

Messages

Exercise 1

1 Your friend Eva; you want to borrow her camera
2 Informal
3 An email
4 Explain why, suggest when you can collect it, say when you'll give it back

Exercise 2

Suggested answers (The useful expressions for explaining, thanking, inviting, suggesting, apologising and asking are underlined*):*
2 I'd like to borrow your camera <u>because</u> my camera (mine) is broken; 3 <u>Thank you ever so much for</u> the two weeks I spent in your house; 4 I know you've never visited my country. <u>Would you like to</u> come and stay in the summer?; 5 <u>Why don't we</u> meet in front of the cinema?; 6 <u>I'm so sorry for</u> forgetting your birthday. I feel terrible; 7 <u>Can you</u> tell me how to get to your house, please?

Exercise 3

1 *Dear ..., Best wishes, All the best, Yours*
2 *Hello, ..., Hi ..., Love, Lots of love, See you soon*

Exercise 4

	A	B	C
1	✗ (The candidate doesn't suggest when he can pick up the camera.)	✓	✗ (The candidate doesn't explain why they want to borrow the camera nor suggest when they can collect the camera so could only get a maximum of 2 marks.)
2	✓	✓	✓
3	✓ (*since* and *and*)	✓ (*but*)	✗
4	✓ (*Dear ... Love*)	✓ (*Dear ... Love*)	✓ (*Dear ... See you*)
5	✓ (41 words)	✗ (This answer is a little long at 50 words. The expressions *How are you?* and *I hope you're fine* are not necessary.)	✗ (This answer is short at 20 words and could only get a maximum of 2 marks.)

Exercise 5

Suggested answers:
A: The answer is well written and organised within the word limit but it could not get more than 3 marks because it doesn't include one of the content points.
B: The answer is a little long but it is a good answer which includes all 3 content points and it would probably be given 5 marks.
C: The message is easy to understand, but it doesn't include two of the content points and it is short. It could only get a maximum of 2 marks.

Exercise 6

Suggested words to underline:
1 You are going to miss (an English-speaking friend's birthday) party tomorrow
2 a note
3 (an English-speaking friend) Ian
4 apologise, explain why, suggest another day

Exercise 7

B: The candidate has included all 3 content points appropriately.
The message is very clear.

Exercise 8

(suggested answers)
A *(6 corrected mistakes are in* **bold***)*
Hello, I am sorry but *(tommorrow)* **tomorrow** I can't go to your party *(becouse)* **because** I have my sister's wedding and she *(live)* **lives** in the USA. I must *(bring)* **take** the train from Lyon and afterwards the *(plan)* **plane** from Paris. Shall we meet next weekend? *(Tanks)* **Thanks**.

C *(changes in* **bold***)*
Hi Ian, I'm sorry for not going to your party *(yesterday)* **tomorrow**. I *(had)* **have** a bad cold and my sister *(had)* **has had** an accident. I *(went)* **'ve been** to the hospital and the doctor *(told)* **has told** her that she *(had)* **has** a broken leg, so I *(couldn't)* **can't** be there. *(I will see you tomorrow)* **How about meeting next week?** Yours,

Part 3
Informal letter

Exercise 1

1 *letter, friend, answering ... questions, about 100*
2 an English-speaking friend   3 They recently had their fourteenth birthday; they were with their family and enjoyed it a lot.   4 What happens when you have a birthday; What you do

Exercise 2

1 *What happens?* He gets excited before it; receives presents from parents, cards and a birthday cake. *What do you do?* Goes out with friends; can do what he likes
2 *Thanks, lots, cool, till, getting, nice, mum, dad, loads of, mates, Anyway, 've got to*
3 Exclamation marks, short forms, e.g. *isn't, there's, it'll.* Very short sentences: *There's a cake, too; Write soon.* Expressions: *take out* (phrasal verb), *the best thing, that's all, All the best*
4 Example: *like a concert.* Reasons: *because it's my birthday, because I've got to go out;* Linking words: *like; because*

Exercise 3

1 *letter, English-speaking friend, (about) 100 words*
2 Your English-speaking friend
3 He or she is going to visit your country next month.
4 More about your country, in particular where to go and what to do there.

Exercise 4

1 1 a̶ ̶g̶o̶o̶d̶ ̶n̶e̶w̶s̶ good news 2 f̶o̶r̶ ̶d̶o̶ to do 3 p̶e̶o̶p̶l̶e̶ ̶w̶h̶i̶c̶h̶ people who 4 y̶o̶u̶ ̶t̶o̶ ̶v̶i̶s̶i̶t̶ you visit
2 No
3 Yes
4 Yes
5 Informal. Short sentences. Vocabulary such as *Hi, Thanks, I can't believe.* Short forms, e.g. *that's, it's.* Punctuation: dash (–), exclamation marks (!).
6 Yes. *Which are the best places to visit?* (second paragraph); *What can I do there?* (third paragraph)
7 *Hi ..., Thanks for your letter, Please write again soon, Best wishes*
8 *because, as, because*

Story

Exercise 1

1 *teacher, story, title, lost wallet, 100 words*
2 title
3 about 100

Exercise 2

1 third person
2 *crowded, busy, upset, angry, nervous, anxiously*
3 a mystery
4 a *was standing* (past continuous), *was stolen* (past simple passive), *realised* (past simple), *had lost* (past perfect)
   b *Upset and angry* (adjectives)
   c *'I believe this is yours'* + reporting verb
   d *looked anxiously inside* without saying yet what he saw
   e *his card, but with someone else's photo*
   f *they had wanted to steal his identity*

Exercise 3

1 *(English) teacher, story, begin, sentence, 100 words*
2 Your English teacher
3 *When the phone rang, I knew immediately who was calling*; at the beginning of the story
4 *phone, rang, I knew, who*
5 first person

Exercise 4

a 2 b 3 c 1

Exercise 5

1 Yes
2 Yes
3 ~~will~~ would (be announced), ~~beleive~~ believe, ~~of~~ in (the world)
4 *Suggested answers:*
Past simple: *thought*; Past continuous: *was taking part*; Past perfect simple: *had completed*; Conditional: *would perform*; Conditional passive: (*would*) *be announced*; Present perfect: *You've won*
5 *immediately, Before, when, After, in two weeks, now*
6 Mainly formal. She uses the full form of verbs: *I had passed, I had completed.* The passive: (*would*) *be announced.* Complex sentences. No exclamation marks or dashes.
7 At the beginning, she makes the reader wait by saying *Before answering, I thought back* and then goes back in time, describing the events leading up to that in the second paragraph. She ends the second paragraph by saying *and now it was time*, and starts the final paragraph with *Nervously, I took the call.* Using the natural pause between paragraphs to create interest is similar to the way writers sometimes do this at the end of a chapter in an exciting novel.
8 She hears this over the phone: '*You've won the National Dance Competition.*'
9 *Nervously, amazed, couldn't bel(ie)ve it, a dream come true, the happiest person (in) the world*

Speaking reference

Part 1

Exercise 1

2 g 3 f 4 e 5 c 6 a 7 b

Exercise 2

~~five year~~ fifth year, ~~at the school~~ at school, ~~so many of the Internet~~ so much of the Internet, ~~as Spain~~ like/such as Spain, ~~We never did~~ We'd never done / We've never done

Exercise 3

2 True 3 False 4 True 5 False 6 True

> **Recording script**   CD2 Track 26
>
> | | |
> |---|---|
> | Examiner: | Now, what's your name? |
> | Emilio: | My name's Emilio. |
> | Examiner: | Thank you. And what's your surname? |

Emilio:	Sánchez.
Examiner:	How do you spell it?
Emilio:	S-A-N-C-H-E-Z.
Examiner:	Thank you. Now, where do you live?
Emilio:	In Santiago. <u>In a district called 'Independéncia'</u>, which is quite near **of** the city centre.
Examiner:	And do you work or are you a student in Santiago?
Emilio:	I'm a student. I'm in my **five** year at secondary school.
Examiner:	And what subjects do you study?
Emilio:	Er … <u>could you repeat the question, please</u>?
Examiner:	What subjects do you study?
Emilio:	Oh, um … maths, science, history, geography … things like that. <u>And English, of course</u>. I do that at **the** school, and I have lessons at home, too, with a teacher that comes to my house.
Examiner:	Do you enjoy studying English, Emilio?
Emilio:	Yes, I like learning it a lot <u>because</u> so **many** of the Internet is in English, and also because most of the music I enjoy is too.
Examiner:	Do you think that English will be useful for you in the future?
Emilio:	Yes, definitely. <u>For instance</u>, I'd really like to travel round Europe and North America, and for that <u>I'll need to know English</u>. Except in countries <u>as</u> Spain and Mexico, of course, where I'll be able to speak in Spanish.
Examiner:	OK, Emilio. What did you do last weekend?
Emilio:	Last weekend … Oh yes, <u>I was at the sports centre</u> on Saturday. We were playing basketball against one of the best teams in Santiago, and in the end we beat them. We never did that before!
Examiner:	Thank you.

Exercise 4

Add more information: *as well as that, also, and sometimes*
Ask someone to repeat something: *could you say that again, please?, sorry, I didn't catch that, could you repeat that, please?*
Give examples: *for instance, like, for example, such as*

Exercise 5

Sorry, I didn't catch that, such as, also, like, for example, and sometimes

Examiner:	What do you enjoy doing in your free time?
Isabel:	Er, sorry, I didn't catch that.
Examiner:	What do you enjoy doing in your free time?
Isabel:	My free time, right. Well, most of all I like doing sports – lots of different ones such as running and swimming. I love swimming, especially in the sea. Also sports that you play with a … er … racket, like tennis and badminton. There's a really big sports centre near my house, where you can do lots of different things. Gymnastics, for example. I really like that. And sometimes I play table tennis there, too.

Part 2

Exercise 1

1   That a classmate is leaving and the rest of you in the class want to get a present for him or her.
2   Discuss the possible presents shown in the picture; choose one of them
3   Six: (set of) books, (digital) camera, (set of) DVDs, mobile phone, (pair of) trainers, MP3 player

Exercise 2

2 Yes   3 Yes   4 Yes   5 Yes, the mobile phone
6 Stella. She deals with the task quite well, keeps the conversation going with her partner and talks quite fluently. Although she makes some mistakes, in general these don't prevent her communicating well and she uses a good range of grammar and vocabulary. Her pronunciation is influenced by her first language, but she can be understood without much difficulty. Lee is weaker on all these points, although he replies to most of what Stella says and knows how to take turns.

Exercise 3

Expressions used: *How about, I'm not really sure about that, You may be right, but, because, I'm not so keen on, Perhaps we should, Yes, that's true, That's a (very) good idea, So shall we … , then?*

Recording script   CD2 Track 28

| Examiner: | In the next part, you're going to talk to each other. I'm going to describe a situation to you. A school friend of yours is going to live in another country. Talk together about the different things the class could buy him or her as a leaving present and decide which one would be best. Here is a picture with some ideas to help you. I'll say that again. |

	A school friend of yours is going to live in another country. Talk together about the different things the class could buy him or her as a leaving present and decide which one would be best. All right? Talk together.
Stella:	OK, er, if I start?
Lee:	Yes, please.
Stella:	How about buying her the books? I know she likes very much to read so maybe they will be nice for her to have.
Lee:	I am no really sure. Very heavy for … er … carry on aeroplane. DVDs better.
Stella:	You may be right, but is difficult to choose for somebody that you … er … not really know very well.
Lee:	Uh-huh.
Stella:	And if we ask what is her … er … favourite kind of film it's not a surprise when we'll give them to her. The same problem with music.
Lee:	Maybe MP3 player, then?
Stella:	Yes, then she can put any music she want. From the Internet. But I think that's not the better thing because she's got already an MP3 player. I'm sure I see her with one the other day, so not that.
Lee:	Uh-huh. Shoes the same.
Stella:	The trainers? Yes, probably she has some and I'm not so keen of them anyway.
Lee:	So which of others we get?
Stella:	Well, she's going to live in a new place so perhaps we should get her the camera? Then she can make lots of photos.
Lee:	Or mobile phone. She can also photo with mobile phone.
Stella:	Yes, that's true. As well she could send the pictures to us here and we can see what is like her new life there.
Lee:	Is very good idea, yes. Shall we do that then?
Stella:	Yes, let's buy her a phone. She'll like that, I'm sure.
Examiner:	Thank you.

Part 3

Exercise 1

(Accept other sensible suggestions)

Photo A: the place, weather, time of day, colours, clothes and activities

Photo B: the place, weather, time of day, colours, clothes and activities

Exercise 2

Sofia talks about the place, the weather, the colours, the clothes, the activities.

Tania talks about the place, the weather, the colours (*dark*), the clothes, the activities.

Exercise 3

Sofia 1 ✓ 2 ✗ There is some range: *a sunny day, trees, mountains* and *there are, I can see, I think* but this is all quite simple. 3 ✗ 4 ✗ (She says *the boy here* which suggests she is pointing at the picture.)
5 ✗ (She stops quickly by saying *That's all*.)
6 ✗ (Her answer is simple and rather short.)

Tania 1 ✓ 2 ✓ 3 ✓ 4 ✓ 5 ✓ 6 ✓ (Tania describes the photo well. She uses a wide range of vocabulary and structure to do this. She describes the location rather than points and speaks for about a minute.)

Recording script   CD2 Track 29

Examiner: Now, I'd like each of you to talk on your own about something. I'm going to give each of you a photograph of people enjoying their free time. Sofia, here is your photograph. Please show it to Tania, but I'd like you to talk about it. Tania, you just listen. I'll give you your photograph in a moment. Sofia, please tell us what you can see in your photograph.

Sofia: Um … er … there are four people in the photograph. I can see a boy, no I think there are two boys and two girls. They all have a … um … a … this. I think they are on holiday. It's a sunny day and the weather it's warm. One of the girls wears short trousers and a red t-shirt. The boys wear … er … er … the boy here wears a shirt. The shirt is blue. They are looking at the trees, mountains and … that's all.

Examiner: Thank you. Can I have the booklet, please?

Examiner: Now, Tania, here is your photograph. It also shows people enjoying their free time. Please show it to Sofia and tell us what you can see in the photograph.

Tania: OK. In this picture, we can see three boys and a girl. I think they could be friends. On the right, we can see a boy wearing a shirt and dark trousers. Next to this boy, there is his friend. He appears to be happy because he's smiling. The other boy is carrying a … a … – it's made of wood and it's used for skating. Er … behind the girl and boys, we can see some buildings and the street so I think they're in a city, maybe New York or London. The weather looks nice and …

Examiner: Thank you.

Part 4

Exercise 1

Free-time activities you do now and free-time activities you'd like to try in the future

Exercise 3

Free-time activities

	now	in the future
Agnes	*meet friends*	
	go to the cinema (very expensive)	
	skiing (once)	*go skiing again*
	playing tennis, beach volleyball	
	travelling	*visit many places, e.g. China*
	listen to music	
	dancing (used to do ballet)	*dancing lessons*
Marcos	*meet friends – have a walk, talk*	
	go to the cinema	
	playing tennis (quite bad), skiing, snowboarding, snorkelling (last year)	*skiing on the water (water-skiing)*
	listen to music, especially rock	*learn to play electric guitar*
	dancing (quite bad)	

Exercise 4

1 ✓ 2 ✓ 3 ✓ 4 ✓ 5 ✓ 6 ✓ Agnes and Marcos are strong PET candidates. They do exactly what is required in this part of the test.

Recording script   CD2 Track 30

Examiner: Your photos showed people enjoying their free time. Now, I'd like you to talk together about the things you enjoy doing in your free time and the things you would like to try in the future.

Agnes: OK. At the weekends, um, <u>I like meeting my friends</u>.

Marcos: Me too. <u>We meet on Saturday afternoon in the … the … town and have a walk or talk. Sometimes we go to the cinema.</u> What about you? Do you like going to the cinema?

Agnes: <u>Yes</u>, but it's very expensive. What about sport? Do you play any sports?

Marcos: Yeah, I agree the cinema is expensive. <u>I like playing tennis</u> but I'm quite bad. <u>In the winter we go skiing</u> to the mountains. I love it. This year <u>I've tried snowboarding</u>. It's fantastic. Have you ever tried it?

Agnes: No, well, I mean … <u>I once went skiing</u> with my uncle but that was two or three years ago. <u>I would like to go skiing again</u> but the mountains are very far. Like you, um, <u>I also like playing tennis</u>, especially in the summer. <u>We also play beach volleyball</u>. There is a place to play on the beach and we have a good time. What things would you like to try in the future?

Marcos: We always go to the islands in the summer. <u>Last year I went snorkelling</u> with my cousins. It was so beautiful to see the fish under the water. You should try it. <u>I would like to try skiing on the water</u>. You know, you have skis and a boat takes you on the water. Yes, I want to do that.

Agnes: Oh, you mean water-skiing. I've never done that. I'm a little scared of the water … I prefer doing things on the land. <u>I really like travelling</u> and <u>when I'm older I would like to visit many places</u>. <u>My dream is to visit China.</u> We have studied so many things about China and I would like to see it. Would you like to travel when you're older?

Marcos: Maybe. I haven't really thought about it. I don't really like cars and planes because I feel … er … I feel not good.

Agnes: Yeah, it's true and sometimes the journey can be long and boring. Don't you think so?

Marcos: Uh-huh. Something else. <u>I would like to learn to play the electric guitar</u>.

Agnes: Really?

Marcos: Yeah. My friend sings really well and there is another friend who can play the drums. We are thinking in making a group. You see, <u>we love all kinds of music but especially rock</u>. Do you listen to music?

Agnes: <u>Sometimes</u>. Well, it depends. If I have to study then I can't listen to music or the TV or nothing but <u>when we have parties I like listening to music</u>. Do you like dancing?

Marcos: <u>Yeah. I love it but I'm quite bad.</u> What about you?

Agnes: When I was younger, <u>I used to go to ballet</u> but I didn't like it. <u>Now I like dancing and I would like to have lessons maybe</u>.

Examiner: Thank you. That's the end of the test.

Both: Thank you.

Authentic past PET paper from Cambridge ESOL

Paper 1

Reading and Writing

Reading Part 1

1 A 2 B 3 A 4 C 5 B

Reading Part 2

6 A 7 G 8 D 9 H 10 E

Reading Part 3

11 B 12 A 13 B 14 A 15 A
16 A 17 B 18 B 19 A 20 B

Reading Part 4

21 D 22 C 23 D 24 A 25 B

Reading Part 5

26 D 27 B 28 C 29 A 30 B
31 C 32 C 33 A 34 B 35 C

Writing Part 1

1 (see/watch) such an // (see/watch) a more
2 (about) having to
3 gave / showed
4 (much) better than
5 end of // referee ended/finished // final whistle of

Writing Part 2

There are 5 marks for Part 2. Candidates at this level are not expected to produce faultless English, but, to achieve 5 marks, a candidate should write a cohesive message clearly communicating all three content points.

Task-Specific Mark Scheme for Writing Part 2

reason why candidate has moved
reference to what candidate likes about new home
invitation to English friend to visit candidate

These are two examples of real PET candidates' answers for Question 6 (Candidate A and Candidate B), followed by the examiner's comments and the marks awarded for each.

Question 6

Candidate A's answer

Dear James

I have moved because my fatheR get anotheR job and my parents hated ouR old flat. I like the football fields and the fantastic tennis couRts. I'd like to invite you to my new home to spend the day together

love

Examiner's comments for Candidate A and mark awarded

> Candidate A
>
> Points 1 & 3 are fine, point 2 is not clearly related to the home, so the communication is successful on the whole.
>
> Mark 4

Question 6

Candidate B's answer

Thanks very much four your letter. It was lovely To hear from you. I'm glad you're enjoying your new job. but That you like Bristol, it's nice The people at work are so friendly.

we're all missing you here in london! Bob and Hilary had a party last weekend and everyone was asking how you were it's was a good party! although I didn't get home Till five in The morning so I spent most of sunday in bed.

I hope you To visit us again here in londo To get much fun TogeThe. The weather is very nice. well no more news for The moment, I'll write again soon.

love

Examiner's comments for Candidate B and mark awarded

> Candidate B
>
> Despite the fluency, this is the wrong scenario and so content points 1 & 2 are missing. Point 3 refers to a repeat visit to the same place.
>
> Mark 1

Writing Part 3

These are two examples of real PET candidates' answers for Question 7 (Candidate A and Candidate B), followed by the examiner's comments and the band awarded for each.

Question 7

Candidate A's answer

Dear John

How are you? I hope everything is O.K. with you and your wife. I feel my town is going to be the same or may be worse in 20 years. Young people leave the town and they never come back. The problem is there is no future for them here. The town is going to become really boring and quiet and only elder people will live here. I think I'll stay here because my entire live is here and my family as well. That's my place and I want to spend rest of my life here.

Take care

Examiner's comments for Candidate A and band awarded

QUESTION 7	Candidate A
ATTEMPT:	Very good
LANGUAGE/ AMBITION:	Ambitious use of language with a wide range of structures, e.g. 'I feel my town is going to be the same or may be worse in 20 years.', 'Young people leave the town and they never come back.'
RANGE:	
ORGANISATION & COHESION:	Well organised and coherent, with appropriate conclusion
ACCURACY:	A few minor errors, e.g. 'my entire live'
TARGET READER/ EFFORT:	No effort required
CONTENT:	On task
BAND:	5

Question 7

Candidate B's answer

Hi Gary

I don't think my town will be like in 20 years ' time there are many changes just 20 years is too shot time for change evrything. The cost is to hight. One the other hand you never know what happen in future. All over the word is still develompment. I don't think I'll alwas live there, but at the moment I have to because I living close to my children shool and work aswell near. I think maybe in future I'll live in country where is quiet live

Examiner's comments for Candidate B and band awarded

QUESTION 7	Candidate B
ATTEMPT:	Adequate
LANGUAGE/ AMBITION:	Ambitious but flawed, e.g. 'One the other hand you never know what happen ... ', 'All over the word is still develompment.'
RANGE:	Adequate range of vocabulary and structure, e.g. 'I don't think I'll alwas live there'
ORGANISATION & COHESION:	Evidence of organisation and some linking of sentences, e.g. 'but', 'because'
ACCURACY:	A number of errors, mostly non-impeding, e.g. 'is too shot time for change evrything'
TARGET READER/ EFFORT:	Requires some effort
CONTENT:	On task
BAND:	3

These are two examples of real PET candidates' answers for Question 8 (Candidate A and Candidate B), followed by the examiner's comments and the band awarded for each.

Question 8

Candidate A's answer

The best decision I'v ever made.

When I want to lering any languag I must my self don't have any thing. the teacher start the decision in the class nessary the student's who understand of me. There are some student's don't asked teacher him what he want. I draice any bady if will aske teacher him instudent is understand the teacher what did he seyed in the class I always ask my teacher about any thing I can't understand of me only because if I asked my teacher any quation about any thing and I don't knew it that is Problem well came. thank you. nice to read you.

Examiner's comments for Candidate A and band awarded

QUESTION 8	Candidate A
ATTEMPT:	Poor
LANGUAGE/ AMBITION:	Severely restricted command of language
RANGE:	
ORGANISATION & COHESION:	
ACCURACY:	Very poor control makes it difficult to understand
TARGET READER/ EFFORT:	Requires excessive effort
CONTENT:	
BAND:	1

Question 8

Candidate B's answer

The best decision I've ever made concerns my studies. When I was 18, I passed the baccalaureat I was studying in the city where I grew. I didn't know what to do, to continue or to begin to work. I was 18, I was very young. I decided to continue and leave in an other city. I chose three cities for the exam that I would like to do. Unfortunately all the answers were negatives. I was really disappointed. My mother told me to try another city but I was not sure because it was really far from my family. Finally, I decided to send my name to this school. When I received the answer I was happy because it was yes!

Today I'm really happy to have sent my name to this school because I passed my exam. I can begin to work and to do what I like in my job.

Examiner's comments for Candidate B and band awarded

QUESTION 8	Candidate B
ATTEMPT:	Very good attempt
LANGUAGE/ AMBITION:	Confident and ambitious use of language, e.g. 'I'm really happy to have sent my name to this school'
RANGE:	A wide range of structures, e.g. 'I didn't know what to do', 'My mother told me to try another city' and vocabulary, e.g. 'concerns my studies', 'really disappointed'
ORGANISATION & COHESION:	Well organised and coherent through use of linking devices, e.g. 'Unfortunately', 'When', 'but', 'Finally'
ACCURACY:	Errors are minor but are non-impeding, e.g. 'leave in an other city'
TARGET READER/ EFFORT:	Requires no effort by the reader
CONTENT:	On task
BAND:	5

Paper 2 Listening

Listening Part 1

1 A 2 C 3 A 4 C 5 A 6 B 7 A

Listening Part 2

8 C 9 B 10 C 11 A 12 C 13 A

Listening Part 3

14 R/roof(s)
15 (the) P/photo(-)graph(s)
16 P/piano(s)
17 (in/the) G/garden(s)
18 September
19 (£)13.50(p)

In Part 3 bracketed words do not have to appear in the answer.

Listening Part 4

20 B 21 A 22 A 23 B 24 A 25 B

Model paper

Recording script CD2 Track 31

This is the Cambridge Preliminary English Test, Number 076.

There are four parts to the test. You will hear each part twice. For each part of the test there will be time for you to look through the questions and time for you to check your answers.

Write your answers on the question paper. You will have six minutes at the end of the test to copy your answers onto the answer sheet.

The recording will now be stopped.

Please ask any questions now, because you must not speak during the test.

PART 1

Now open your question paper and look at Part 1.

There are seven questions in this part. For each question there are three pictures and a short recording. Choose the correct picture and put a tick in the box below it.

Before we start, here is an example.

Where is the girl's hat?

Mum:	Where's your new hat, Sally? I hope you haven't left it on the school bus.
Sally:	Don't worry, Mum. I put it in my school bag because I was too hot.
Mum:	Are you sure? I can't see it there. You probably dropped it in the road somewhere.
Sally:	Oh, here it is – hanging in the hall. I forgot to take it this morning.

The first picture is correct so there is a tick in box A.

Look at the three pictures for question 1 now.

Now we are ready to start. Listen carefully. You will hear each recording twice.

One.

Which band will the girl watch?

| Girl: | I'm going to hear my favourite band play tonight – you know – The Arctic Blues. |
| Boy: | Oh, I know them. There are three of them, aren't there? I really like the drummer. |

Girl:	Oh, he left – they don't have a drummer any more. <u>But the singer and the guitarist are still the same</u>. And they've got a keyboard player now.
Boy:	Oh, well I might come along.
	Now listen again.
	TAPE REPEAT
	Two.
	Where does the boy feel pain now?
Doctor:	Tell me what happened exactly.
Boy:	Well, after I fell off the rock my back felt a bit sore for a time, then it seemed to be all right. But I woke up yesterday with <u>this bad pain in my left leg, and it still really hurts</u>.
Doctor:	I see. Have you had any other pain, a headache for example?
Boy:	Well, I did have a bit of a headache after I fell. I think I hit my head on the rock. But it's fine now.
	Now listen again.
	TAPE REPEAT
	Three.
	Where is the computer now?
Woman:	I didn't really want a computer in the house, but my son does need one for his homework. Of course, he wanted it in his bedroom, but I said no – it's for all the family to use. <u>First we tried it in the sitting room</u>, but there's not much room in there, so then we put it in the room my husband uses as an office. But he wouldn't let anyone else use it, so <u>now it's back where it was before, and we've moved the sofa a bit</u>.
	Now listen again.
	TAPE REPEAT
	Four.
	How does the woman recommend travelling around the island?

Woman:	Now the island is easy to get to by plane, and when you get there, you'll find there is a local bus system so you don't have to hire a car, although they're available if you want. Some visitors in past years have hired <u>bicycles</u>, which they enjoyed very much. They're cheaper than a car and they do mean you can get to those parts of the island which are off the main bus routes. So, <u>as long as you can ride one safely, I'd say that's the best idea</u>.
	Now listen again.
	TAPE REPEAT
	Five.
	What do both girls decide to wear to the disco?
Karen:	What are you going to wear to the disco tonight? I'm going in <u>my green T-shirt</u>, jeans and white jacket.
Lisa:	Oh, <u>don't wear that T-shirt, it's the same as mine</u>. I'm going to wear that one, but with a skirt. I'm not taking a jacket, though, it'll be too warm.
Karen:	<u>It doesn't matter if we go in the same clothes</u>. I haven't got anything else I want to wear anyway.
Lisa:	Oh, all right. I suppose it's not important. See you later.
	Now listen again.
	TAPE REPEAT
	Six.
	Who gave the man the CD for his birthday?
Brother:	Thanks very much for the birthday present. I've always wanted to read that book.
Sister:	That's OK. Hey – I went round to <u>Dad's</u> yesterday. <u>Did you like the CD that he bought for you</u>?
Brother:	Yes! Great choice! How did he know I wanted that one?
Sister:	I think he had some help from our little brother – they went shopping together last weekend.
	Now listen again.
	TAPE REPEAT
	Seven.
	What is the man going to order?

Man: Is that apple pie you've got? Mmm … I think I'll have some of that. I'll get you another piece too, if you want.

Woman: I'd love another piece, it's delicious. Only I'm afraid this was the last one. They've got chocolate cake, though. Why don't you have that?

Man: Never mind. I just thought the apple pie looked good, that's all. I'll <u>get some coffee</u>, anyway. I need something before the film starts. <u>Should I get you one</u>?

Woman: Oh, <u>go on, then</u>. We've got time – the film doesn't start for another twenty minutes.

Now listen again.

TAPE REPEAT

That is the end of Part 1.

PART 2   CD2 Track 32

Now turn to Part 2, questions 8 to 13.

You will hear the pilot, Kate Gingford, talking about the last few days of her flight around the world in a small aeroplane.

For each question, put a tick in the correct box.

You now have 45 seconds to look at the questions for Part 2.

Now we are ready to start. Listen carefully. You will hear the recording twice.

Kate: So last week when I was talking about my flight around the world, I'd got as far as Norway. This week I'll tell you about the last part back to London.

When I landed in Norway, two friends were there to meet me. We stayed together in a hotel and talked a lot about my trip and the route I'd chosen. Next morning, we were given a wonderful cooked breakfast and then <u>my friends helped me get into the suit I have to wear when flying over water</u>. It's really tight.

I hadn't slept much, but I was excited and felt really wide-awake on the flight to Denmark. <u>My son, who is also a pilot, called me on the radio</u>. He was flying a plane in Germany at the time and we chatted for a few minutes. I was flying across the sea in thick cloud so I couldn't see much, but I arrived in Denmark safely on the Sunday evening.

On Monday I was worried about the plane. <u>There was a problem with one of the front wheels</u>. I knew I could still take off and fly, without any fear of an accident, but I knew that if I made a bad landing I could damage the plane and so not be able to continue. I called the airport in Holland, my next destination, to arrange some repairs, and fortunately I managed to land there without any problems.

That night I stayed with some friends on their farm in Holland. Next morning it was so foggy that I couldn't fly, but it <u>was</u> good to have a break. It was difficult to sleep so I walked around the farm instead. I hadn't spent any time in the countryside for months, and <u>I'd forgotten how much I missed the sound of birds</u>.

When the fog lifted in the afternoon, I was pleased to learn they had repaired my plane, and I took off within minutes. My next destination was a flying club in the north of England and <u>I knew it would be impossible to land there once the sun had gone down</u>. But fortunately it was a lovely sunny evening, and I arrived in good time.

I left early again on Thursday for London. I felt nervous because it was my last day of flying. Then, when I finally landed, <u>I felt wonderful – the long, difficult journey had been worth it</u>. It was lovely seeing my family who were all there to meet me. I promised I wouldn't make another long trip like that again.

Now listen again.

TAPE REPEAT

That is the end of Part 2.

PART 3   CD2 Track 33

Now turn to Part 3, questions 14 to 19.

You will hear a recorded message about a tourist attraction called The Grand Palace.

For each question, fill in the missing information in the numbered space.

You now have 20 seconds to look at Part 3.

Now we are ready to start. Listen carefully. You will hear the recording twice.

Tour guide: This is the Grand Palace information service. We are pleased to announce that the Grand Palace is now open again. The emergency repair work on the <u>roof</u> is now complete, but work is still in progress to repair the outside walls of the building, which were damaged in storms last year. Visitors may like to look at an exhibition of <u>photographs</u> in the entrance hall, which show how this work is done. The exhibition is near the gift shop, where you can buy postcards of the Palace and slides of some of the paintings.

The Palace was built in the 18th century as a holiday home for the King and his family, and decorated in the classical style. You can admire the beautiful painted ceiling in the music room, which contains the Queen's <u>piano</u>. Upstairs are the royal bedrooms, containing 18th-century furniture. Visitors can also walk through the palace kitchens and into the dining room, where the table is laid for forty guests, with silver dinner plates and beautiful glasses.

If you want refreshments, home-made cakes, sandwiches, tea and coffee are served in the Queen Anne tea-room. On fine days, refreshments are also served in the <u>garden</u>.

The tea-room is open every day from 3.00 to 5.00 p.m., or 5.30 p.m. during July and August. The Palace itself is open every day, from 10.00 a.m. to 6.00 p.m. in the summer season, that's June to <u>September</u>, and from 10.00 a.m. to 5.00 p.m. from October to May.

There is an entrance charge of £5.50 for adults or £3.50 for students and children under 14. There is also a special family ticket available for <u>£13.50</u>. It's for 2 adults and 2 children, so you save £7.00.

If you would like further information, please call us on 01293 567488 during opening hours. Thank you.

Now listen again.

TAPE REPEAT

That is the end of Part 3.

PART 4   CD2 Track 34

Now turn to Part 4, questions 20 to 25.

Look at the six sentences for this part.

You will hear a conversation between a boy, Tom, and a girl, Jemma, who are studying in different parts of the country.

Decide if each sentence is correct or incorrect. If it is correct, put a tick in the box under A for YES. If it is not correct, put a tick in the box under B for NO.

You now have 20 seconds to look at the questions for Part 4.

Now we are ready to start. Listen carefully. You will hear the recording twice.

Jemma:	Hi Tom, I haven't seen you since we left school.
Tom:	Jemma, <u>what are you doing here? I thought you were at university</u>.
Jemma:	I'm back home with my parents for the holidays. I couldn't afford to stay in London.
Tom:	Do you like city life? You must find it very noisy and busy after this village?
Jemma:	Well yes, but there's always something happening. Not like here.
Tom:	There's the cinema in Kingsford.
Jemma:	Yes, but it's 20 kilometres away. Where I live in London there are lots of cinemas with all the latest films, just round the corner.
Tom:	Lucky you! <u>By the time the films reach Kingsford cinema everybody else has forgotten about them</u>.
Jemma:	The trouble is, London's so expensive. At weekends I usually go to a club or a restaurant with my friends. That can cost more than £30.
Tom:	<u>Really! I can't believe that</u>. An evening out round here never costs me more than £20. How do you afford it? Have you got a part-time job?
Jemma:	Not yet. I've done a course at the local swimming pool to get a certificate in life-saving. <u>I had to pay for the course</u>, but it means I can be a pool life-guard when I go back to London. I'm going to work early in the morning before my classes start.
Tom:	<u>It won't be very exciting, just sitting watching people swimming</u> up and down.
Jemma:	Maybe not, but the money's good. That's the main thing.
Tom:	Actually, I've got a job in a children's holiday camp near here for the summer. I'm going to organise their sporting activities.

Jemma: Really? Can you give me the phone number? Perhaps I can get a job there too, while I'm at home!

Tom: <u>You're probably too late</u>. I applied five months ago, and I had to have an interview and a health check. But you can try.

Jemma: Well, there's nothing else for me to do here.

Tom: OK. I'll find the number.

Now listen again.

TAPE REPEAT

That is the end of Part 4.

You now have six minutes to check and copy your answers on to the answer sheet.

You have one more minute.

That is the end of the test.

Acknowledgements

The authors would like to thank Annabel Marriott and Jane Coates personally for all their input, efficiency and good humour. Many thanks also to Chris Williams (senior production controller), Michelle Simpson (permissions controller), Guy Brook-Hart (for permission to adapt the Grammar reference section from *Complete First Certificate*), Hilary Fletcher (picture researcher), John Green (audio producer), Tim Woolf (audio editor), Kevin Doherty and Marcus Fletcher (proof-readers).

Emma would like to thank colleagues and students at Lacunza – IH San Sebastián for trialling some of the material. She would also like to thank family and friends for all their support and encouragement. Very special thanks to Mikel, Sara and Alex for their patience and understanding.

The authors and publishers are grateful to the following for reviewing the material during the writing process:

Jane Coates, UK; Caroline Cooke, Spain; Ellen Darling, Italy; Stephanie Dimond-Bayir, UK; Sarah Hellawell, Spain; Joanna Kosta, UK; Peter McClaren, UAE; Karen Saxby, UK; Amanda Thomas, UK.

Development of this publication has made use of the Cambridge International Corpus (CIC). The CIC is a computerised database of contemporary spoken and written English which currently stands at over one billion words. It includes British English, American English and other varieties of English. It also includes the Cambridge Learner Corpus, developed in collaboration with the University of Cambridge ESOL Examinations. Cambridge University Press has built up the CIC to provide evidence about language use that helps to produce better language teaching materials.

Key: l = left, c = centre, r = right, t = top, b = bottom, u = upper, lo = lower, f = far

For permission to reproduce photographs: Alamy/© Richard Arthur p. 53 (br), /© blickwinkel p. 98 (F), /© Corbis Premium RF p. 26 (2), /© DK p. 89 (cr), /© Jason Friend p. 35 (t), /© imagebroker pp. 18, 31 (uc), 62 (3), /© John MacPherson p. 27 (C), /© Tina Manley/Asia p. 17, /© Aivar Mikko p. 40 (4), /© Paul Panayiotou p. 22 (r), /© PCL p. 112 (l), /© Real World People p. 26 (1), /© Colin Underhill p. 62 (1), /© vario images GmbH & Co.KG p. 26 (6), /© Aram Williams p. 98 (A), /© WoodyStock p. 33 (c); B&C Alexander/ArcticPhoto p. 39 (br); Aquarius Collection /© Walt Disney p. 70 (t); Corbis p. 171 (t), /© Walter Bibikow p. 33 (tr), /© Comstock Select p. 55 (r), /© Dean Conger p. 39 (bl), /© cultura p. 34 (5), /© Randy Faris p. 58 (bl), /© Ole Graf p. 52 (b), /© Image Source pp. 47, 58 (tl), 85 (2), /© Image Werks p. 54 (bl), /© Inspirestock p. 31 (Locl), /© Catherine Karnow p. 171 (t), /© Rainer Kiedrowski/Arcaid p. 10 (bl), /© Bob Krist p. 34 (7), /©Leonard Lenz p. 87, /© LWA-Sharie Kennedy p. 8 (tl), /© Simon Marcus p. 55 (l), /© John Miller/Robert Harding World Imagery p. 40 (3), /© Reuters p. 35 (b), /© David Stoecklein p. 34 (3), /© SYGMA p. 74 (l), /© Thinkstock p. 31 (Locr), /© Cesár Vera p. 94 (B), /© Steven Vidler/Eurasia Press p. 40 (5), /© Westend61 p. 145 (r); Getty Images/AFP pp. 62 (4), 70 (bl), 85 (3), /AFP/SAEED KHAN p. 154, /altrendo images p. 34 (2), /Aurora/Curtis Johnson p. 89 (b), /DK Stock/David Deas p. 31 (cl), /Grant Faint p. 32 (tl), /First Light/Spyros Bourboulis p. 83 (C), /GK Hart/Vikki Hart p. 59, /Hola Images p. 54 (br), /Iconica/John Giustina p. 58 (br), /Iconica/José Luis Pelaez p. 150 (t), /Iconica/Bambu Productions p. 150 (b), /The Image Bank/Stephen Derr p. 71, /The Image Bank/Andy Rouse p. 98 (G), /Jupiterimages p. 107, /Evan Kafka p. 52 (4), /Lonely Planet Images/John Banagan p. 67, /Lori Adamski Peek p. 80 (bl), /Panoramic Images p. 41, /Photographer's Choice/Patti McConville p. 34 (6), /Photonica/Troy Aossey p. 44 (5), /Photonica/Philip J Brittan p. 112 (r), /Justin Pumfrey p. 26 (3), /Joe Raedle p. 28, /Riser/Jenny Acheson p. 32 (br), /Riser/Edgardo Contreras p. 90, /Riser/Joanne Dugan p. 150 (c), /Sports Illustrated p. 85 (1), /Stone/Tim Flach p. 98 (B), /Stone/Judith Haeusler p. 31 (b), /Stone+/Alistair Berg p. 83 (B), /Taxi/Gregory E Betz p. 21, Taxi/Peter Pinnock p. 85 (4), /Taxi/Jacqueline Veissid p. 150 (uc), /UpperCut Images/Keith Brofsky p. 16 (C), /Workbook Stock/Scott Areman p. 32 (bl), /Yellow Dog Productions p. 16 (E); The Kobal Collection/LucasFilm p. 39 (t), /Universal/Working Title p. 52 (5), /Vinet, Pierre/New Line /Saul Zaentz/Wing Nut Films p. 74 (r); Masterfile/Aluma Images p. 53 (tl), /Raoul Minsart p. 15, /Brad Wrobleski p. 32 (tr); "Courtesy NASA/JPL-Caltech" p. 100; Photographers Direct/BinghamPhotography.com p. 16 (B), /Alex Segre Photography p. 8 (br); PhotoLibrary.com/age fotostock/Thomas Dressler p. 27 (D), /age fotostock/Wojtek Buss p. 40 (2), /age fotostock/Joseph De Sciose p. 44 (4), /age fotostock/James McLoughlin p. 80 (tl), /Aflo Foto Agency/Koji Aoki p. 62 (6), /Aflo Foto Agency/Masakazu Watanabe p. 80 (tr), /Aflo Foto Agency/Mark Newman p. 98 (H), /All Canada Photos/Josh McCulloch p. 27 (B), /arabianEye RM/Celia Peterson p. 106 (B), /British Council/Allan Stanley p. 103, /Cultura/Dev Carr p. 54 (tr), /Chad Ehlers p. 33 (br), /F1 Online/Carol Buchanan p. 98 (C), /Flirt Collection/Larry Williams p. 44 (2), /Flirt Collection/ML Sinibaldi p. 44 (3), /Flirt Collection//Warren Faidley p. 62 (5), /Wayne Fogden p. 13, /Imagebroker.net/Günter Flegar p. 10 (tr), /Imagebroker.net/Jochen Tack p. 11 (bl), /Imagebroker.net/Winfried Schäfer p. 52 (2), /Imagebroker.net/Sabine Lubenow p. 94 (A), /Juice Images p. 33 (bl), /Kablonk/Kablonk! Kablonk! p. 49, /M.E.N. Media p. 93, /Nordic Photos/Gunilla Lundstrom p. 26 (4), /Nordic Photos/Hans Wretling p. 34 (4), /Pacific Stock/Ariyoshi Rita p. 40 (1), /Photoalto/Corinne Malet p. 44 (1), /Photoalto/Zen Shul/Patrick Sheindell OCarroll p. 58 (tr), /Photononstop/Christian Arnal p. 80 (br), /Photononstop/Tibor Bognar p. 94 (C), Photo Word Ltd/Poole pp. 10 (c) 11 (t), /Pixland p. 145 (l), /Radius Images p. 33 (tl), /Somos Images p. 22 (l), /Superstock/James Urbach p. 98 (D), /WESTEND61 p. 62 (2), /White p. 8 (bc), /White/Colin Paterson p. 34 (1); Press Association Images/Niall Carson/PA Archive p. 106 (A), Rex features/© Everett Collection p. 52 (1), /Henry Lamb/BEI p 70 (br), /Ken McKay p. 52 (3), /NBCUPHOTOBANK p. 52 (6), /Peter Price p. 27 (A), /Solent News p. 29, /© 20thC.Fox/Everett Collection p. 70 (cl); ShutterStock Images/Matt Antonino p. 31 (tr), /Atomi p. 88 (c), /Stephen Bonk p. 32 (c), /Tiago Jorge da Silva Estima p. 98 (E), /dwphotos p. 26 (5), /dyoma p. 88 (b), /Gregory Gerber p. 88 (t), /Jaroslaw Grudzinski p. 106 (C), /hamurishi p. 66, /ImageryMajestic p. 15, /Tischenko Irina p. 89 (cl), /Monkey Business Images p. 150 (Loc), /Khoroshunova Olga p. 83 (A), /Tatiana Popova p. 88 (Locl), /Stephen Aaron Rees p. 88 (cr), /Elena Schweitzer p. 89 (tl), /Stepanov p. 89 (tr), /Jozsef Szasz-Fabian p. 88 (ucl), /Tobik p. 88 (Locr), /Timage p. 16 (A), /Tonis Valing p. 53 (tr), /WizData, inc. p. 16 (D), /Yellowj p. 88 (cl), /ZTS p. 88 (ucr).

We have been unable to trace the copyright owner for the image on p. 107 (br) from *China Daily*.

Recordings produced by John Green, TEFL Tapes edited by Tim Woolf at ID Audio, London.

Illustrations:

Javier Joaquin pp. 86, 144, 153, 160, 161, 162, 169

Kveta pp. 8, 17 (m), 18 (m), 19 (m), 20, 35, 39, 40, 50, 57, 68, 73, 74, 76, 82, 88, 90, 93, 104, 111, 173

Rob McClurkan pp. 48 (br), 77, 92, 101, 106, 112

Andrew Painter pp. 17 (b), 38 (tl), 64, 106, 110 (l)

Aleksandar Sotirovski pp. 10, 20, 48 (t), 57, 69, 91, 94, 104, 110 (br), 146, 173, 174

David Whamond pp. 12, 30, 31, 38 (tr), 46, 89, 92, 113

Cover design by Wild Apple Design Ltd

Designed and typeset by Wild Apple Design Ltd